My Father's Roses

My Father's Roses

A family's memoir of three generations
divided by fate and united through love

NANCY KOHNER

with a Prologue by Bridget McGing

HODDER &
STOUGHTON

First published in Great Britain in 2008 by Hodder & Stoughton
An Hachette Livre UK company

First published in paperback in 2008

1

A CIP catalogue record for this title is available from the British Library

Hardback ISBN 978 0 340 96024 0
Trade paperback ISBN 978 0 340 96025 7

Typeset by Hewer Text UK Ltd, Edinburgh
Printed and bound by Clays Ltd, St Ives plc

Hodder & Stoughton policy is to use papers that are natural, renewable
and recyclable products and made from wood grown in sustainable
forests. The logging and manufacturing processes are expected to
conform to the environmental regulations of the country of origin.

Hodder & Stoughton Ltd
338 Euston Road
London NW1 3BH

www.hodder.co.uk

For Daniel, Bridget and Grace

Contents

Foreword and Acknowledgements xi

Prologue by Bridget McGing xvii

1 Paternity 1

2 Valerie and Heinrich 14

3 Two Single Beds 20

4 High Hopes 22

5 If You Carry On Like This . . . 28

6 Bukwa 32

7 Swimming Lessons 35

8 The Sea 40

9 Professor Novak's Ultimatum 42

10 Have You Heard . . . ? 44

11 Saaz and the House of the Schochet 46

12 Rudi in Prague 51

13 Savouring Names 55

14 Der Garten 57

15 Franz in Leitmeritz 60

16 Krakow 64

17 Being British 77

18 Small and Safe 79

19 The Stucker 85

20 Travelling 92

21 Baking 94

22 Putte 101

23 Home Leave 105

24 The Attic 111

25 Hans 113

26 The Patriarch 115

27 A Jewish Brothel 123

28 Becoming a Man 124

29 All It Is Is War 130

30 Sewing Lessons 138

31 The Problems of Defenestration 145

32 The Anniversary 147

33 Bilin 154

34 What Happened to Maxl 156

35 The Wheelbarrow 157

36 Deutschtum and Jewishness 160

37 Adolf Girschick 162

38 The Balcony: 27 August 1922 164

39 Die Goldige 167

40 Palestine 171

41 Breakfast in the Garten 178

42 You Are My Father 183

43 Playing with Huberman 189

44 Quiet and Tender 192

45 Edithlein   196

46 Vote for SHF   203

47 The Telephone   211

48 Der Tag   213

49 The Welcome   216

50 All of Us   220

51 Berta   227

52 The Sound of Breaking Glass   229

53 Bitter Sorrow   230

54 Opapa   233

55 Staying Beside Her   235

56 The Earth Goes Round and Round   238

57 A Birthday in Prague   243

58 Hansi   247

59 An Effort of Love and Will   253

60 The Messepalast   261

61 Theresienstadt   264

62 The Handbag   266

63 Omama   269

64 Russell Square   270

65 The Journey   273

66 Your Hand in Mine   278

Foreword and Acknowledgements

I have been waiting to write this book for most of my life. Since it is a family history and I did not intend to include myself in it, I may have sensed its prospect even as a child. As a teenager, I waited with cheerful optimism. In my twenties, I began to research, to read, converse, discuss, debate. I began to bore my friends.

When my children were born, motherhood made me less certain. And as my uncertainty about my purpose grew, so my possibilities decreased. I had no spare time, but in any case, I no longer knew what or why I was writing.

When my father died, grief made me frantic to write and unable to lift my pen. Instead, I spent time with my father's brother's wife, Edith Kohner, who talked to me about my father, his family and the past. She opened box after box of jumbled letters, diaries and photographs, and although I was hampered by the old script and my limited knowledge of the languages used, I began to sort and catalogue them and familiarise myself with their dates and origins. I added them to some documents that had turned up after my father's death. I recorded lengthy conversations with Edith, who was sympathetic and generous. A clumsy understanding began to grow.

A friend, Alix Henley, hearing of the collection of letters and my desire to have them translated, put me in touch with Peter Heller through her mother, Lotte. Lotte and Peter had been colleagues at the Foreign Office, and before that, Peter had worked for the BBC and, during the war, for the Monitoring Service.

I spoke to Peter on the phone and we arranged to meet. I think we were both a little wary. I was about to show a stranger some very personal documents that contained . . . I knew not what. He had been warm and interested on the phone, but I wasn't sure whether I would be able to back-track if, when I met him, I felt that he was not the right person for the task. Peter, for his part, must surely have wondered whether this was a sufficiently professional undertaking.

When we met, my misgivings were overcome. The coincidences were extraordinary. Peter had grown up not far from my father's home and had lived and worked in Bohemia. Like my uncle, he had been a law student in Prague. He was steeped in the same culture and was expert in all the necessary languages – not just German and Czech but even the particular form of shorthand used in some of the letters and diaries. He could read the handwriting, which for me was, and still is, indecipherable. He knew the geography and the social and political history; he knew the music and the literature; he knew about the schooling, the humour, the clothes, the food . . . all the minutiae of my family's life in Bohemia. He was also the child of a Jewish mother and, like my father and uncle, he had made a lucky escape in 1939.

But what convinced me that Peter was the right translator for the job was not so much all of this (although it was astonishing good fortune) but the fact that, even at that first meeting, I knew that he understood an enterprise that as yet I hardly understood myself, and that he would support me in it.

Peter has translated many hundreds of my family's letters and diary entries: it has been a Herculean labour, stretching over many years. He has done it with meticulous care, great good humour, and not a single complaint. He has never imposed his own ideas but has supported mine, at the same time gently offering me the advice that only someone with such a vast store of experience and expertise could offer. And he has produced something more than mere translations, for he has peppered his typescripts with his own explanatory remarks and illuminating comments, and in this way has added immeasurably to my understanding and knowledge.

Gradually we became friends as well as collaborators. We travelled to Prague together and I learnt a little more about Peter's own life. It was typical of his professionalism that, although he had his own stories to tell, he never muddled his own history with the one he was making accessible to me.

I owe an enormous debt of thanks to Peter, and both my family and I also owe thanks to Jill, his wife, who has unfailingly supported him – and me and my children too.

Once Peter's translations made the letters and diaries readable, I had to re-think what they meant and what could be done with them. More time passed. I was now clear about the personal meaning of the material, but uncertain about its public significance. I showed a few of the letters to one or two friends. One Sunday, Andrea Levy, to whom I had lent one of the files of letters, rang me unexpectedly and asked if she could come over to see me straight away. An hour or so later, she walked into the house, sat down at my kitchen table, and spoke to me about how much the letters had excited her. I shall always be grateful for her spontaneous, convincing affirmation that the letters had meaning and value beyond the purely personal.

But it was only when I could free myself of other work, re-assess my response to my father's death, and allow myself to write not just for my family, the archive, and a wider audience but for myself as well, that I could begin to write, and write freely.

My friends supported me. It is useful to have a ready-assembled group of English literature graduates to hand, and my fellow students of thirty-five years before all rallied round with their very varied, sometimes conflicting, always stimulating commentaries. They have made the writing a pleasure – and also greatly improved it. Jenny Cuffe's praise, criticism, practical wisdom and above all her enthusiasm, Kate Jameson's clarity and stern encouragement, and Felicity Rosslyn's impressive knowledge and sensitive insights have sustained me through every uncertainty. They have all given up days of their time to read my drafts, and despite what surely must have been strong temptation, they have never once told me to stop talking and either get on with it or give up. My dear friend Ali Leftwich has similarly encouraged and reassured me, and I have depended on her steadiness and understanding. Having a very different background herself, she has been able to tell me what it is like to read this kind of personal history without any contextual knowledge, and has pulled me up when I have assumed too much. Ruth Bender-Atik, burdened by being one of my few Jewish friends, has endured many a conversation revealing my ignorance of Judaism outside my own cultural inheritance. She too has read and commented, and her different perspective has been welcome.

My cousin, Billy Kohner, as the son of one of the main protagonists, Franz Kohner, has had most reason to interfere – and has not done so. He has been supportive from the start and I thank him especially for that. It has been a particular pleasure to share memories of our similar upbringings. Our fathers had much in common, and that is a delight – and a source of amusement – to us both.

Many of my friends (Celia Fisher, Isabel Jameson, Avril Maddrell, Gill Mallinson, Lesley Moreland, Jake Phelan and Jill Russell) have generously given their time to read and talk to me about the book.

During the course of my research, I came across a number of people who were helpful beyond what was required of them: Peter Brod, Jiři Fiedler, Martin Gutzer, Ron Herrmann and Keiren Phelan.

Another contact came about by chance. One evening, my phone rang and a female voice I did not know asked for me by name. When I identified myself, she explained that she had come across the name of Kohner in a list of Jewish inhabitants of a Czech town called Podersam. Could I be any relation? I confirmed that I was, and asked her for her own story. Her name, she said, was Carol Noble, but her father's original name (he had come out of Czechoslovakia on a Kindertransport), and therefore her grandfather's, was Löbl. On the other side, her grandmother's family was called Mühlstein. Both were Podersam families.

It so happened that the name of Mühlstein featured in one of my father's often repeated favourite stories. I asked her if she was a relative of Walter Mühlstein's, and she said he was her great-uncle. 'I can tell you, then,' I said, 'that your great-uncle used to throw dried horse shit at my father.' Maybe it wasn't quite the connection she had been hoping for, but this was the beginning of a great collaboration. We were both seeking the same information; we both wanted to learn about the community in which our families had lived. Some years later, we travelled to Prague, Podersam, Saaz and Theresienstadt (Terezin) together, and without Carol's energy and tenacity, I would not have managed to acquire the information I did from the Czech museums and archives.

The greatest pleasure has been to work with my daughter, Bridget McGing, and to her I owe the greatest thanks. There is no task she hasn't shared with me and made a delight. Together, we've pored over documents and photographs, organised and re-organised them, read, re-read and discussed them, and transferred them painstakingly to albums and to the screen. We've travelled together and penetrated the mysteries of the Czech archives, wandered through museums, and sat on the dark, deserted platforms of railway stations whose names we could not pronounce. As a historian, her knowledge and skills have been invaluable, and her perspective has been a foil and sometimes (though not without argument) a corrective. Above all, she has made writing this seem both important and possible, and I have been able to accept her optimism because she also knows how hard writing is.

NHK
February 2006

Picture acknowledgements

The majority of photographs are from the author's collection. Additional sources: p. 81, postcard of the Ringplatz and p. 83, Podersam synagogue, both from the photo archive at Podbořany Town Hall; p. 215, extract from the *Gedenkbuch für die Stadt Podersam*, from the Státní Okresní Archiv, Louny; p. 215, photograph of the invasion of Podersam, printed in *Podbořany: Dějiny města a okolních obcí*, Smetana, Jan, (Podbořany, 2001).

Prologue by Bridget McGing

I grew up with an archive of epic proportions. In fact, 'with' is not quite the right word. I grew up *in* an archive. My childhood home was filled with a general miscellany of objects brought out of Czechoslovakia in 1939. The linen was on the bed, the glass on the sideboard, the china in the dresser. I played from the sheet music, ate with the cutlery and walked on the rugs. Thanks to the many photographs, I grew up (quite literally) surrounded by members of the family. Franzi, Berta and Rudi kept watch over the hall, a young Opapa guarded my mother's bedside table, while an older one kept a watchful eye over her desk, and Omama sat on the sideboard – keeping track of all our comings and goings. The past was simply an integral part of my childhood. There was never one particular point of discovery, no moment when I became aware of my family's history and understood it. Instead, I grew up alongside it, with full knowledge of everything that had happened, encouraged to speak about it freely and passionately.

From a very young age I saw this family inheritance as something special and exclusive, magical even. My mother's passion for it was infectious and I willingly joined in. I remember sitting with her on the floor of her office, documents spread out around us, meticulously dating, identifying and ordering, gradually transforming the hoard into an archive. I remember poring over photographs and negatives with a magnifying glass, carefully scanning and preserving the increasingly familiar images. I remember our many travels – gathering information, quarelling with archivists, discovering buildings, records and stories.

I remember arguing, although arguing is not quite the right word. The beautiful and totally illegible handwriting of my ancestors was always hotly contested – that's a 'u', no, it's definitely an 'a', or is it an 'o'? The photos were another source of intense debate – is that Opapa in the back row? Or a stranger? Is that taken in the *Garten*? Or is it in Saaz? When my mother started writing the book, these debates become more frequent. My mother was an English graduate, I am a history graduate, and two disciplines did not always coexist happily – my mother enjoyed creating stories, painting pictures with words, I was more concerned with historical accuracy. 'You can't *assume* that letter was from Berta.' How do you *know* that Omama cooked that?' Always eager to deliver that sharp kick to bring my mother back to unsentimental reality.

I vividly remember laughing: at the hats that Valerie wore, at the mandatory dog that would turn up in every other photograph, at Heinrich's pompous and patronising letters, at Rudi and Franzi's tendency to take their tops off at every opportunity. I remember laughing at my obsession with Onkel Edward, at our attempts at pronouncing Czech, and at our pitiful struggles to cook dumplings. And I remember how laughing could so easily turn to hysterics when standing on Czech railway platforms in the middle of nowhere.

But I also remember crying. My mother never attempted to hide the tragedy of our family's past and she never felt ashamed of expressing that sadness. In fact, my mother's propensity to cry – at the reading of Omama's last letters, at the recordings of Opapa playing the violin, at the site of the train station at Terezin – taught me more about my past than any research could. Such willingness to share emotions and instincts so openly and candidly is not a trait often found in this area of family history, and it is one that I am profoundly grateful for. She enabled me to feel a natural continuity and connection with my heritage – a connection I know she had not received so straightforwardly from her father, and that she had struggled to create for herself.

So although this book was only written two years ago, I feel I have lived with it all my life. When I was small I would listen to my mother talk about it with her friends, explaining how the letters and diaries she had inherited could tell her family's story in their own words. As I grew up and started to read the letters myself, I too could see the potential, and I began to share her enthusiasm for the project. But her other work made even beginning the book an impossible task, and I could sense her frustration as countless other Holocaust memoirs and stories were published while hers remained unstarted.

In my first year at university she wrote a chapter. It was not a long chapter, and she was not happy with it, but they were words on paper, a beginning. I loved them, I read them to anybody I could make sit still for long enough, willing or otherwise. It was a chapter about her father, and it was the first time I had seen her memories of him written down. I tried to encourage her to write more. But in my second year of university my mother was diagnosed with cancer, and we embarked on a seemingly endless run of hospital appointments and treatments. I spent much of that year rushing between home and university (often with books and a half-completed essay in my bag) to try and help her through the worst times. She was on her own, and she was scared. And the book disappeared from view at the very time when it felt most urgent.

The diagnosis that the cancer was terminal came just half an hour after I emerged from my last exam in my final year. From that June in 2005, until her death in March 2006, my mother wrote constantly. In the very worst circumstances, and in increasing pain, she wrote 75,000 words, finally fulfilling her ambition and completing the long-awaited book. She would sit in armchairs, in bed, in hospital waiting rooms – writing, reading, deleting, re-writing, moving, editing. It was a labour of love in the very truest sense of the words, and she died only one week after finishing it. It was an incredible achievement, and one I still find difficult to comprehend. It was not how she wanted to write it, and it was not the book she had imagined it would be, but she had written it.

If it was not the way my mother was expecting to write the book, it certainly wasn't the way I was planning to spend my first year out of university. I had hopes of continuing my studies, of pursuing my own project on the past. But all such hopes were abruptly suspended during one phone call to my mother on a sunny day in June. So I put my life on hold, and focused on the year ahead. As my mother's carer, I concentrated on making the last months of her life as bearable as they could be. With my brother and sister I fed, washed, dressed, drugged and entertained her. I cleaned the house, walked the dogs, cooked the food and collected prescriptions. I walked with her, slowly supporting the daily progress from the bed to the chair, from the chair to the garden, from the garden to the bed. I made endless notes – which drugs to take when, what food she wanted (what food she didn't), who to call for help. I arranged visits from her friends, and postponed them when she couldn't see them. I argued with people who weren't being helpful, and I thanked those who were.

Sometimes I felt bitter. Watching my friends rush ahead, pursuing jobs and theses and travels, it was easy to feel both left out and left behind. I felt stuck between two starkly contrasting worlds, and at times it made me resent them both. But any bitterness, of course, led swiftly to guilt. How could I possibly think that I should be doing anything other than looking after my mother? I loved my mother, but I also genuinely enjoyed her company. We were friends – the very best of friends. So what on earth was I doing thinking I would rather be somewhere else?

But looking back at that year, through any bitterness or associated guilt, my over-riding emotion is one of simple admiration. My mother made a miserable and frightening year somehow feel special. We sat together in pastel green hospital armchairs, drinking powdered tea from plastic cups and surrounded by drips and machines, and she made it feel special. She did so by remaining unashamedly herself – her brilliant sense of humour, her sharp intellect and her sheer stoicism prevailed. And it was when she was writing that she was most herself. When she wrote she ceased to be a cancer patient, she was, as she had always been, a writer. The book absorbed her into another world, to the point where her laptop and a folder of the family's letters could provide the same, if not greater relief than the regular doses of morphine. So I simply helped in any way I could.

Sometimes she needed documents hunting out, or something researching in the library. Sometimes she needed to talk through the latest chapter, or the one she still wasn't sure about several chapters back.

Sometimes the help I could provide was purely practical. My mother had been a writer all her adult life, and I was used to her office and desk being part of the house. But now she could no longer sit in her office and substitute desks had to be set up around the house. One in the bedroom, one in the sitting room, one (for particularly fine weather) in the garden. When we had to leave the safety of the house for the regular chemotherapy sessions, the substitute desk would come too. We would arrive at the hospital with several large bags packed with her laptop, letters, draft manuscripts, photographs, documents, pillow, hot water bottle and blanket. We must have looked an odd pair, sitting in the corner of the ward talking through Heinrich's route to the *Garten*, or Berta's orchestra rehearsals in Saaz.

As the year went on my mother's writing gained momentum. She began to write faster, with a real (and understandable) urgency. She didn't always need me to discuss the next chapter, and as she needed more and more care, there was not always time for me to do so. I started to have less to do with the content of the book, and more with just making it possible. It wasn't a role I was used to. Up until that point, my family's past had been a joint project that my mother and I had shared. But towards the end of 2005 it was clear that our wonderful collaboration was coming to an end, and that I occupied a new position watching from the sidelines. The completion of the book itself could only belong to my mother – *she* had to finish *her* book and try to make sense of her relationship with the past. I had a different task ahead. I had to concentrate on the present, and find a way to stay with my mother until the end. I had to hold onto her while I still could, and try to prepare myself for a life without her. That was not something I could do by looking backwards. It was not something that my family's past would help me with. I had to sit with her, watch her and hold her hand.

Now, two years after her death, I am left having to put down in words my experiences of that year and my feelings towards what remains. To be honest, I no longer know. The wonderfully familiar archive that I have grown up with suddenly feels very different now it is sitting in *my* kitchen. My mother's extensive handwritten notes no longer feel like the gems of information they used to, but reminders that she is no longer here. I am wary of research that might uncover information she would have wanted to know, or documents that only she would know where to file. The china, glass, linen and furniture somehow don't feel the same when squeezed into every corner of *my* house. The photos seem more remote when there is nobody with whom to laugh about them. Above all, the very size of the archive, the size that originally made it so powerful, seems almost overwhelming now I am left to carry it alone.

And so it is only now that I am aware that the archive and what it represents might, or even could, have a separate meaning for me. And it is only now I realise that this meaning may, by necessity, be different to my mother's. I feel I am beginning to understanding the concept of 'responsibility', or even 'burden'. Will I ever know as much as my mother? Will I be able to take care of everything as well as she has? Is this even something that I want to do without her? Is that a choice I have? And I know these are feelings my mother would understand, and I know they are feelings she would not want me to have.

This book now joins the archive it originated from, as my mother's contribution to the inheritance that was so important to her, and I must begin, slowly, to build my own relationship with it all. I am left with what my mother taught me – the discipline of research, the art of writing, the emotion of discovery. She taught me how to respect and to treasure. But most of all she taught me to be proud. Her love of, and commitment to, these characters enabled me to love them in a way their letters, diaries and photographs could never have done on their own. And so my starting point will be this manuscript. What it contains, quite simply, is my mother's voice.

Paternity

*M*y father was Czech, but when I was a schoolgirl in the north of England in the 1950s and 60s and I had to fill in forms that asked for my father's nationality, there was confusion. For he was born not in Czechoslovakia (not yet formed in 1905, the year of his birth) but in the Austro-Hungarian Empire. He was named Rudolf, the name of Emperor Franz Josef's son, and his older brother was given the name of His Royal and Imperial Majesty himself. On at least one form, I can remember writing 'Austro-Hungary' as my father's country of origin – which may have bewildered the officials in Bradford Town Hall.

In fact, as far as I can remember, he never referred to himself as Czech, and as a boy he would almost certainly have thought of himself as German. He was born in the small town of Podersam (in Czech, Podbořany), about fifty miles west of Prague in the area of western Bohemia bordering on Germany. He spoke German, his culture was German, he was educated in German, and he learnt Czech, with difficulty and little lasting success, as a second language at school. When I was a child this all seemed perfectly straightforward to me: I thought that everyone in Czechoslovakia spoke German as their native language.

But with the advent of the Second World War, he could no longer think of himself as German. He arrived in England as a Jewish refugee in the summer of 1939. Hitler had invaded his homeland and was soon to destroy his family. He was no longer German: he was Jewish. Yet in the 1950s, when I was a child, I was barely aware that he was Jewish. The word was hardly mentioned. I knew we were not the same as other, indigenous Bradford families. But Jewish? I didn't think so.

My father was a piece of exotica. He never lost and never concealed his foreignness, and I loved it. He looked different to other children's fathers – taller, darker, and in my eyes twice as handsome, with a high, broad forehead, an impressive nose and a black moustache. He dressed well, was something of a peacock in fact, and in summer wore a freshly cut rose in his buttonhole. No other father I knew indulged in his fascinating ritual of filling with water the special metal reservoir that held the rose, selecting and picking the rosebud fresh from the garden in the early morning, and placing it to advantage in the buttonhole of his jacket before leaving for work. No other father I knew, in those days before men's toiletries became acceptable and most men restricted themselves to aftershave and Brilliantine, used the lotions and potions that scented my father's morning wash and shave. The Odol mouthwash, Dr Dralle's Birkenhaarwasser, and the mysterious Musk Ox Essence were accepted occupants of our bathroom cabinet. No other father I knew, in a time when English beds were made with sheets and blankets, and English food was unadulterated by foreign influences, slept under a feather quilt, or ate gherkins, salami, dark rye bread and yoghurt, which he and I bought together from the Polish shop in Bradford market on Saturday mornings.

Of course, all this is no more than any child of a foreign parent experiences and I am uncertain as to why, looking back, it seems so special to me. Perhaps life in a post-war northern town was particularly drab – though I didn't find it so. I liked the unforgiving character of the place. The Bradford of my childhood still preserved its sooty connections with the Victorian industrial past, and the countryside around, the moors and dales, was hard and unspoilt. More likely, the reason was that my father made these foreign eccentricities seem particularly exciting, and made them his own. He added to them, embellished them, played to an audience. He was a gentle, reflective man, but he also often played the extrovert and was excitable, funny and passionate.

He spoke fluent and highly literary English, but he never lost his accent and would often accentuate it. This was particularly so when he wished to haggle over a price or charm a woman. He was a great flirt and, when younger, was given to clicking his heels and bowing when introducing himself to women. After he died, the contents of our attic were found to include a package of photos of attractive women, sometimes posing with my father, sometimes alone, with messages written on the reverse: 'With tender regards, Helene'; 'Sincerely yours, Mary'. The package was labelled in my father's European hand, and with a touching attempt at English slang, 'All sorts of ragging. Nothing serious'. One of these women, Fraülein (or maybe it was Frau) Zentner-Stein, entered the mythology of my childhood as the woman with whom my father, then in his late twenties, had run away. His disapproving family, so it was said, had sent his brother Franz to retrieve the errant pair and take my father on a Mediterranean cruise to cool his ardour. This was such a favourite, funny family story that it was a surprise when I later discovered it to be true.

The language of my childhood was scattered with foreign expressions, some in German ('nicht in den Wind pissen' was a favourite), some in Yiddish or the local Egerlander dialect, and some in a mixture of all three. We used these sayings freely in family conversation and they became mixed with linguistic inventions and collected sayings of my father's, which he relished for their ludicrous or euphonious sounds. Schicklgruber, for example, the original surname of Hitler's father, did service as a swear word. 'He's there!', which we would shout on dog walks to encourage our terrier to chase after rabbits, was conflated to become 'Iddair!', mimicking my father's problems with the English 'th' sound. We always and deliberately mispronounced the word 'yacht', putting in a short 'a' and a German 'ch' sound, because that is how my father had once mistakenly pronounced it.

Raucous German songs also featured in family life. One, sung to the robust tune of the *Radetzky March*, began with the puzzling words 'Wenn die Katze und der Hund über Eckstein springt' ('When the cat and the dog jump over the cornerstone'). Later verses were apparently so rude that they could not be revealed to me, though it is hard to see the potential in the opening line.

3

My father had a great capacity for seeing the humorous side of life. He liked to act the fool and make people laugh, often embarrassing my mother, who bore his lack of inhibition patiently. Yet he was also a serious man. Through my teenage years and early adulthood he wrote me lengthy letters that reflected on my own life and his in ways that never failed to interest, amuse and support me. More recently, reading the letters written to him by his own father, long letters filled with pompous sayings and homespun philosophy, I have wondered whether to an outsider's eye my own father's philosophical musings would appear just as tedious. I don't think so. But then, perhaps my grandfather's letters didn't seem pompous to my father.

My grandfather Heinrich's letters show he was not an uneducated man, but he cannot have received much of his education at school. He attended a grammar school near Pilsen in west Bohemia, but he was not there long before his father Abraham decided it would be more economical to apprentice him. And since, as it happened, Onkel Mann required an apprentice, Heinrich's education was brought to an abrupt halt, including, to his lasting regret, the violin lessons he had only just begun.

Heinrich resolved that his own sons would have what he had been denied, and as a result my father was well educated – although that prim English term, with its class connotations, is inappropriate. In his later life in England, much of the content of his Germanic education was of little use to him, but his time at the Deutsches Staats-realgymnasium in Prague gave him more than a good grounding in the necessary subjects and skills. Simply to be a school boy in Prague (he was in lodgings during term time) in the early years of the twentieth century was enough to provide him with a cultural education unlike anything contemporary England had to offer. Culture was in the Bohemian air he breathed.

Not surprising, then, that he was musical. Well, it was more than that. For my father, music was a necessity, like food and drink. His taste was broad, but Germanic and orchestral in the main, with a particular and predictable love of Mahler. I learnt little from him about the shape and structure of music, the names and dates of composers, musicology in general; but I learnt much that was infinitely more exciting and mysterious – about how to listen, respond and find meaning in what I heard. When music moved him, he showed it. Sometimes, listening to the cheerful nostalgia of Strauss's Viennese waltzes or the grandiose sentiments of a Wagner chorus (he was not averse to Wagner), he would turn up the volume to the maximum, open the windows wide and sing with the music. Listening to music with him, sitting on his knee and held close, I would feel him catch his breath and sob when the music became tender or sad.

On Saturday nights my father would take my sister and me to the subscription concerts in Bradford's St George's Hall. These were the days when the Hallé Orchestra flourished under Sir John Barbirolli. In the restrained English audiences of the 1960s, my father would be the first to get to his feet to applaud and loudly cheer. Afterwards, at home, intoxicated by the music, he would take out his violin and play, bending, swaying, moving around the room, leaning towards us and drawing away, playing by ear or from dog-eared, yellowed music that had come with him from the old country.

There was no fussy preamble to his playing. He would take his violin from its case and, with head on one side, listening attentively, make a few strong sweeps of the bow across the strings. Chords were tried, pegs quickly adjusted, and a black velvet cloth tucked against his neck. The transition from preparation to playing was hardly noticeable.

He played with passion, and I learnt to think of the violin as one of the most expressive of instruments, a voice for the feelings. Sadly, my prosaic violin teacher, who was aptly named Miss Sawyer and with whom I was incarcerated once a week throughout my schooldays, failed to instill the necessary technical expertise. For some years I played with great feeling but no facility at all. Looking back, it seems strange that my father took little interest in my lessons. Perhaps, having learnt as a boy under a very different system, he felt he should leave teaching to others. His own teacher had rapped his knuckles if he played a wrong note.

He loved gardening but he was an eccentric gardener. Roses were his great love and it was usual for his hands to be covered with scratches from working among the bushes and climbers. He said his roses were like women – beautiful, desirable, but with sharp thorns to wound and hurt. These roses were pampered. A bucket and shovel were carried in the boot of the car at all times, and if my father spied a likely-looking pile of horse manure on the road, he would stop the car, jump out and gather it up. We often had smelly journeys home. Once the roses were in full bloom, he would invite me out into the garden and show me the flowers he especially loved, remarking on their beauty, asking me to savour the scent, pronouncing (often mispronouncing) their names with relish – Josephine Bruce, Nevada, Masquerade, Zéphirine Drouhin, Mermaid, Danse de Feu.

In those pre-garden centre days, we would go into carefully chosen spots in the countryside at weekends to collect leaf mould. Pretending to be on a dog walk if other people came by, we would crouch in the earth, scrape away the surface layer to reveal the decomposed leaves below, and scoop up the friable dark earth. My father would shoulder the sacks to the car and, once back home, spread the leaf mould lovingly where he felt it was most needed. He was also an avid compost maker and particularly enjoyed the job of turning our large compost heap, creating a nectar-like smell, usually just as my mother was serving Sunday lunch.

He created the garden himself. The house I was born in was my parents' second married home, the first being rented, the second built to their specifications. The land around formed a good-sized garden and my father designed the flowerbeds, lawns, hedges, paths, drive and garage. He must have derived great pleasure from doing so, for his father had done the same thirty years earlier, making a garden where there was none before.

My father told many stories about his childhood, but the stories were anecdotal, piecemeal and funny; they did not make a history. He dwelt mainly on the good times. He only gradually came to understand my desire to know about his family and his past, and much was still untold when he died. The tragedy that had befallen the family in the Holocaust was never actually concealed, but little was made of it, and as a child I witnessed without realising it his continuing guilt and grief. One could sense the past on him like a suit of clothes, but few explanations were ever given, and even as I grew into my teens I had little understanding of what had taken place.

My cousins, Franz Josef's children, were more in touch with their past and I rather envied them. My own background was mixed. My mother, Olive, was English. She met my father after he came to England, and they married in 1943. She never learnt German and didn't seem to take much interest in my father's past. Franz, on the other hand, who was six years older than my father, had married before the war in the early 1930s. His wife Edith was also a Czech Jew, and their first two children, Dinah and Ruth, were born in Czechoslovakia. In 1939 the family of four escaped together to Belfast and made their home there. We visited them quite often – at least every summer on our way to family holidays on the deserted, rainy beaches of southern Ireland.

Franz would have disputed that he was like my father, whom he regarded as too cautious. It is true that Franz was louder, larger in personality, more extrovert. He was impatient and uncompromising, a risk-taker; my father was exactly the opposite. Nonetheless, to me the two men possessed the same charm, the same passionate but thoughtful engagement in life. Franz was a favourite relative of mine and I, I think, of his, although I have to admit that he had the gift of making each person he met feel particularly favoured, so that looking back, I suspect I may have been deceived.

What I loved most about Franz was his extraordinary generosity. He was the most giving of men, and everything was done to extremes. On one Irish holiday I fell ill and was in bed feeling sick when Franz and my youngest cousin Billy came to visit. Marching into my hotel bedroom, Franz threw onto my bed not one, not two, but a huge heap of chocolate bars which, regardless of my bilious condition, were offered to make me better. They did, of course. Grand gestures like these have a magical quality in a child's eyes, but my mother found it hard to approve. Franz's love of excess could not be squared with her own comparatively austere upbringing, and there was always a slight tension between the families, Franz and Edith disapproving, in return, of what they saw as my mother's English restraint.

It must have been hard for my mother sometimes. Speaking to Franz or Edith on the phone, my father usually lapsed into German. I found it exciting but it must have made her feel excluded. What is more, my father never, to my knowledge, visited my mother's parents; instead he would despatch her with my sister and me in tow, for an annual summer trip to Kent while he remained at home.

On special occasions throughout her married life, my mother laid out the old Czech table linen, polished the silver, and washed with painstaking care the Bohemian glass and china. She continued to use the Czech bedlinen, which fastened with separate button strips and made changing the beds a complicated and time-consuming business. She accompanied my father to concerts and operas which were more to his taste than hers. She even tried, with limited success, to cook Czech specialities for him. But then, she had fallen for him head over heels, and it was a wartime wedding.

When my father died in 1987, his small diary for the year of 1939 was at the top of the pile of papers lying on his desk. Really, it was no surprise. As he grew older and his mental grasp deteriorated, the past increasingly reclaimed him. He wrote of it to me more often, and also more sadly than before. His feelings of guilt and regret grew stronger. He had fewer people around him with whom he shared his past.

The 1939 diary says very little and there are many blank pages. But silent as it is, it speaks to me of the misery of a year in which, finally, everything was lost. On 15 July of that year, my father boarded a train at the Masaryk Railway Station in Prague, bound for the Hook of Holland. On the evening of Sunday, 16 July, he arrived in London. He never returned to Czechoslovakia.

The diary was no surprise to me, but an old photograph given to me soon after my father's death, was. The photo is tiny, grey, with the appearance of a still taken at random from an ancient home movie. My grandmother, Valerie, is wearing a bathing costume and is standing up to her knees in water. She is laughing and splashing water at my grandfather, who stands, also wearing a swimsuit, to one

8

side. They are not young – I suppose my grandmother must be in her early fifties – and no one could call them good looking. They are a middle-aged couple, bathing in a lake somewhere in Czechoslovakia, one summer in the early 1930s, and they are transparently happy.

Until I looked at this photo, I don't think I had ever seen a picture of my grandparents that showed them relaxed and unposed. Asked to describe his mother, the adjective my father chose was 'beautiful'. I think he meant this more in a spiritual than a physical sense, although she is indeed beautiful in some of the photos I have of her. In her twenties and thirties she was large, dark-eyed, heavy, but as she grew older, she became statuesque and elegant. And as the bone structure of her face becomes, photo by photo, more prominent, her features become more clearly defined, her expression more intense and reflective, and yes, to me too she seems beautiful.

Beautiful – but not someone I could see as my grandmother. Until I saw her, on that faraway, sunny day in the 30s, up to her knees in water, laughing and splashing my grandfather, and he splashing her back. And when I look at that picture, I can see in the figure of my grandmother the ordinary reality of her life – her love affair and marriage, the birth of her children, the hard work in the house and in the family shop, all the joys and worries of her life. I can see her making *Apfelstrudel*, brushing her children's hair, talking with customers, choosing that new coat with the huge fur collar, trying to ease the aching tooth, the pain in her back. I can see the Prague ghetto,

Theresienstadt, and the train on its slow, slow journey, across Czechoslovakia, into Poland, and so at last to Treblinka and the gas chamber.

Forty years after my father fled from Prague, the wooden crates and trunks that fled with him were still piled on top of one another in our garage. The lists of what they had once contained, meticulously typed even in the chaos of departure, were still pinned inside the lids. Packed in those crates, and despatched from Prague before my father even knew whether he would be permitted to follow them, was antique furniture, oriental rugs, Bohemian glass, monogrammed linen, silver, china, pictures, jewellery. Somehow, who knows how, this precious cargo survived a hazardous journey across a Europe then on the eve of war, and arrived safe and sound in a northern English town.

So I grew up in a house part-furnished and decorated with the uprooted contents of my grandparents' home, and with artefacts treasured by my father to the point of reverence. Edith, Franz's wife, claimed that after 1939 possessions meant nothing to her any more. 'I could leave all this tomorrow without a backward glance,' she would say, indicating her own treasures. And I think my father was guiltily conscious that he attached undue importance to these material things.

But of course it was the loss of the people he loved that caused my father to cling to what he had. He spoke often – too often – about 'that swindler Matouschek', a Gentile who in 1939 was asked to look after some of the family jewellery. He concealed it in his Prague flat, in the urn containing his wife's ashes, but neither Matouschek nor the jewellery were seen again. Experiences like these rankled, and in old age my father became miserly about his possessions, making inventories, listing and re-listing each item in his sloping hand. He found it harder and harder to part with things. Loss had made leave-taking difficult.

But although my father treasured what had been so miraculously preserved, there was also a disjunction, a fracture of continuity between the past, present and future. He came to England, worked hard, met and married an English woman. She was, in those desperate refugee years, all that he could hope for: gentle, kind and loving. And she created for him a home, a family and a secure life. But to do that, the past had to be left behind, or at the very least placed where it would not get in the way.

Along with the china, glass and linen in those wooden crates there came an infinitely more valuable inheritance. Unlike the glass displayed on the sideboard, or the china and silver brought out at Christmas, this other inheritance was mostly ignored. Disordered piles of letters, and cigar boxes filled with crumpled photos, lay neglected in our attic and garage. At my uncle's house, there was a still larger collection, not just letters and photos but also journals and notebooks, newspaper cuttings, bills and receipts, school reports, certificates, scraps of verse, invitations, birth, marriage and death notices, recipes, maps, menus, medals, concert programmes . . . From before the First World War until the end of the Second World War and beyond, the family must have saved thousands of documents. They hoarded everything, and when they lost their home and country, they took with them what they had hoarded and never threw it away.

When my father died, a wave broke and deposited this memorabilia at my feet. The wave receded, my father was dead, and there was no one who could explain the meaning of what was left behind.

My father's brother Franz had died fifteen years earlier and the hoard he left behind was now in the hands of his wife Edith. Together Edith and I spent long hours sorting through documents and photos, she trawling her memory but unable to offer much that related to the time before she met Franz in the 1930s.

At first I was excited. I had never before seen my grandmother's handwriting and now here it was. I had never seen pictures of my great-grandparents and my great-uncles and aunts. Here they were. I had never been told of my uncle's experiences in the Austro-Hungarian army. Now I could read about them in his own words. A door I had been knocking on for years had suddenly swung open. The extent, variety and richness of the record was overwhelming. There was even the X-ray of my uncle's leg, shattered by a grenade in 1918; and a delicate, printed invitation to my great-grandparents' wedding in January 1874 – at one o'clock in the synagogue in Saaz, followed by lunch at two.

But then, what does one do with such an inheritance? Part of me wanted to leave it as it was – not quite to close the door on it, but to leave the disorder undisturbed. On the other hand, I was desperate for knowledge. I needed to discover everything this unlooked-for archive could tell me. And above all, I wanted to honour the people whom I loved but had never met.

So I began to put it in order. I spent long months carefully listing letters and placing them in chronological order. I pored over un-certain postmarks, identified handwriting and signatures, and re-united the pages of letters that had become separated. I spread out the photos and grouped them, searching with a magnifying glass for the tiniest shreds of evidence to help me attribute time and place. I bought files and albums and carefully preserved the evidence. I took what I had been given and added to it by reading and researching. I made contacts with other refugees and their families, attended lectures, travelled to Prague and toured the archives and museums. It was a labour of love that is still unfinished.

Sadly, in the process, a slow change happened. It seems to me now that the meaning of the documents as I first received them has been obscured and they no longer speak in the same way. They have become self-important, carefully preserved in their plastic wallets, filed in meticulous order, translated, annotated, explained. I look at them with pride but a little despair. A similar feeling sometimes strikes me in museums, where objects carefully, hygienically and oh-so-tastefully presented for inspection become harder, not easier, to see. I long for some subjective knowledge, to see the pen taken in the hand, the hand passing across the page, my grandmother seated at the table, the tilt of her head as she bends to her task, the smell of baking drifting in from the kitchen. I long to see the paper crisp and new as she bought it from the shop, the colour of the ink as it flowed from her pen, the stamps as the tobacconist sold them to her, and the expression on her face as she licks and seals the envelope.

Instead, the past is forever faded ink, worn clothes, and a battered leather suitcase that was once brash and new.

When I was young and watched films about the Holocaust and the death camps, I would scan the faces on the screen, hoping to see my grandmother. In the stumbling lines of anxious, unknowing people, among the hopeless faces gazing from the trains, among the naked, shaven, unidentifiable bodies, I hoped to see some sign that this one, no, this one perhaps, was *my* flesh and blood, so that through some additional knowledge about time and place, when and where and how, my sense of the dreadful isolation of her death would somehow be lessened.

Now, as an adult and a mother, I hope I will not see her. For what would I see? And what would I then know?

But my eyes still scan the faces. I am as intent on gathering knowledge as I ever was – more so, for I have discovered that each piece of new knowledge changes the old knowledge my father gave me, and changes too my relationship with my father, and my relationship with the past, so that the task becomes gargantuan, and the question is no longer what to know but where to stop.

2

Valerie and Heinrich

*T*he year is 1896. The place, Libotschan, a village on the western edge of Bohemia. Here, in a house in the Judenringl, lives Jakob Herrmann, a smart man with a goatee beard, the keeper of a general store that also stocks seed and tools for the local farmers.

Jakob's wife Berta died seven years ago at the age of thirty-seven, leaving him eight children: Valerie, Oscar, Kamill, Adele, Franz, Anna, Karl and Ida. Ida, the baby, was just one when her mother died.

Valerie, the oldest, is now twenty-two years old and Jakob depends on her more, perhaps, than he is prepared to admit. She not only cares for the family, but does much of the work in the shop too, often rising at three or four in the morning in winter to serve the men who had been hacking and pulling ice from the river.

Now Valerie is being courted by her future husband, Heinrich Kohner, who comes from the nearby town of Podersam. Heinrich is also a smart man, and he too sports a fashionable goatee and a moustache with the tips twirled slightly outwards.

As for Valerie, she has a strong face, abundant dark hair caught up in a chignon, watchful eyes, and by her own admission, she's not prepared to look at a man unless he can write well. She won't consider Herr Zentner, for example, no matter how determined he is to marry her, because his love letters are riddled with spelling mistakes.

Despite this rule, Valerie has had plenty of suitors before Heinrich Kohner. There was Karl Kussi, for example.*

> VALERIE: Karl Kussi once came to Libotschan on horseback, just to show me he could ride. People in the village laughed when they saw him and one man shouted out to him, 'Herr Karl, Fraülein Valli said I was to give you her regards.' And Karl believed him! Once he was thrown off his horse right below our window. I laughed, and he said, 'Fraülein Valli, do laugh again. It's lovelier than a whole opera.'
>
> One day I dropped a coin. Karl picked it up and begged me, 'Fraülein Valli, please may I keep it?' And the next thing I saw he had it on his watch chain. I was cross about that but he asked me not to be angry and proposed to me. It was just before I got engaged to Heinrich, and I said, 'I can't.' He said, 'I would treat you so tenderly, not even the smallest stone would hurt you.' Afterwards, Karl found out that I was about to get engaged. It was hard on him. He loved me so much that once he pretended to have become engaged himself, and even had the engagement announced, just to upset me. He named his first child Valerie.

It is Heinrich Kohner, not Karl Kussi, who will be the man for Valerie, and the people of Libotschan approve of her choice. They make fun of all her suitors except for Heinrich. He is their protégé. But her father, Jakob, is less impressed.

---

* This conversation between Valerie and Heinrich took place in the 1930s. Franz, their eldest son, prompted them to talk and recorded what they said in his diary.

VALERIE: Father was strict and he made a fuss about letting me go out on Sundays. First I had to do the dusting and clear up. I was pleased if I managed to get away by three o'clock. One Sunday there was a concert at the Nightingale Inn and Heinrich was there. He introduced himself as, 'Kohner, from Podersam,' and seated himself next to me. But he kept pulling at his stockings because the stockings wouldn't stay up, and afterwards Father asked, 'Who was that young man? It was dreadful, the way he was constantly fiddling with his stockings.'

After the concert, Heinrich sent his first letter to me, with a poem by Baumbach in it: 'Bin durch die Alpen gezogen . . .'

Later, I went to a ball in Podersam. It was my first ball. I wore a red dress, Empire style. I went with Tante Albine.

Before the ball, I felt sick. I'd eaten a piece of cake with coffee cream. Mrs Menschek, the seamstress from Saaz, who had come to do our hair, said, 'Wipe your eyes with your shirt tail.' But it didn't do any good. Then Onkel Karl gave me some soda water and I was sick on Tante Albine's carpet.

At the ball, I felt sick again and Heinrich took me to a room, brought me some brandy and kissed me. I felt awful. Someone kissing me! Then I was sick again.

HEINRICH: Then we danced all evening. The kisses brought her back to life! I said straight away, 'Fraülein, I'd like to marry you!'

VALERIE: The next day, Heinrich gave me a book of Baumbach's poems as a present and we arranged to meet in the park.

Despite this promising beginning, it is some time before Heinrich and Valerie are formally engaged. Time passes, and Valerie begins to feel it will never happen.

VALERIE: Before our engagement, we didn't see or write to each other for months. I was very unhappy. I thought we'd never be able to marry. For my birthday, I got a bouquet as big as a wheel from Heinrich. But from that October to the following March, there was nothing. Then Heinrich arrived and said, 'Now then, do you want to marry me or not?' I didn't know any longer whether I should or I shouldn't, but I said, 'Yes,' and a week later we got engaged.

Even so, I always believed I couldn't leave Father, and Heinrich's mother was very jealous. She thought I would deprive her of Heinrich's affection.

Jakob was not generous about his daughter's dowry. Maybe the business was not doing well, or maybe the matter of the stockings still rankled. Maybe the prospect of his own abandonment, as a widower with a business to run and seven children to care for, caused him to be mean-spirited.

> HEINRICH: Before we got engaged, Jakob said he would like to give Valli more money as a dowry. I said, 'I don't want any money, but my parents would.' So then he offered five thousand Floren. My father said, 'That's not a lot.' But I said, 'I'm satisfied. I'd marry her without money.'

Valerie and Heinrich were married on 20 May 1897 at the synagogue in Saaz. They went to live with Heinrich's parents in the flat above the Kohners' shop, ten miles away in Podersam. The shop, on a street just off the main square, is a stone's throw away from the Hotel Rose, the setting of the ball and their first kiss.

———

Jakob was not altogether correct in describing his daughter's suitor as a 'young man'. Heinrich Kohner was already thirty-five years old when he and Valerie became engaged, some twelve years older than her and only fifteen years younger than Jakob himself. But neither Valerie nor Heinrich mention their difference in age. Instead, Valerie is concerned that her father will not be able to manage his large family without her. And she is right, because within a couple of years of her wedding, Jakob sells the house in Libotschan, moves to a larger property in nearby Saaz, and invites his wife's sister Anna to come to live with them, run his house and care for his children.

Anna Ehrlich is middle-aged and looks as solid as they come. She has three grown-up children of her own and since she is also recently widowed, she is glad to take up this offer of a new role and a comfortable residence in Saaz. To Valerie's younger brothers and sisters she becomes not, as one might expect, 'Tante Anna' but 'Tante Ehrlich', and from now on she rules the household with a firm hand.

Valerie should not need to worry about them but, sadly, the new arrangement isn't completely satisfactory. In Valerie's opinion, it would have been better for everyone if Jakob had remarried and sent Tante Ehrlich and her children away. Her oldest child, Hugo, is a particular cause of bitterness. 'He bought three wagon-loads of lentils in Russia and we had to throw them out because they were bad. He ruined our horses. He was nasty with Kamill and Adele. Once he attacked Kamill with a chair.'

But Valerie's attention must now be elsewhere. Heinrich is now her first concern.

What sort of a man is he, this Heinrich Kohner, Valerie's new yet not-so-young husband?

Heinrich is the man who stands astride history, one foot planted in the nineteenth century, the other stepping energetically forward into the twentieth. He is the man who bursts into the light from an ancestral world made obscure by distance and difference. He is the man who moves from survival to success.

His father, Abraham, would surely have liked to have claimed that role, as would Abraham's father Moises, and Moises' father, whose name is unknown, before him, each in turn striving to better himself and his family, to secure a name, a reputation and a good living. But it is to Heinrich Kohner that the honour falls. And that is at least in part because, when Heinrich was no more than five years old and not yet dreaming of success, the Austro-Hungarian government in faraway Vienna granted full economic, social, personal and legal rights to all its Jewish people.

The Jews in Podersam began to flourish as they had never been able to before. The town flourished too. New breweries and distilleries grew up, increasing the demand for hops from the local farmers. A brickworks, and china and pottery factories were established. The railway arrived. Podersam was booming, and the door that had been closed for Abraham and Moises now stood open for Heinrich. He only required a modest amount of ambition, a generous helping of luck, and a dash of arrogance to carry him through.

So in the closing years of the nineteenth century, when Heinrich brings his bride back to the premises above the shop in Podersam, he already knows that the world is his for the taking. He has a successful business, the possibility of wealth, a position in the town, and a beautiful woman by his side – a woman with whom, incidentally, he is deeply in love.

3

Two Single Beds

*M*y parents' bedroom was divided into two territories. They did not have a double bed but slept continental-style in two single beds pushed together, and where the two beds met was the territorial dividing line.

My mother's bed was made up as most English beds were at the time with sheets, a blanket, an eiderdown in winter and a further blanket over the foot end of the bed to hold the eiderdown in place. Beneath the pillow lay her full-length nightdress with lace at the collar and cuffs. My father's bed, on the other hand, had two large continental-sized pillows and a puffy feather quilt. He used the linen that he had brought from Czechoslovakia: smooth damask, with button-strip fastenings. He wore a capacious white linen nightshirt with his initials embroidered on the pocket.

On my mother's side of the bedroom there was an English wardrobe filled with English clothes. There were tweed skirts, blouses and cardigans; a two-piece costume for special occasions with a brooch pinned to the lapel of the jacket; summer dresses with belted waists and knife-pleated skirts; slacks, a windcheater, and a collection of headscarves. Next to the wardrobe was a low dressing table on top of which my mother kept her Mason and Pearson hairbrush, a bottle of Yardley's English Lavender eau de toilette, and a pot of face powder. The pot had a bee in bas-relief on the lid.

On my father's side of the room there was furniture brought from the old country. A low wardrobe, contradictorily referred to as a tallboy, had hanging space for suits and shelves where carefully folded shirts and underwear were stacked. Since my father threw so little away, many of the shirts still bore labels revealing their foreign origins. On top of this wardrobe, he kept his violin. Its brown leather case, like the wardrobe, was compartmented inside to provide soft, lidded spaces for his rosin, mute and spare strings.

A large oak chest stood under the window. Inside the chest was another small, lidded compartment containing small treasures: lengths of lace and ribbon from the Podersam shop, an ancient silk scarf with fringes, a broken gold and enamel ring. In the main body of the chest was bed and table linen, a few German books, a fake-fur rug, a tiny silver travelling mug that folded, concertina-fashion, into a black leather case, and a strange hat, very old, moulded like a small rounded box to fit snugly over a bun on the back of the head, and covered in silver filigree and tiny silver beads – a Czechoslovakian wedding bonnet. Who knows who had worn it.

In the 1960s, when it became the thing to have every possible piece of furniture on castors, my parents put castors on the legs of their beds in order to make it easier for my mother to make them. One Sunday morning, hearing a crash, my sister and I ran to our parents' bedroom to find my father on the floor between the two beds. They had rolled smoothly apart as he, presumably, had rolled smoothly towards my mother. An unsuccessful border crossing.

4

High Hopes

*N*ow she was married, Valerie had a husband to care for, a house to manage, and a shop to run. And over the next six years, she had three children.

Franz Josef was her firstborn, in 1898; Berta Elise came two years later; then a gap of four years and, in 1905, 'our charming little Rudi Oscar'. Valerie recorded each birth in her prayer book.

The two boys were circumcised and given their Hebrew names – Jizchok ben Isroel for Franz, David ben Isroel for Rudi – on the eighth day after birth. Rabbi Rudolf Rychnovsky officiated, and for each ceremony, Heinrich walked the short distance from the house and shop up the gentle hill to the synagogue, proudly bearing his new baby in his arms.

Franz was born in late December when there was snow on the ground and every night brought a hard frost. Inside the Kohners' house, the water pump on the landing had to be covered with straw and sacking to prevent it freezing. Valerie worried about keeping the baby warm enough, but he was strong and healthy and gave no real cause for concern. When Valerie was busy in the shop, her mother-in-law, Grossmutter Marie, sat by the stove in the tiny kitchen on the floor above, rocking Franz in her arms.

He was a handsome baby with a smooth round head covered with silky stubble, irresistibly inviting a brush with the cheek or lips. His eyes were large and dark beneath a high forehead. They said he looked like his father, but those dark eyes were Valerie's. Gazing at him seated on her mother-in-law's lap, she saw herself looking out at the world a second time.

When Franz was nine months old, Valerie took him to the local photographer, Fritz Ideler, to have a portrait photograph made. She changed and dressed him, laid him in the large perambulator, and made her way up the hill to the grandly named Atelier Ideler. Fritz's wife greeted her at the door and, cooing over the baby, led her into her husband's studio.

It was chilly in the studio but at Fritz's suggestion, Valerie undressed Franz and laid him, stomach-down and naked, on a fur rug provided for the purpose. Franz pushed himself up on his forearms and kicked his legs. He liked being the centre of attention – and maybe the fur rug felt good on his stomach. There were no tears or complaints. Fritz stood by the camera and Valerie stood behind, calling softly to Franz so that he would look in her direction.

In this way, the photo froze for the future the look with which Franz responded to his mother's call.

By the time Rudi was born, Franz had already started elementary school in Podersam. And by the time Rudi started at the same school, Franz had left and was living in Prague, attending the Deutsches Staatsgymnasium in den Koeniglichen Weinbergen, a grammar school in a Prague suburb. Two years later, Berta followed Franz to Prague, and it must have seemed to Rudi that he would always be the last, the one left behind, the little brother. He sought comfort from his geese, a small flock of friends whose welfare was temporarily placed in his hands before they were killed for their meat, fat and feathers. His favourite was the one his father had named *die Jungfrau*, the Virgin. When in due course it was Rudi's turn to be sent to school in Prague, it was his beloved Jungfrau whom he missed the most.

Valerie and Heinrich had high hopes of their first son. From the moment of Franz's arrival in Prague, letters of exhortation and admonition travelled regularly from Podersam to Franz's lodgings.

They had found him accommodation with an old friend, Marie Rychnovsky, the widow of Rabbi Rychnovsky, the Podersam rabbi. Rabbi Rychnovsky had died two years before at the early age of fifty-five and Frau Rabbiner Rychnovsky (it was the convention to recognise her husband's status when addressing her) had moved to Prague, where she kept house for her son. Since Franz was learning the violin, and Valerie and Heinrich were determined to provide for his cultural as well as his academic education, it was an added bonus that Frau Rychnovsky's son was none other than Dr Ernst Rychnovsky, respected music critic of the *Prager Tagblatt* newspaper. Ernst Rychnovsky had studied musicology at the German University in Prague, and now, still only in his early thirties, he had already produced three works on the music of Bohemia and had begun to research the book he would later write on Smetana. In the small flat, it can't have been easy for him to pursue his academic interests, and he may not have welcomed the arrival of a young lodger, yet he seems to have taken Franz to concerts and the opera, and although Franz expressed no particular affection for either Herr Doktor or Frau Rabbiner Rychnovsky in his journals or memoirs, the arrangement seems to have been successful. Frau Rabbiner was kindly, and cooked and cared for Franz *in loco parentis*, receiving in return for her pains supplies of fruit, butter and other goods from the country, sent by Heinrich and Valerie. Only Frau Rabbiner's *Buchteln* – a sweet pastry usually stuffed with jam, which she instead filled with sauerkraut – proved more than Franz's good manners could bear. He would slip them unnoticed into his trouser pocket then dispose of them later on his way to school, dropping them through the grating in the pavement above a basement flat.

As a young man at the end of the First World War, Franz returned
to live in Prague and chose to lodge once again with the Rychnovskys.
But this is September 1909, and Franz is only ten years old when he
arrives on the Rychnovskys' doorstep for the first time.

26th September 1909
Heinrich to Franz

Lieber Franz

I know you're of good character and have a sense of honour and
you'll make every effort to please your teachers and us. You'll be a
good boy and attentive. It's easy for you because you are lodging
with a good family and all you need do is follow the example of
Herr Doktor who you should think of as taking my place. If you
turn out even half of what he is I'll be perfectly satisfied. You
know how hard it is for me to earn the money that's needed to
keep you there. Later you'll understand it better. But I'm fully
prepared to make every sacrifice. Just you be good and industrious
and never forget your loving father

Heinrich

30th September 1909
Valerie to Franz

Mein lieber Franzi!

We're glad to hear you've settled down so quickly and you have
such good intentions. I hope you won't forget to carry them out. I
was very annoyed that my big boy, of whom I'd like to be proud,
is so forgetful. Remember, you must wash every day. Don't think
you can let the odd day go by without it. And pay attention at
school and don't chat with your friends when you should be
listening. It's not like school in Podersam!

Rudi misses you terribly. Yesterday our apprentice in the shop wanted to give him a hand with something, and he told him, very emphatically, 'I'll do that myself, I'm no longer a child!' A little while ago he asked me, 'Mamma, have you ever been drunk?' in a tone which made me roar with laughter. He's a darling boy.

Bertl has started violin lessons. I am curious to hear what Herr Wolf will say about your playing. Please play only what Herr Doktor allows you to. And practise! Altogether, don't make it too difficult for Herr Doktor and the good Frau Rabbiner to get along with you. Be obedient and don't wake Herr Doktor from his morning sleep. It's time enough for you to get up at seven. My greetings to the Herr Doktor and Frau Rabbiner. I am writing this letter in the shop and it is very busy.

Valli Kohner

5th October 1909
Valerie to Franz

Mein lieber Franzl!

Your letter this week has not given us the pleasure we hoped for. The way you write shows you are writing only because you have to, and you haven't made up for what you omitted in the previous letter. We've no idea how you're doing at school and what you do with the rest of your time. Also, you must not be so immodest! You talk offhandedly about 'going to the theatre' but the fact is you can only go because the Herr Doktor is kind enough to take you. If I were in your position and allowed to see such a lovely performance, I'd have said: 'It was very beautiful', but you simply say it was 'quite good'. We're also surprised that you didn't fast for Yom Kippur like last year. I am sorry to have to tell you off, but it's got to be. You really have it so good. Few other children could say that of themselves and you must therefore show your gratitude by carrying out your good intentions.

Don't make it too hard for good Frau Rabbiner to get along with you, or else I'll come, and then you'll be in for something!

Your faithful Mamma

15th December 1909
Valerie to Franz

Mein lieber Franzi

Christmas is drawing near and since, as far as we can judge, you've tried to be a good boy you'll probably come home next week. Take care when you are on the train. Don't go near the door, or an open window, stay quietly in your seat. When you get to Saaz, don't leave any of your parcels behind. Please don't bring any unnecessary things, but do bring the pressed paper soldiers for Rudl. He's been dreaming about them for so long. Also you must find something small for Bertl, and perhaps a few sweets, which are appreciated so much more when they come from you. I've sent you a tie so you don't have to look shabby, and if your shoes are torn, bring them home. Rudl talks of nothing else but your homecoming.

Greetings from your Mamma

Heinrich adds:

Now that you've got a grade one in Latin, I'm happy to give you permission to come home for Christmas and am looking forward to seeing you here, cheerful and in good health.

5

If You Carry On Like This . . .

*I*n February 1910, Franz received his first written school report. At the top of the imposing document, his class teacher, Franz Egerer, had inscribed *sehr gut* in a flourishing hand. Only against 'Handwriting' is there anything less than *gut*, and in that subject Professor Egerer, had he but known it, was fighting a losing battle. If Professor Egerer had been more successful in teaching his pupil to write legibly, perhaps the wealth of letters and journal entries that Franz produced throughout his life would have been the cause of less frustration to his descendants.

No matter what the school report said, Valerie and Heinrich continued to worry, and they expressed their concerns in their letters – although 1910 begins in a quieter vein.

19th January 1910
Heinrich to Franz

Mein lieber Franz!

I am pleased that writing letters is no longer such a headache for you. We want to know how you are getting on. A pupil in your class told Onkel Siegmund that you are always embarrassed when the Herr Professor asks you a question. But you don't have to be worried. You know your stuff, and you are working hard at home, so I don't think you need be anxious.

You must also remember to say your prayers. It's a good thing and pleases God. You are, after all, staying with God-fearing people and they'll be much fonder of you and everything will be much easier for you if you follow their ways. Once you get used to praying, it'll become a need, like eating. When I sometimes don't get round to saying my morning prayers, I feel something is missing all day long. Keep well, dear boy.

Tata

26th January 1910
Valerie to Franz

Lieber Franzi!

Since your schoolmarks were not as good as they should have been, it was a reasonable punishment that Dr Rychnovsky didn't take you with him to the concert.

How is your Czech getting on? Any progress? You must learn it, though you find it hard. It's necessary to know both national languages these days if you want to get on.

On Sunday, dear Tata and I went for a walk about six in the evening. I suddenly saw a shining yellow star with a long white tail. It was Comet 1910A. You can imagine how proud I was of my discovery! Today one could see the comet again but it was much paler, even though its trail was longer than on Sunday. Everybody was out on the streets to see this rare phenomenon in the skies.

Your faithful mother,
Valli Kohner

13th June 1910
Heinrich and Valerie to Franz

Lieber Franz

If you carry on like this you'll see what happens. Where is your sense of self-respect and your promises? We fulfil every one of your wishes, you live like a prince, and learn nothing. Instead of advancing, you are falling back. I'd expected better of you. I am very angry and hope you'll repair the damage.

[Valerie adds]: Yes, going to the theatre, outings etc, you like all of that, but to make a bit of an effort when learning doesn't come so easily, you never think of that! Pull yourself together so we needn't be ashamed when Herr Baumgaertl or anyone else asks how you're progressing.

[Heinrich concludes:] To get a '3' in maths is due to nothing but slovenliness in my view, for you know your sums well, here at home, all of them. You're getting better and better! Franz! Franz!

22nd October 1910
Heinrich to Franz

Mein lieber Franz!

I am sorry to learn from Frau Rabbiner that you are no longer as good a lad, nor so industrious, and that you have a temper and are stubborn. You can imagine that this made us very sad. I shouldn't have believed it if I hadn't noticed these things during your holidays. I often punished you for it and you promised to improve, but is this how you keep your word? If sometimes you think you are being wronged, you are mistaken, for when you are good, everyone recognises it and praises you. I think you have had enough opportunity to notice what we have to put up with in the shop, how we are wronged and even offended, yet we can't afford to lose our temper. I've made up my mind to have you brought up as a decent, efficient human being who'll be of use to God and the world. At home here you've had enough occasion to see how, through industry and perseverance, modesty and kindness, one can become a real man. Learn from that! So far I've achieved everything I set out to do, though it hasn't always been easy. I wish and advise you, Franzl, to make an all-out effort to fulfil this my most heartfelt wish – otherwise you'll see what your Tata is capable of. I hope you'll take these admonitions to heart.

H Kohner

6

Bukwa

---

*T*he summer after Franz completed his first year at school in Prague, Heinrich planned a family outing to Bukwa, a small hamlet to the west of Podersam where Count Czernin, later to be Austro-Hungarian Foreign Minister, had a country residence. Countess Czernin would sometimes visit the Kohners' shop to buy dress material or some trimmings for a new hat. She had an account at the shop, and Valerie would note her purchases in the large, leather-covered account book. Heinrich, who teased and flirted with most of his female customers, would welcome the Countess instead with a formal greeting and an elegant bow, and charge her a little more than normal prices.

Perhaps it was this aristocratic connection that caused Heinrich to choose Bukwa as the destination for their trip. It was picturesque, set in rolling countryside on the forest edge, and the parkland surrounding the Count's mansion was perfect for a summer afternoon's stroll.

For the journey of some twelve miles, Heinrich hired a coach, complete with coachman, from Emil Killian's coach and wagon hire business in Schlossgasse, to ensure that the outing would be a great occasion.

The chosen day was a Sunday, and as the Kohners drove out of Podersam, there were plenty of people on their way to church, who stopped and waved. The open coach was a grand affair, pulled by two horses, with room for everyone to sit in comfort. Rudi, who was then five years old, was allowed the privilege of travelling next to the coachman. From this position, he had a commanding view, and could savour the smell of the leather reins, the horse blankets and the bag of oats tucked under the coachman's seat.

They travelled west through the village of Pomeisl, then on to Teutschenrust, the village where Heinrich was born. It was a hot day. The coach wheels gently stirred the dust on the unmade road, and only the sound of the horses' hooves disturbed the peace. In Bukwa, they stopped outside the small inn. They ate bread with home-made butter and Heinrich drank beer.

In the afternoon, Heinrich had arranged for a photograph to be taken, a formal, outdoor picture of the family group. Perhaps it was Fritz Ideler, the Podersam photographer, who received the commission. If so, he would have had to have made his own way from Podersam to Bukwa, carrying his heavy camera and tripod with him.

The photograph has an odd significance. The family, unsmiling and serious, are grouped around a bench, each person slightly separate from the rest. Heinrich, seated on the arm of the bench, his hands folded over a carved walking stick, has adopted a patriarchal pose. There is a wild flower in his buttonhole and a cigar, in a holder, in his mouth. His expression is one of self-conscious satisfaction. Next to him, his daughter Berta is demure in a pale lace dress and black woollen stockings. She holds a small wicker basket decorated with painted flowers. Rudi, whose boots only just touch the ground, wears (probably at his mother's insistence) a straw hat to keep the sun off his head. He is der Kleine, the Little One. Franz, der Grosse, wears the corduroy jacket he normally wears for school, and a shirt and tie that must have been uncomfortable on such a hot day. His watch, attached to a leather strap, sits in his breast pocket. Only Valerie, holding a small bunch of flowers, does not look at the camera but glances distractedly into the middle distance.

It was 1910, a golden time. There is a sense of ambitions achieved and promises fulfilled. The family business is flourishing. The family itself is thriving. Does it matter (Heinrich thinks) if Franz sometimes gets a lower mark than expected? Everyone can see he is a bright, talented boy. He will find his feet. And Berta, who practises the violin so assiduously: she is a good daughter and will surely be a good wife. And charming little Rudi, a late baby and so welcome, what does it matter if his mother spoils him a little? All is for the best in this best of all possible worlds.

7

Swimming Lessons

There were three rooms in the Rychnovskys' flat, serving as living, sleeping and music rooms, plus a kitchen, where the maid slept on a folding bed, and opposite the kitchen the 'kumbal', a windowless cupboard of a room which should have been the maid's accommodation but which was instead given to Franz. The door had to be left slightly open for air, so at night Franz had easy access to the maid herself – a source of solace to them both.

The flat was in a desirable, middle-class area of Prague that had in earlier times been the site of the royal vineyards. The Rych-novskys themselves were typical of the cultured, German-Jewish society of the area, and the maids they employed were Czech country girls on their own and in a large city for the first time in their lives, who worked from early morning until late at night for low wages.

Throughout Franz's time with the Rychnovskys, the assault of his parents' letters continued. They wrote at least once, sometimes twice a week, devoted, loving, anxious letters, often written in snatched time while working in the shop, always relentlessly urging him on to work harder, behave better and achieve more. They do not hold back from telling him how his younger sister and even little Rudi are getting high marks and excellent reports, and how fortunate he should consider himself to have parents who work so hard for him and spend so much money on his education. They themselves, they tell him, did not have the opportunities they are providing for him and it is his job to make the most of all they are giving him and not waste their money as he sometimes seems inclined to do.

One would have thought that such parental ambition, so clearly expressed, would be stifling and that Franz would have rebelled, become cynical perhaps, or fallen a little out of love with his parents. But not at all. He accepted their demands and reprimands, and although there are few of his own letters preserved from this time, his later writings express nothing but unreserved admiration, gratitude and love. And gradually, as Franz's school years go by, Heinrich and Valerie's letters begin to voice more openly the love and concern they had at first concealed.

During 1913, Valerie became unwell. She had a bad back and was physically exhausted. In May, she saw Franz briefly in Prague, staying overnight on her way to the fashionable spa town of Bad Gastein, where she stayed for a month to recuperate. So it fell to Heinrich to make the first response when Franz announced his intention of learning to swim.

4th June 1913
Heinrich to Franz

Mein lieber Franzi!

I agree that it would be sensible for you to learn to swim but you must be very cautious. Don't attempt any 'dares', and don't catch cold. You're sometimes like a little child without any common sense, and you don't think how you upset others. Be punctual for your lessons, and even more punctual when you go home so that Frau Rychnovsky doesn't worry unnecessarily. Even very skilled swimmers are exposed to many dangers, and many a swimmer has drowned, including our Onkel David in Nachod, because he went in the water when he was too hot. So I urge you once again to be sensible. Don't swallow water. But there again, don't be frightened. I learnt to swim without an instructor. I don't think Mama will gladly let you learn, but I think you'll soon master it, because

you're a good gymnast. You don't have to jump from the board, it
often leads to accidents . . .

Love
Tata

It seems, though, that the idea of swimming was soon abandoned
once Valerie returned from Bad Gastein.

27th June 1913
Valerie to Franz

Mein lieber Franzl!

I greatly enjoyed my stay in Gastein, but I am glad to be at home
once again and with dear Tata after such a long separation. I
received your letter with the news of your good marks in maths,
and I hope you will now be one of the top pupils. I am so glad
you will not be learning to swim in Prague. I should always have
worried that you might pick up some disease. I think Tante Ida has
told you that there is now a swimming pool in Saaz where you
could learn. Now if one was able to learn in the Salzkammergut
lakes, then I think even I could learn to swim.

   We're looking forward to having you at home again soon, and I
expect Frau Rabbiner will be glad to have a break from you . . .
We've got flowers in all our shop windows, mostly Alpine flowers
which I picked myself in the mountains and sent home.

   The new maid is turning out all right. There isn't any other
news.

Your faithful Mamma

The following year, Franz found the courage to broach the subject of
swimming again, and this time he received a more encouraging reply.

It's to be hoped he had the tact not to remind his mother of her previous letter.

21st March 1914
Valerie to Franz

My dear Franzl

You are a silly ass. Of course you can learn to swim at once. I think I told you that before. At least you will be able to make use of the skill in the summer. But don't overdo it. More than an hour is too much, I think, to start with, and you must not stay at the swimming baths, don't hang about, but go home straight away. I'm also glad that you want to learn English. When you come home for the holidays, you'll have to pass some of your great knowledge on to me. Dear Tata thinks you ought to have some long trousers made to go with your blue suit. If Frau Rabbiner is of the same opinion, go to Herr Glaser and ask whether he's still got the material.

Kisses from your Mama

Late in life, Franz recorded in his memoirs that he had been a weakling and a coward at elementary school in Podersam, and teachers were relieved when he did not take part in games because he invariably got hurt. For a time after his arrival in Prague, he didn't do any better. His school was accommodated in a row of old houses, joined together by narrow passages and stairs, with no facilities for physical education. Twice a week the boys would be taken to a nearby school for physical training under the direction of Professor Reinhold Michel. Michel, a tall, impressive German, chided Franz at first for his lack of manliness. Yet it seems as time went by, Michel gradually succeeded in encouraging him to enjoy his physical strength and agility. Later, Franz revelled in strenuous physical exercise and encouraged younger boys in the Jewish gymnastic clubs to do the same.

In 1919, following the First World War, a newspaper clipping reported the suicide of Professor Michel at the age of forty-four. He had enlisted at the beginning of the war, been taken prisoner by the Serbian army, and had returned to his homeland in 1918. The newspaper reporter stated that the reason for his suicide was unknown, but Franz felt sure his pride had been crushed by his experiences during the war. Michel was the only one of his professors whom he remembered with gratitude and respect, and he wrote: 'I owe Michel an awakening of my strength and pride, and I am sad to this day that his was broken.'

8

The Sea

~~~~~~~~~~

My grandmother never saw the sea. She visited and loved the lakes of her homeland, but she never knew what it was like to stand at the rim of a continent and watch the waves roll in from a watery horizon. Her sons, on the other hand, crossed seas, holidayed by the sea, and Franz eventually bought a house that looked out on to the sea, the shore not three hundred yards from his front door.

On our annual Irish holidays when I was a child, my father insisted that we swim in the sea every day. My mother did not join us and would remain on the beach or, in bad weather, in the car with a book.

But whatever the weather, my father would lead my sister and me, at a run, across the pebbles or the ridged sand (no matter if the tide was out and the race a long one) and, without hesitation or pause, into the waves. If we were lucky, we had sun, though it was rarely hot. But we also swam in drizzle and mist, in pouring rain, in gusting winds, and in full-blown storms. We almost always had the beaches to ourselves.

Once in, my father would stand with the water up to his waist and first splash and rub his upper body and face, exhaling

noisily, before striking out for an energetic swim. My sister and I, clad
in our 1950s swimsuits and with unbecoming swimming caps clamped
on our heads, swam less certainly, but we shouted out with the thrill
of it all – the stunning coldness of the water, the vastness of the waves,
the terrors of the creatures lurking below. And we gradually turned
blue with cold.

Afterwards we would race back to the car, where my mother would
greet us with towels and our clothes. It was almost impossible to dry
ourselves or dress with our numb and trembling hands, and before we
could get into the car, my father would insist on vigorously brushing
our bare feet and legs to get rid of the sand. He kept a brush for the
purpose in the boot of the car, with stiff bristles that scratched our
cold skin. Once decontaminated, we could get into the car and my
mother would give us chocolate.

This wasn't just about enjoyment of physical exercise: it was a
philosophy. The same philosophy required shallow, cool baths, or
cold showers, and vigorous rubbing down afterwards with a rough
linen towel. I cannot remember my father ever relaxing in a deep hot
bath, or succumbing to the pleasures of a large, soft terry towel.

On a later, continental holiday, probably in Austria, we came
across an outdoor exercise area with a high bar. While my sister and I
played on the other equipment, my father gripped the high bar and
began to pull himself up, then lower himself again, body held straight,
legs together, arm muscles bulging, counting each lift as he did it. We
watched in amazement. This was a side of our father we had never
known about. 'Stop!' cried my mother, seeing his gritted teeth and
reddening face. 'More! Keep going!' my sister and I urged. 'Seventeen,
eighteen, nineteen . . . twenty!'

9

Professor Novak's Ultimatum

*I*n the summer term of 1914, when Franz was fifteen years old, Professor Novak, Deputy Director of the Deutsches Staats-real gymnasium unexpectedly summoned Heinrich to the school for an interview. Franz was brought out of class. Ignoring Franz and speaking only to Heinrich, Professor Novak asked that Franz be moved to another school. Otherwise, he explained, he would be expelled.

When Heinrich asked for a reason, Professor Novak presented a letter he had received accusing Franz of visiting the red-light district behind the famous Pulverturm in the centre of Prague. The letter was anonymous.

Heinrich looked at his son and cried.

3rd May 1914
Valerie to Franz

I have received your nice letter and was very pleased. Do not worry, my dear boy, about this despicable thing they have done to us. I was very shaken, believe me, but I didn't for a moment believe those nasty things in the letter. I know you too well for that and am sure you are incapable of wickedness. Also I know you are being looked after by Frau Rychnovsky. Naturally, the big city presents many temptations and if one is not strong and gets into bad company, it is of course possible that nasty things may happen. But not with you, Franz; surely we can rely on you. You have always been a good son and will remain so.

Now let's say no more about the matter. Forget it, as dear Tata and I shall. That's the best thing.

10

Have You Heard . . . ?

*F*ranz's fall from grace coincided with a larger world event, which took place five hundred miles away.

On 28 June 1914, Archduke Franz Ferdinand, heir to the Austro-Hungarian throne, visited Sarajevo to inspect army manoeuvres. Serbian nationalists who had been plotting his assassination threw a grenade at his car as he travelled towards a reception at the city hall. Unharmed but indignant, he interrupted the Mayor's welcoming address: 'What is the good of your speeches? I come to Sarajevo on a visit, and I get bombs thrown at me. It is outrageous!'

Later, the imperial indignation was silenced. Gavrilo Princip, one of the three men detailed to assassinate Ferdinand that day, was sitting outside a café in Franz Josef Street when the cavalcade drove past. He fired from a distance of five feet, shooting the Archduke in the neck and his wife Sophie in the stomach. Both were killed.

Rudi and Berta, both at home in Podersam, lost no time in writing to Franz.

29 June 1914
Rudi to Franz

Lieber Franz

Have you heard about the heir to the throne and his wife? It's terrible. We've put notices in the shop window.

You'll be coming home soon. I hope you'll be bringing a good school report.

Love from Rudi

29 June 1914
Berta to Franz

Liebster Schwanz!

I bet there was a bit of a to do in Prague today. Everybody was agitated here too; people were standing around in groups everywhere. Lots of telegrams have been published and black flags are flying everywhere.

Yesterday we were in Saaz. Mammalittl has put on four kilograms!

Love and kisses from your faithful sister

Austro-Hungary declared war on Serbia on the day of the assassination. Yet Heinrich, adding a quick note to Franz on the back of Rudi and Berta's letters, makes no reference to either the assassination or the conflict to come, saying simply that he has refrained from writing recently because he does not want to distract Franz from his schoolwork. He could not know, but might perhaps have been thinking, that the war would provide distraction of a different kind for his eldest son.

11

Saaz and the House of the Schochet

As requested by Professor Novak, Heinrich took Franz away from the grammar school in Prague and sent him instead to a grammar school in Saaz, the provincial town not far from Podersam where Jakob Herrmann, Valerie's father, had set up house with Tante Ehrlich shortly after Valerie got married.

So Franz exchanged the sophisticated, highbrow atmosphere of the house of a rabbi's widow for lodgings with the family of a 'schochet' – the ritual slaughterer of the Saaz synagogue. Herr Wiener was a fat, shapeless, uncouth man, with a small, shrivelled wife who had one significant skill, the cooking of fatty Jewish food. Franz, now fifteen and used to the manners and customs of the Rychnovsky establishment, watched in disgust at mealtimes as the meat fat trickled down from the corners of Herr Wiener's mouth, staining the bulging waistcoat below. Before long he had asked to take his meals in his own room.

The Wieners had two daughters. The younger slept with her parents, but in a strangely provocative arrangement, the older daughter, Annie, occupied a room that led off the bedroom allocated to Franz. She was a few years older than Franz, who was, after all, still only fifteen, but an affair between them seemed inevitable and continued for the next two years with, astonishingly, no awkward consequences. At the same time, Franz's outward life was all that Germanism demanded. He belonged to the *Deutsche Wandervogel*, the young hikers' movement, and sang German folk songs. He read and wrote German poetry, and when the Saaz grammar school celebrated the Emperor's eighty-sixth birthday in 1916, Franz (with help from the

Professor of German) composed a eulogy, which was published in the local newspaper. He also wrote more intimate and sentimental eulogies in the style of the post-Romantic German poets for the blue-eyed, blonde-haired daughter of the Primarius of Saaz's general hospital. She never saw them – because he never showed them to her. When they passed each other in the evening corso (when the local population would promenade in Saaz's large main square), both would blush and neither spoke.

Franz disliked Saaz, and the Saazer Staatsgymnasium in particular. He was determined not to fit in. He had tasted the delights of Prague, and Prague was where he wanted to be. So it wasn't long before an argument began between him and another boy in his class, Matouschek. Franz, talking with one of the girls in his class and wanting to impress her, referred slightingly to the boys in the class as 'Plebejers', or plebs. The girl promptly passed the insult on to Matouschek and there was a fight. Afterwards, and in recognition of the bloody nose that Franz had administered to Matouschek's friend in the skirmish, Franz was ostracised by the boys. No one spoke to him, and he endured six months of this estrangement before Matouschek approached him one evening in the corso and apologised. It is some measure of Franz's arrogance – and, perhaps, his feelings about Saaz – that he turned down the chance of reconciliation.

The Wieners' house adjoined the synagogue on a street not far from the town square, and on one corner of the square, under the arched colonnade, were the offices of Franz's uncle, Karl Herrmann, Valerie's younger brother. Karl had been a young boy of ten when Valerie married and left home. Now he was in his late twenties and making a success of the business his father Jakob had begun all those years before in the nearby village of Libotschan. Jakob had run a village store, which also supplied the local farmers with seed. Now Karl was a successful seed merchant, with an office and a *Magazin* (storeroom) in

central Saaz, and a large open car in which he toured the neighbour-
hood, dealing with the wealthy farmers. In the *Magazin*, he stored not
only corn, grass and other seed but also saltpetre, which was imported
from Chile and used in the local tanning trade. In the office, Karl's
sister Ida helped to run the business, tapping out letters, orders and
invoices on her typewriter. When little Rudi was brought to visit,
Tante Ida, of whom he was very fond and who often told him jokes,
would allow him to play on her typewriter, the first he had ever seen.

In 1914, the year Franz arrived in Saaz, Karl and Ida were still living
there with their father in the family house. It stood in a small cobbled
square, only a few minutes' walk away from the family business in
Marktplatz and from the synagogue in Langegasse. Their siblings had
married and moved away, but this self-contained, intelligent pair
continued to inhabit the house long after their father's death the
following year. It was Onkel Karl who supported Franz in his feud
with Matouschek and friends. 'Let them bite on diamond,' he advised.

198 Schünitzplatz. That was the address. One photograph, probably
taken around this time, shows the house, large, square and solid. It

stands large, square and solid to this day, battered and abused but hardly changed. The bricks and mortar look so immutable that the human stories acted out within the walls seem elusive in comparison. Nonetheless, every time I look through the windows, I still expect to see figures from the past, moving jerkily as if in an old film. And at any moment, I imagine, I may see Onkel Karl, with his bald head and gentle eyes, emerge from the front door and set off towards the town, looking quietly prosperous in a suit, his watch chain looped across his waistcoat.

There are squatters in his house now. The children play noisily in the square and ask to have their photos taken by the tourists – which is what I am. My father, Rudi, was the same age as these children when he was taken to visit the house, and though he also knew it as an adult, he always remembered it through the eyes – and nose – of a child. The Herrmanns let out the ground floor to a teacher, Herr Fleischer, and lived themselves on the floor above, so to reach their front door one had to walk along a tiled passage, up the stone stairs, then through a glass door. And here was another corridor, with a strange pungent smell and doors leading to rooms on either side; and between the dining room and the neighbouring bedroom, hanging from the door frame, was a swing. And Rudi, pushed by Tante Ida, could swing from room to room, forwards into the dining room, backwards into the bedroom. He never tired of the game until Tante Erhlich, old, short-tempered and resplendent in shiny taffeta, put a stop to the fun.

198 Schünitzplatz has many stories to tell, but is stubbornly silent. The children running in and out of the broken front door are deaf to the voices in the walls. The children want to talk, but not about the past. They want to talk about our shiny car, about where we have come from (Germany? America? England?), about their brothers and sisters and friends, and where we can buy good ice cream. They can speak a little English and want to try it out.

Here is one story they do not know. On a dark evening in November 1926, Onkel Karl returned to this house from Prague.

He had been away for a little over a fortnight, and it had been a happy time. His sister Ida, at the age of thirty-eight and to the family's surprise and delight, had that month married Otto Robitschek, a widower with a farm near Aussig. So 198 Schünitzplatz, which had once been so full, was now empty. And Karl sat that night alone in the house and recorded his sister's remarkable marriage in the family Bible, writing in a spidery hand,

> On 7 November 1926, my dear little sister Ida, who was the cheerful spirit of our house, married Otto Robitschek in Habrovan. May the blessings of our Lord be with them. Written on 23 November when, on my return from Prague, I entered the utterly deserted house for the first time. Karl.

And these children playing in the square do not know that after sixteen years together, Ida and Otto were also together on 28 July 1942 when they travelled on Transport Aay from Terezin to Baranovici. Their ultimate destination was Minsk, and the train should have arrived there on 30 July, but over two days, 28 and 29 July, Wilhelm Kube, General Commissar for Belorussia, carried out a 'grand action' in Minsk in which 10,000 Jews were killed. So it seemed more efficient to stop the Aay transport at Baranovici railway station and liquidate the Terezin prisoners there.

Ida and Otto were ordered off the train along with everyone else and were asked to bring with them their utensils for lunch. The SS and the collaborating local police then marched them to a wood three miles away near the village of Kolpenice, and there they were shot. A group of prisoners from the nearby Koldichev camp buried the bodies in prepared pits.

Three miles is a long walk for lunch.

12

Rudi in Prague

In the black-and-white and sepia worlds of the oldest family photographs, no one appears as anything but dignified. There are no funny expressions, no tricks, no wrong moments. There is no drama; there are only tableaux. The faces stare out from the faded pictures, full of meaning yet so motionless that the meaning is obscured.

Later photos are more dynamic. There is expression, movement and context. Instead of holding me at arm's length, these photos are more generous and invite me in. But no sooner do I try to enter than the door slams shut.

The greatest barrier is the monochrome tint. I cannot imagine this world in colour, and the lack of it creates a distance far greater than time. I long to see the varying shades in my grandmother's hair, to know the colour of Berta's new dress and the paint they chose for the garden gate. The Kohners' shop window has no colourful merchandise, and the town itself, recorded street by street in numerous pictures, is dull on even the sunniest day.

To colour in the pictures of the past, I turn to the objects that have survived. The Bohemian glass decanter is a deep wine red; a glass goblet is sapphire blue. The divan cover is in subdued blacks and browns; the rugs are the colours and tones of a della Francesca mural. The white china tea service has old gold edging and a pattern of olive green leaves. The woven woollen shawl echoes the same golds, greens and reds.

I try to picture my family's home, full of these colours when they were new. So I imagine the lace that has aged to ivory as newly white, and the monogrammed bedlinen, which has been washed to near-transparent thinness, with a new damask sheen. I try to imagine the furniture unmarked and the violin music unyellowed, uncreased and untorn.

When I first visited Podersam and walked over the ground that had once formed part of the *Garten*, I picked up a conker in its broken shell. It had fallen from one of the horse chestnut trees that had bordered the *Garten*, and I knew that my grandmother might have picked up just such a conker, and that the deep rich brown of the nut and the milky whiteness of the shell lining would have been the same to her eyes as to mine. Yet it is still hard to believe, because the monochrome evidence of the old photos, and the harsh technicolour of my modern world, persuade me otherwise.

Sometimes I like to think about these old photographs in other ways, and instead of scrutinising them for every detail of their content, I think about them instead as events. For often what is most interesting about a photograph is the simple fact that it was taken. Behind every photo lies the intention to take it, and the idea that what it will record should, for whatever reason, be recorded. And looked at in this way, my large collection of photos from the past appears less random, less chaotic, and becomes a series of contiguous, significant moments in the lives of those I love.

On 28 June 1916, an unknown photographer was hired to record fifty small boys sitting the entrance examination to the Deutsches Staatsrealgymnasium in Prague. Near to the back, seated at a shared desk, Rudi Kohner looks fixedly at the camera. He is eleven years old and he knows that if he succeeds in this examination, he will at last be entering a world he both longs for and dreads. If he succeeds (and he is a clever boy), then he will follow his older brother's footsteps to a grammar school in Prague. All the intellectual and cultural resources of a high-class metropolitan grammar school, and indeed of Prague itself, will be at his disposal. And even now, at the age of eleven, he knows that Prague is an extraordinary city.

But he does not want to leave home. Prague is exciting, but he loves the secure, enclosed world of Podersam. He loves his first-floor home above the shop, his mother's cooking, his own bed, the roomy attics where the laundry is hung to dry, the warm stove in the kitchen where in winter Grossvater Abraham, now white-whiskered and blind, passes his days. He likes to sit on the balcony Heinrich has built at the back of the house, looking down on the yard of the Hotel Sonne and watching the coaches come and go, the horses harnessed, unharnessed, watered and fed. He likes the shop with its dark wooden drawers and shelves laden with boxes, and the *Kontor*, the office-cum-storeroom where, as a little boy, he would be tucked up to sleep when Valerie and Heinrich worked late. He loves his visits to the shop of Alois Lorber, the eccentric bachelor watchmaker with the thick black moustache, whose narrow shop stands opposite the Kohners' and where he sits for long hours in the dark back room, watching Herr Lorber at work. He is used to his morning walk to school, across the town square with its linden trees, war memorial and the statue of the Emperor Josef II, up the hill that leads towards the station, and so to the imposing Knaben Volks-und Bürgerschule. These days he does not even mind so much when Walter Mühlstein, old adversary but fellow Jew, lies in wait and throws dried horse dung at him.

But there was no going back. Rudi passed the examination, and one has to hope that it did not rub salt into still open wounds when he sent the photo of the examination, conveniently produced by the photographer in the form of a postcard, to his exiled older brother in Saaz, inscribing in ornate handwriting on the back, 'Beste Grüsse'.

13

Savouring Names

I have inherited a feast of names. I roll them over and over on my tongue to taste them all.

My grandmother was never 'grandmother' in my mind because during my childhood she was always referred to as Omama. Other children had grandmothers, who were generally cosy, benevolent and, most important, in evidence, and I had Omama.

But long before Valerie became my Omama, she acquired a plethora of other names with a wild variety of free spellings. She was Valli, also Walli, Wallei, or Walhi. She was Mama, or Mamma, and at the end of her letters the adjective that so often precedes that loving name is 'faithful'. Mamma became Mammalittl. In his letters home throughout the First World War, this is the name that Franz uses most often. 'Liebste Mammalittl,' he writes. 'What a sweet, dear and beautiful Mammalittl you are.'

Towards the end of her life she became 'Standuhr'. I will never know for certain why she was likened to a grandfather clock, although she was surely the steady mechanism at the family's heart.

Heinrich, Tata, Ta. And always, in Valerie's letters to the children, 'unser lieber Tata'. Franz, Franzi, Franzl, Franzele, Affenschwanz, Schwanz, Schwanzerl, der Grosse . . . Berta, Bertl, Berterle, Blümele, Putte . . . Rudolf, Rudi, Rudl, Ruderle, Bübl, Bübele, der Kleine, and sometimes, Schnopper.

The sounds of these names are soft to my ear. I grew up with German sounds, which seemed to me euphonious and gentle. The debasement of the German accent through Nazi caricatures on film and television had not yet occurred, and I had no reason to associate

German sounds with violence or fear. I heard my father speak a language of love and laughter, a language that was all the more expressive because, to my ears as a child, it had no literal meaning. Listening to my father speaking German, I heard a hidden part of him give voice.

14

Der Garten

*I*n August 1916, Heinrich concluded a business deal that had long been a dream of his. He bought a plot of land.

He bought it from the estate of the Podersam lawyer, Dr Schneider, whose office was just round the corner from the Kohners' shop, opposite the Mühlsteins' leather shop on Saazerstrasse. During his university days, Dr Schneider had been an enthusiastic member of the duelling and drinking student fraternity, the right-wing *Schlagende Verbindungen*. As a result, he returned to Podersam with the traditional sabre scars on his ruddy cheeks and a large beer stomach. Having continued to fuel his paunch in the bars of the Hotel Rose and the Hotel Sonne (both a stone's throw from his office), he died young, leaving a wife and small son. When Frau Schneider and her son moved away, Heinrich, seizing his chance, bought the land which was to become the *Garten*.

It is impossible to anglicise the word to 'garden' and keep its meaning. When as a child I listened to my father's descriptions of its glories, it was always the *Garten*. If a translation has to be made, then 'Paradise' might be a more suitable word. My father called it an 'Island of Happiness'. The capital letters were his own.

It did not adjoin the house, but was not far distant and could be seen from the first-floor rear balcony. There was about half an acre of land in all, edged on two sides by an imposing red-brick wall and bordered on the third by the *Sauerbach*, a brook so called because of the slime and smell it picked up from the boggy meadows and the absence of a proper sewage system in the town. The fourth side was formed by the wall of the big barn belonging to Friedrich Löwy, the

Jewish grain merchant. Within these perimeters there was mature land, which Heinrich employed a landscape gardener from Saaz to improve, lay grass and paths, plant trees, roses and shrubs, and build a summerhouse with a pergola in front and a divan inside where he could rest.

Heinrich loved the *Garten* with a passion. It was land, territory, kingdom; the jewel in his Jewish crown. He loved it as land, for connection and growth, and he loved it as a symbol of rootedness, recognition and identity. He loved it, too, simply as a family place, where he and those most dear to him met, ate, talked and played, returning to it summer weekend after summer weekend, even after the children had grown and left home.

Through the *Garten*, Heinrich founded a dynasty of gardeners. Many years later, when my father walked out into his own English garden each summer morning to pick an early rose for his buttonhole, he was doing no more than his father had done before him. In Podersam, people judged from Heinrich's buttonhole whether he was in a good mood and it would be wise to come shopping that day.

It was impossible then to conceive of a universe that did not contain the *Garten*.

The *Garten* stood, and for me still stands, for the small world my family inhabited and loved. Heinrich swore to his children that if, after his death, they even so much as considered selling the *Garten*, he would personally descend from the clouds to prevent it.

In the end, this wasn't necessary. Heinrich was removed from his *Garten*, not it from him. Later, the land was appropriated and built over, and now it lies under concrete. I like to think, however, that the soil that meant so much still rests in a quiet, moist layer beneath the noise of the modern traffic, an earthy seam of memories of loving, passionate people struggling to establish eternity in Eden.

15

Franz in Leitmeritz

───────── ❦ ─────────

*I*ncreasingly, the war began to make claims on the family.

Heinrich's younger brother Eduard was already a professional soldier. Valerie's brother Kamill left his home, wife and two small sons to fight, and was taken prisoner on the Russian front. Herrmann Mandl, husband of Valerie's sister Adele, was posted to Hungary as a radio operator. Onkel Karl exchanged the seed trade for the administration of an army hospital, leaving the house and business in Saaz in his sister Ida's hands.

Eduard was in his forties, Herrmann and Kamill in their late thirties, Karl was just thirty. But Franz was seventeen years old, and in his view, Gavrilo Princip had done him a good turn. He could not wait to enlist. This was to be his escape from provincialism, his entry into the adult world. Two years after his unwilling arrival in Saaz, he was released from the Staatsgymnasium to queue with other men and boys for the *Assentierung*, the medical examination for military service, held in the dance hall of the Hotel Rose in Podersam. When the commission of officers and army doctors declared him fit, he was so overjoyed that he ran naked from the hall, shouting jubilantly, and had to sneak back later to retrieve his clothes. He returned home in proud anticipation of becoming an *Einjährig-Freiwilliger*, a one-year, voluntary officer cadet. It was a misnomer, of course. In 1916 there was nothing voluntary or one-yearly any more.

Shortly afterwards, Franz left for Leitmeritz, an elegant, prosperous town fifty miles north-east of Podersam, for a six-month course at an officers' training school. He hoped for a fine uniform, but Heinrich had other views and insisted on the basic uniform supplied by the state, conceding only the addition of some calf-leather boots.

A larger and more practical problem was the need for a horse. Heinrich was no judge of horse-flesh and took the advice of the regimental vet, who sold him a small, lively, short-legged horse called Lola. Lola already had a festering saddle sore on her shoulders, and the strenuous exercises in the riding school each morning, when the cadets swung themselves on and off their horses at the gallop and performed all kinds of horseback gymnastics, slowly deepened the wound until the poor horse screamed with pain. She was declared unfit for military service  before Franz's first month of training was out, and had to be retired. So, to his disappointment, Franz found himself riding horses used and abused by generations of recruits until a new horse could be bought.

The regime at Leitmeritz was strenuous: gymnastics and marching from 6 a.m. to 7 a.m., work in the riding school 7 a.m. to 9 a.m., dry, clean and stable the horses 9 a.m. to 10 a.m., exercises with the heavy cannon 10 a.m. to 12 a.m. Lunch, then classes all afternoon, taught by the officers, on tactics, ballistics, geography, anatomy and diseases of the horse . . . At 6 p.m. the horses had to be fed and watered before the cadets themselves could eat. The horses, of course, came first.

Feldwebel Fritsche, heavy-set with a thick red moustache, gave the orders. He bullied the thirty young cadets through the day, swore at them, cursed their ineptitude and weakness – and mothered them tenderly. Finding Franz's thighs raw from rough riding, he showed him how he should piss into his cupped hands and rub the urine into the wounds to close and harden them. The next morning, he was roaring at Franz again as he failed to achieve a hundred knee bends with his rifle held horizontally in front of his chest. 'Sau civilist!'

Maxl was the name of Franz's second horse, a tall brown gelding, once a colonel's horse, extrovert and spirited. They made an arrogant pair, and for the first time in his life, Franz found himself in love.

Franz Diary Entry autumn 1916

We went out today with our Oberleutnant who was riding Perle, a slim, lively hunter. There were about a dozen of us cadets, and the Oberleutnant led us out over the training ground and up onto the mountain ridge that runs behind the barracks. After a sharp trot, he commanded us to gallop, indicating that we could let our horses have their heads. The Oberleutnant was ahead of us, but at his command, I tucked myself down behind Maxl's arched neck, whispered in his ear, and relaxed the reins, and within seconds, I had left the others behind and passed Perle. The Oberleutnant shouted 'Halt!' but I couldn't pull Maxl up. He was flying over the turf, his belly almost skimming the ground, and his blood was up. It took me half a mile to rein him in so that I could return to the group, and I was sentenced immediately to eight days' detention in the barracks guard room.

But when we returned to the officers' mess, and I had spent two hours rubbing Maxl down with straw, I was forgiven.

16

Krakow

When Franz enlisted, he had the chance to apply to a regiment of his choice. Wildly excited and overambitious, he favoured an infantry corps with a reputation for daredevilry, maybe the Viennese *Hoch-und-Deutschmeister* 73rd. But Heinrich intervened. One afternoon, he called on Frau Direktor Hossner, the widow of a distinguished Podersam schoolmaster, whose son was a captain in a heavy field artillery regiment. After a quiet talk in her elegant apartment, strings were pulled and arrangements made for Franz to join Captain Hossner's regiment.

In November 1916, having passed the examinations at the end of his training course with just 'adequate' marks, Einjährig-Freiwilliger Corporal Kohner, Franz Josef was detailed to join the *Kaiserliche Koenigliche schwere Landwehr Feldartillerie-Regiment Nr 26, Batterie 4*, then positioned outside Krakow, 250 miles away in Galicia. Filled with apprehension, Valerie and Heinrich travelled from Podersam to Leitmeritz to see him off. The men slipped and slithered their way from the barracks to the railway station, the damp snow forming balls under their horses' hooves. At the railway station, two railway cars awaited them; one, carrying oats and hay for the horses, was also where the privates would sleep; the other was reserved for the officer-cadets. And while Franz, conscious of his new responsibilities, officiously examined every bale of hay, checking there was no wire to cut the horses' legs, Valerie sat in the station waiting room and wept.

26 November 1916
Franz to Heinrich and Valerie

Meine Lieben

We're likely to stay here for several weeks. Please could you send me a light green shirt, a raincoat, a couple of towels, and some money for Krakow? I expect we'll be going to Krakow a lot because there's nothing to do here in Lublin and it's an hour's trip on horseback into the centre of town. I could also do with some bread, but Maxl is all right and doesn't need oats.

We are living four or five of us to a room in the officers' quarters of the Rakowicz cavalry barracks – or what qualifies here as officers' quarters.

Krakow is a very beautiful city, like Prague, old with attractive churches, towers and cafés, the occasional Jewish rag-trader, and some big shops. There are lots of troops. Our commander, Leutnant Maly, seems a fierce man, much feared. He is on leave at present.

Franz

29 November 1916
Valerie to Franz

Mein lieber Franzl

I'm relieved to hear you have arrived in Krakow after your long journey, and that you are not at the very front line. We have arranged for parcels to be sent to you with food and money, and we are making enquiries about the raincoat you need. Meanwhile I hope your fur coat will do to keep out the damp.

How did you survive that endless journey? Did your supplies and good spirits last out to the end? Was there any heating? I expect Maxl was glad to get out of his box.

You'll all soon recover from the hardships you've endured now that you're in Krakow. I suppose it's a pleasant town. It wouldn't be too difficult for us to get there, and that would be nice, but then parting again would be hard, so maybe it's better if we stay at home.

Rudl keeps getting 'I's' in his German work, so you see he is following your good example. Doesn't that please you? By the way, Popuda, who used to patch your trousers, died suddenly yesterday. Otherwise, there's nothing new here.

A thousand kisses from your ever loving faithful
Mama

29 November 1916
Heinrich to Franz

Mein lieber Junger

We accompanied you in spirit on your long journey. Use your time in Krakow well, have a look around, but don't go out on your own. Take care. There are good and bad people everywhere, honest people and thieves.

We will send you the raincoat you need, and a fur collar, either from Prague, or we will have one made in Vienna. We are also sending a hundred Kronen. Get yourself some food so you stay strong and healthy. Keep off smoking and drink, and beware of certain women, they come cheap in Galicia but they are also dirty and diseased. Do try and remain a bit of my boy, and be good. It will give me joy.

Fondest love
Your Tata

2 December 1916
Franz to Heinrich and Valerie

Liebste Eltern!

I have just given the orderly two Kronen for some bacon he's brought me from town, so now I'm down to my last ten Kronen note. I've no option but to ask you for some money. Krakow is an expensive town – except for food which is cheaper than at home. What we get in the officers' mess is very good, ample and cheap, but one still can't manage without all sorts of extra expenses. I only had 140 Kronen with me, and the journey here was dear, so now I've got through it. Hosch and Buxbaum had 300 Kronen and they've ended up with a hundred. Even our virtuous comrade Schmidt's finances have run down from 180 to 20 Kronen. So, please send me money as soon as possible for this damned Krakow, or else I'll starve, or worse, I'll have to borrow.

If they'd sent me straight to the trenches, I'd have been spared these problems.

In a few days our battery commander Leutnant Maly is coming back from leave, and all we'll need then are our artillery pieces before we move out. If I haven't got a raincoat from you by then, I'll buy it here, that is if I've any money.

Maxl is doing all right, only he's in the same boat as me so far as food goes. He hasn't got enough. But my crafty orderly, Smacylo, managed to get some oats.

Less important than money, but very welcome, would be a piece of butter and a bit of bread and chocolate.

Hope you're all well.
With love from your grateful son.

2 December 1916,
Berta (in Prague) to Franz
[The Emperor Franz Josef
had died on 21 November 1916].

Liebster Schwanzerl!

Yesterday I went to a concert with Rudl. Today I met him coming out of school, looking a terrible mess from eating bread with Povidl [plum jam], with a few bits still in his pocket, unwrapped of course and horribly messy. I advised him to eat them, which he then did with great relish!

All week there have been ceremonies in the churches, synagogues and schools. Mimi Lenhart even went to the funeral in Vienna.

I must be off to school now.

A million kisses from your faithful
Bertl

2 December 1916
Valerie to Franz

Liebster Franzl!

Today Frau Direktor Hossner was with me in the temple, and yesterday I went with her to church for the mourning ceremonies. How sad that our good Emperor was not able to live to see a victorious peace.

Your Mamma

4 December 1916
Heinrich to Franz

Mein liebster Junge

We've sent you two food parcels and a hundred Kronen, also a
parcel for His Majesty Maxl. I hope you received it, and the
shirt from Leitmeritz. We are neither writing nor sending
anything that is not allowed, for we are good Germans and
Austrians and hope that our just cause will soon lead to a
happy end.

Fondest love
Your Tata

5 December 1916
Valerie to Franz

Mein lieber Franzl

We were grieved you had money and food problems for a few days
in Krakow. Unfortunately we couldn't speed things up here.
Everything takes such a long time. I hope by now you have
received the parcels we have sent. We are still trying to obtain the
raincoat.

I could smack myself for not having sent you far more food,
money, and supplies for Maxl too. But you didn't want it then, and
we could not foresee that everything would be used up in the
journey to Krakow. Well, no more of that.

As I write, a bunch of children are just rushing past the
house. It's St Nicholas's day today. Do you remember how
you used to put out a stocking when you were a child? I
wish those days were back and you were a little boy
again. How happy and carefree we would be. Your
rocking horse and wooden sword were your entire armoury

then. But with God's help even these dark days will pass, and all the evil things will be but a bad dream, and you will be back with us safe and sound and cheerful. May God let it be so and protect you for our sake too. This is what your faithful, loving Mama is praying for every day and every hour.

13 December 1916
Franz to Valerie and Heinrich

Liebste Eltern!

I'm writing this in the dug-out, which we found ready for us, complete with a table and bench and little stove. There are a lot of cracks between the boards of the hut, and it is still without turf to cover the windward side, but it's quite nice and warm, though sometimes your eyes sting from the smoke and you can hardly see the packs hanging on the wall or the radio on the shelf. Most of the space is taken up with three beds, which are partly home-made. Mine consists of a birch tree base with wires drawn across, which I rescued from an old flooded dug-out. I have hay in canvas as a mattress, and my sleeping bag, plus blankets, lie on top. As you can tell, very comfortable. Next to me there is Schmidt's bed. I am good friends with him, as is Maxl with Schmidt's horse Selma. They've become an inseparable pair. But I'm disappointed with the other two men. Hosch, whom I sometimes prefer, lives here. Buxbaum has annexed a tiny old dug-out for himself. As I'm writing, Hosch and Schmidt are playing chess by candlelight, and now and then a machine gun rattles or the sound of some heavy guns echoes like thunder.

Please don't send me anything that needs boiling in water, because it stinks even when it's cooked. Butter, sausage, bread are all welcome. If I've got something to drink, I can stomach even bacon. I also have another request: a pair of warm knitted gloves.

Maxl is fine. He's in a stable which is temporarily only covered with brushwood, but it's due to be roofed soon.

With fondest love from your son
Franz

16 December 1916
Franz to Valerie and Heinrich

Meine Lieben

Please don't think I'm cheeky for sending you a list of things I want. I'm only doing it so that you don't send things that won't be any use. I'd also like to ask you to keep any letters in which I paint a picture of my life in the field. One day, if I get back, I'd like to read them.

Yesterday I was in the trench. Until I get to know the lie of the land, I've been detailed to the telephonists, and yesterday we laid a cable to an observation point through the woods, across barbed wire entanglements, until we reached an open field which was within enemy sights. It's a weird feeling to hear rifle fire for the first time. The shots are presumably aimed at me yet are nothing but bangs and a brief whistling sound. I was fired at but only heard the bang, not the whistling. I ran along the trench for a long time and there was Russian gun fire as well as our own. It was very interesting. In the afternoon, I rode as orderly with the first lieutenant to headquarters. Maxl was very sprightly, though he often sank in swampy places. Once, when the road was interrupted by a stretch of water, the lieutenant's horse wouldn't cross. So I was given the order, 'You, try!' So I rode in and Maxl sank up to his belly but then seemed to get a foothold on firm ground and managed to struggle out, shake himself, and off we went at a merry trot.

With fondest love from your son
Franz

—————— ∿   ᴄ⌐——————

18 December 1916
Franz to Valerie and Heinrich

Liebste Eltern

Today I'm in the foremost trenches. As I'm writing this, I'm getting telephone signals through my headphones and the bullets and guns whistle and bang in front of us and behind us. After each salvo, the sand trickles in through the chimney. I've just been reading some novels, and I'm very well. After 48 hours' duty, I'm looking forward to two days off. I'm going back to the battery, and it would be wonderful to find a parcel from you. Please could you send me some wool and a needle for darning?

   People in the hinterland imagine everything here is far worse than it is. I hope you're not worrying when I say how things are. Mostly I am just terribly bored. When I'm freezing cold, I know I'll be able to sit by a stove in a few hours' time, and when I'm hungry, I can eat. So despite war and winter, I'm doing better than a lot of others, and I get so many things from you in your parcels, I can't thank you enough.

Franz

—————— ∿   ᴄ⌐——————

22 December 1916
Valerie to Franz

Liebster Franzl

I have just sent off all the things you asked for, but I don't yet
know whether the things I have sent to Krakow have reached you.
Of course, one can't get much into these small boxes, nor can we
send more than two or three each day, but I hope they help to fill
a gap in your supplies.

All your letters and postcards are being kept in a box, and one
day when you read them, it will seem like a fairytale and you will
hardly be able to believe you lived through so much.

Grossvater says he really doesn't have any business being here
on this earth any more, but he thinks he had better wait until his
Franzele returns.

A thousand kisses from your
Mama

23 December 1916
Franz to Heinrich and Valerie

Liebste Eltern

I'm doing all right. We're rebuilding our dug-out and improving
the roof. Leutnant Krause is bringing us food from the officers'
mess and so far we've had a bottle of wine, a tin of cherries and
a tin of greengages. Maxl is fine, but he isn't being ridden so he
is very wild. The weather's wonderful too, with snow and
sunshine.

I need some washing soda, and a box to keep matches in, but
please don't send too much other stuff. You say you are sending
one or two parcels a day and I dread getting too much. Don't
worry unnecessarily or spend too much.

I have just finished my last stint on telephone duty. The communication centre is a dangerous place and often means six hours of detonations and all round din. Telephone service further back from the front is less dangerous and worrying. But now I'm going to be detailed as an aide-de-camp. The major says it's an honour and he hopes he'll be able to rely on me. I'm due to report tomorrow morning.

I hope you have a good rest during the Christmas holidays.

Your grateful son

25 December 1916
Rudi to Franz

Liebster Franz!

I got lots of things for Christmas. From Tata, a fine paint box; from Herr Koponasek and Tante Ida, books.

I've been given a violin, but only for practice for the moment. If you get a fiddle from Herr Kohout, you can give me yours. I played it today and I nearly kept it.

Dear Mamma is always agitated if a day passes without a letter or card from you. She's busy now preparing supper, and because Herr Lenhart is coming, all the fine crockery is being laid out.

I hope the war is over soon and you come home to tell us all about it. I must stop now because Mama wants to get at the table. Keep well and take care you're not hit by a shell. Shoot lots of Russians.

Kisses from your brother Rudi

25 December 1916

Berta to Franz, added to Rudi's letter

Lieber Franzerl!

I don't know what Rudi has said but just in case, I'll tell you that
Herr Lenhart is coming and dear Mama is very worked up about
being hostess. Yesterday we all played cards, following Rudl's
ingenious rules, which meant that as usual we first swore at each
other and then gave up.

Ten thousand kisses from
Bertl

25 December 1916

Franz to Heinrich and Valerie

Meine Lieben!

Last night I went out to our guns. It was a strange evening with a
few bright clouds and the wind whistling through the black trees
like on other evenings, but this time the men were leaning against
the gun carriages talking of going home and their friends at home.
In one of the tents there were three of them, and it was the
birthday of one, which they celebrated with a bit of army-issue
wine and played on the mouth organ and the violin. I listened till
darkness fell. As long as one doesn't start thinking, it's all right,
but if you once let yourself start to think, all kinds of memories
crowd in. I can smell all the different aromas of home – the smell
of the big room, and the hot air on the ground at midday, and I
can hear footsteps on the stair carpet, and Tata whistling.

Maxl's stable is right next to my hut at present. I'm with him all
day. I let him out first thing to graze and watch him conducting
his love affairs!

With fondest love from your son
Franz

25 December 1916
Heinrich to Franz

Mein liebster Franzl!

All our thoughts and talk are about you and we all have but one wish: to embrace you again in good health. I know, my dear boy, that thousands are out there, and that all their dear ones at home have the same wish. I know what war means, I don't forget it for a moment. We are all patriots, and we've never missed a chance of proving it, which is why I gladly make this sacrifice, but I never believed it would be so hard. Do your duty, help as much as you can to win the war, for we must and will win. But Franzl, you are still a child. Don't get carried away. There's no need for acts of bravado, or doing things that are against regulations. Thousands have lost their lives that way without benefiting anyone. Don't rush into danger. Let people older than you teach you what to do, obey your superiors, and you'll see you'll be able to face many a danger, and one day you'll become a smart, strapping officer.

Here we have a lot of visitors. But we are missing our Franz.

Fondest love
Your Tata

17

Being British

'*I*'m backing Britain,' sang Bruce Forsyth in 1968,

'Yes, I'm backing Britain,
We're all backing Britain
The feeling is growing
So let's keep it going
The good times are blowing our way.'

In Bradford's local newspaper a photo appeared, showing a local businessman in his office, sporting a Union Jack badge. His name was Mr Rudolf Kohner. He and his staff of three, he said, were going to work an extra half hour a day without pay in support of the 'I'm backing Britain' campaign.

At that time, my father was a successful area manager for a national company selling industrial heating and ventilation units. He was an established local businessman, a high earner with a large company car and a pleasant detached house on the edge of Bradford that he had built himself. He worked long hours, was committed to improving not just his own but also the company's performance and profitability, and believed in the economic and national importance of small-scale British business activity. Perhaps on the surface he was not such an unlikely candidate to support Harold Wilson's campaign to promote British standards, British jobs and British investment.

It was not that he wanted to be more British than the British. It was not that he had adopted a new persona, a new nationality (although by this time he was a naturalised British citizen), or new political allegiances. I don't believe it was even gratitude to the country that had accepted and sheltered him. But my father had a capacity for fierce loyalty, and what may look like cheap chauvinism was in fact, I think, something deeper and more strongly felt.

Heinrich and Valerie felt just as deeply about their place within the Empire, and their feelings were perhaps the stronger because as Jews they valued their liberties and their potentialities highly. For them and their kind, it had not always been like this. It had not been like this, in fact, in living memory. So, during the First World War, they knew it to be their duty to support the Austro-Hungarian army and its cause, and their letters never question the necessity and utter right-ness of the conflict. If it causes them hardship, if they are beside themselves with anxiety about the fate of their son, and if they long for peace, they are still unshakeable in their belief that this has to be. And they want to play an honourable part.

As a boy, my father was less enthusiastic about the war. He was often hungry as a schoolboy in Prague and developed boils on his legs. In later life he still mentioned these and would display the (I thought rather faint and disappointing) scars. But he imbibed from his parents a powerful combination of duty and fervent patriotism, and maybe it was that which was still alive in him in 1968, re-channelled into Gannex-mac politics.

Or maybe he simply saw a good business opportunity. A bit of publicity, his photo in the paper, his company's name associated with a national campaign, the good times blowing his way. My father was nothing if not a salesman. A persuader, a publicist, a closet politician. A 1960s spin doctor with a European accent and a Union Jack badge.

18

Small and Safe

*P*odersam.

At first, I didn't know the town had a Czech name as well as its German one. It was simply Podersam, the place where, long, long ago, my father had been born, grew up, lived and worked. The place where my grandparents had their home and business, lived and loved, argued and cried, and raised their family.

Even long after my father had left Podersam far behind, he still spoke of it often, with affection and sadness. He conjured it in my imagination with words like 'small' and 'safe'. I held small, safe pictures in my head to illustrate his stories of his childhood.

It was not safe, of course, as it turned out. But certainly, in the first decades of the twentieth century, it was small, having fewer than 4,000 inhabitants, and it was a vigorous, thriving town, a centre for the district, with successful businesses, flourishing industries, and prosperous hop farms in the surrounding countryside.

I was right to think of it as German. The majority of its inhabitants were German and only a small minority were Czech. The Jewish community was smaller still, numbering about 100 – yet this was a substantial community, proportionately larger than Jewish communities elsewhere in Bohemia, and larger by far than Podersam's Protestant population. The great majority of Podersam inhabitants were Roman Catholic, and the Catholic church of St Peter and Paul, with its terracotta onion tower, dominated the town. A short distance away down the hill, customers to the Kohners' shop knew the time by the striking of the church clock.

There are parts of Podersam that I have known all my life yet never saw until I visited the town forty years after my father left. And what I saw then was not what I had thought I knew, and was not even what my father had known, because in towns like Podersam, the spirit of their early-twentieth-century heyday has evaporated under the long, slow onslaught of war and violence, expulsions and reinstatements, Communism and depression. The revivalism that is now under way, the recreation of belief in the town itself, pays respect to its past, but does not connect with it. I, for one, am grateful that there is interest in the town's history. But it would be whimsical to think that the present-day inhabitants of Podbořany either have or can make any connection with my family or their world.

In my mind's eye, I can walk the streets of Podersam, hand-in-hand with my father or his parents. I know my way from here to there, I know the landmarks, I know the buildings and the streets, who lived where, who did what.

I can imagine myself standing outside 284 Ringstrasse, the Kohners' shop. Above me, the sign above the large windows reads 'A. Kohner'; the business, founded by Grossvater Abraham in 1856, will always retain his name. It is a hot, sunny day, so the awnings have

been pulled out over the windows to shade the beautifully presented display – Heinrich's own work, for he likes the windows to look enticing, and Valerie is too busy with the more immediate demands of family and customers.

I press my face to the window to see the goods through the darkened glass. Fabrics are artistically draped over stands, and pictures suggest the fashionable dresses they could become. Rolls of lace in different widths, ready-made lace collars, cards of buttons and braid, show the trimmings that might be added. A wide selection of collarless shirts occupies almost an entire window, with a row of socks and stockings lined up across the bottom. This window is testimony to the work of Fräulein Stanek, an elderly lady with a mouth set at a slant, who makes these shirts at enormous speed. She lives *am Berg*, on the gentle hill that leads up towards the Catholic church, and Rudi often makes the journey to her house to deliver the material for her shirtmaking.

If I turn round, I can look across Ringstrasse to the Hotel Rose, which boasts a pavement seating area where customers can drink, eat, meet and talk, and watch the Podersam world go by. I would like to sit there for a while. Some years before, in the early evening, I might have

seen Valerie, stately in pale-green brocade, and Heinrich, ebullient with a fat cigar, come arm-in-arm towards me across the road, on their way to a dance at the Hotel Rose. And I might have seen them pause for a moment outside and wave to little Franz and Grossmutter Marie, both leaning out of a first-floor window above the 'A. Kohner' sign to watch them go, Franz a little uncertain because he knows he must now go to bed without his mother's goodnight kiss.

From here, I have to crane my neck a little to see the writing at the top of the high building next door, which advertises in fancy lettering, '*Buchbinderei, Papierhandlung*'. It is Karl Pfaff's bookbinding and stationery business and up, in the main square, Herr Pfaff has a book and stationery shop. He, like Heinrich, is an important member of Podersam's business community. And like Heinrich, Karl Pfaff is German, but unlike Heinrich he is not Jewish, and twenty years from now he will therefore see the Kohners leave Podersam as the invading German army arrives, and he, unlike them, will survive the war in the place where he has lived and worked for so long. Yet in 1945, when the Germans are defeated and the Czechs come to power, Karl Pfaff, white-haired and elderly, will be taken out into the fields on just such a hot summer's day as this, and shot. And I cannot say whether there was reason, if there could be reason, for such a shooting, since there is nowhere any evidence that Herr Pfaff was a Nazi.

If I walk to the bottom of Ringstrasse and turn right, I am in Rathausgasse, and passing the town hall on my left, I can walk up the hill, turn into Tempelgasse, and stand outside the synagogue. It is not old or beautiful. It was built in 1873 and the architecture is surprising – stark, with a white stucco front and three elongated arched windows. Still more surprisingly, there is no door, and if I want to go in, I must enter through the *Volkshaus* next door where there is a meeting room, an office for the rabbi, classrooms, and a matzo bakery. This is Rabbi Ignatz Duschak's domain. He came to Podersam on Rabbi Rychnovsky's death and he, and his wife and children, will be here until they, with the other Jews, must leave.

Or, if I was to walk along Ringstrasse in the other direction, I would come into the large, open square, the Ringplatz, with its Linden Allee,

The Podersam synagogue

the formal avenue of linden trees where people can stroll on summer evenings. The Hotel Sonne fronts onto the square, and Heinrich, drinking a beer or coffee there after lunch, has clinched a deal with its owner, Herr Bärtl, and secured some advertising space high on the hotel wall. So postcards of Ringplatz, the most photographed part of the town, now also advertise, in yellow lettering on a large black board, 'A. Kohner. *Leinen- Tuch- Schnitt- und Mode-Waren.*'

From Ringplatz, I can stroll on up the hill, past the *Volks und Bürgerschule*, past the Löbls' house and farm on Bahnhofstrasse (we are on the edge of town now), and so to the station. And passing through the station's entrance hall, I come out onto the single platform and take a seat. I might, if I wish, catch a train to Prague, and travel with my father on his journey to school. Or I might travel with Valerie to Saaz, where we will visit her father Jakob, and Onkel Karl and Tante Ida in the house in Schünitzplatz, and Karl will speak to us passionately about Zionism, and Ida and Valerie will disappear together into the kitchen and produce *Kaffee* and *Kuchen* – a *Striezl* or *Apfelstrudel* – which we will all enjoy together. And afterwards, Jakob, who is an old man, will smoke a long, thin Virginia cigar.

But Podersam will always be a town of exteriors. I long to go inside the shops and houses but the doors are forever closed to me. I long especially to enter 284 Ringstrasse, not by the shop door but at the side, where stone steps will lead me up to the first-floor living quarters, past the pump on the landing into . . . I don't know which room. I do not know the layout of the house, and my imagination, which seems so ready in other cases to supply a convincing fiction when fact fails, hesitates to create it. So I am left standing in the street, and above me, Berta looks out of a window, leaning on the sill, smiling but silent, and Opapa comes to the shop door to see a customer out and, looking out onto the street, does not see me.

19

The Stucker

The school chosen for Rudi in Prague is not the school that Franz attended. After Franz's ignominious departure, further contact would have been embarrassing. Rudi's school is in the very centre of the city, in the splendid Kinsky Palace in the Old Town Square, and his lodgings are not far away on the famous shopping street, the Graben. This is where Ida Pichl lives, in a flat at the back of a shopping arcade called *Die Schwarze Rose*, and Ida and her mother Kathi (soon to assume the honorary titles of Tante Ida and Tante Kathi) will look after him and do their best to comfort him when he is homesick.

September 1916
Heinrich to Rudi

Mein lieber Bübl

Have you settled at school? Do you understand everything the Herr Professor tells the class, and are you paying attention? The first form in grammar school, mein Büb, is like building a house. Elementary school is digging the foundations, then comes the first form at grammar school when the walls begin to be built, stone by stone. But beware of any gaps in the wall, because if there are any gaps, the second and third floors could collapse, bringing down the whole building and often burying the builder too. So, mein Büb, study hard, pay attention to everything, even the smallest detail. It could be very important later.

Love and kisses from
Your Tata

Rudi hardly needs this advice. He is determined to study hard and it is his nature to pay attention to the smallest detail. He is anxious to please his parents and earn their praise. Besides, he is very unhappy. He is eleven years old, and he does not know anyone at the school he now attends. He feels banished, and he knows he will not see his parents, his grandparents, Herr Lorber the watchmaker, Robert and Rudolf the shop assistants, Maria the maid, or his geese, until Christmas. True, Mama and Tata say they will visit, but he knows they are busy, it is wartime, and their attention is focused on Franz.

Rudi's answer to his unhappiness is to work. He wants to get the best marks possible, then everyone will be happy.

As well as Tante Ida and Tante Kathi Pichl, there is one other person in Prague on whom he can depend. Berta, now fifteen years old, is also in Prague, at least some of the time, and for all that she is moody and self-absorbed, she loves Rudi and looks after him. They see each other frequently. Sometimes they spend time at each others' lodgings; sometimes they visit Richard Lenhart, the wealthy friend of their parents who has a large shop at the bottom of Wenceslaus Square and whose sons, like Franz, are fighting; and sometimes, best of all, they go together to a concert or the theatre.

Rudi counts the days through his first term and returns home for Christmas with relief, carrying with him an impressive report. But January comes too quickly, and when he takes the train back to Prague, he is in tears. Berta, concerned about him, sends a card with some sisterly advice, and Rudi writes back to her:

19 January 1917
Rudi to Berta

Liebe Berta!

I loved your card and thank you sincerely for how you told me things. I see it all now. One can't always be at home. One's got to see life from another angle, and not allow oneself to be overwhelmed by homesickness. The more one thinks of home, the greater the longing, and one neglects other duties. But I've got back onto the right road.

Lots of kisses from your brother Rudi

On the same day, and in the same determined tone, Rudi also writes to Valerie and Heinrich:

Liebste Eltern!

I'm not so homesick now because I've got used to life here again. It was just the first few days till I settled down. Like starting an engine which hasn't been in use for some time. It's always a bit of a problem at the start. However, I've been very lucky indeed. I got a 'I' in history, natural history, religion and geography in the orals, and a 'I' in Latin and German homework, which means a total of six well-earned 'sehr gut' marks. I hope this gives you pleasure.

I went to see Herr Lenhart this week and told him I'll have my Bar Mitzvah next year and would like to have some lessons. He recommended me to Dr Deutsch, the rabbi at the Jubiläums-synagoge, who'll arrange everything for me. I need a tallith, a pair of tefillin, and I think I'll also need a new suit and hat because the one with the breeches has nearly had it – it's tight, torn, the trousers are dirty and the lining is wearing thin. My other suits, except for the grey one, aren't too big either. The same goes for my winter coat.

For my Bar Mitzvah, I'd like visiting cards, a collar protector, notepaper, a seal, and a book. But I'm not suggesting you should give them to me as presents because I think others will do that. And you can give me the money for the Bar Mitzvah lessons when you come.

The day before yesterday, there were big workers' demonstrations. Food is in short supply here. I'm lucky to have my own supply, although my butter, the apples and the smoked meat are nearly gone. I finished the loaf only today: it's still in my stomach!

My oldest shoes won't last much longer. They're too small and bursting all over the place. I'm not wearing them for the moment because they cramp my feet and then my toes freeze. Anyway, I've got my new ones.

Now I've told you everything I have to say. What's new in the shop? How's Herr Lorber? Grossvater and Grossmutter? I had a card from Franz today. Have you? Write soon about everything.

Lots of greetings and kisses from your son, who owes you so much gratitude.

When they are not worrying about Franz, everyone in the family, including Franz himself, is now worrying about Rudi. Valerie writes to Franz about him, Franz writes to Berta, Berta writes back to Franz, and only Heinrich strikes a note of optimism, asserting that it will all come right in the end. Valerie is proud of Rudi's achievements at school, but his homesickness starts up a corresponding ache in her own heart: she misses him too. Franz is convinced that Rudi is becoming a *Stucker*, a swot, a boffin – although Rudi himself claims that all he wants is to follow in Franz's footsteps. Berta is inclined to agree with Franz, and both write letters to Rudi, giving stern advice of which their father would have been proud. Rudi replies with disarming honesty:

27 January 1917
Rudi to Franz

Liebster Franz!

It's going to be Tata's birthday on February 8th and I'll give him my report as a present. I hope it's a good one. I want to please him and become a good pupil. I had a sore throat this week and I'm missing Mamma and Tata very much. Soon it will be my birthday and it will be the first time I celebrate it away from home.

Since I've been in Prague, I've got more courage. I'm a different person here. But to go for a walk with my friends like you suggest isn't possible. I've got no time, and also I've got no friends. I get on with everybody, and chat to people, but if I go out, I like it best if I can go with Berta. And there isn't enough time, which is why I want to opt out of singing lessons. I could get my work done in a couple of hours, but once I've learnt something, I'm not really satisfied until I've been over it once or twice more, and so time passes. And I don't want to go for walks in the evening. Besides, there's violin and French.

I've got to study a bit more now.

Kisses from your brother, Rudi

There are other reasons too for the family to worry. It is not a peaceful time in Prague. As Rudi has not held back from telling his parents, there are frequent and sometimes violent demonstrations because of the food and coal shortages, and Rudi's walk to school takes him through the centre of the city.

26 January 1917
Rudi to Valerie and Heinrich

Liebste Eltern!

On Tuesday there were huge demonstrations. You've probably read about them. There was some rioting, especially in the Old Town Square. It was impossible to get from the Graben to the Square because police were blocking the way. The demonstrators had it in for the Germans, and it wasn't safe to be on the streets. Today all the shops are shut because yesterday windows were smashed and shops were looted, especially in Weinberge and at the Café Nizza and at Heine's.

When are you coming to Prague? Please write and say, even if you only have a rough idea of when it might be. I look around outside school every day in case I miss you.

Lots of kisses from your grateful son Rudi

The war made life uncomfortable in other ways too. February was a particularly cold month, with temperatures falling to fifteen or twenty degrees below zero. The shortage of coal meant there was no heating in the school, and the boys sat in lessons in their overcoats. Trams stopped running, and cinemas and theatres closed. And although Valerie and Heinrich sent food from the country, shortages were affecting them too and sending food to Franz came first. Rudi often went hungry. He wrote to Franz and asked whether he was getting enough to eat. 'If not, I'll send you a flea salad, paper dumplings and an inkpot. Bon appétit!'

Still, it seemed that when the occasion demanded it, the family could still pull out all the stops. On 3 March 1917 it was Rudi's twelfth birthday.

4 March 1917

Rudi to Valerie and Heinrich

Liebste Eltern

A lot of my presents arrived on Friday, but Tante Ida didn't give them to me. On Saturday I went to school and all the boys congratulated me. When school finished at 11.00 a.m. I ran home, and Tante Ida told me there hadn't been a single letter or anything else for me. I tried to console myself and went to my room, and there were all these lovely things on the table! Tante Kathi congratulated me and then I started to have a good look at it all. First the magnificent box of pastries. I can't tell you what a joy that was. And so tasty! I could hardly believe that it was all for me. Then the nice little Striezel. And of course the potato dumplings with meat. They must have been Tante Ida's idea. Or dear Tata? Then the tie with the mirror, and the box of apples, and the cakes. I had a whole box of nuts from Saaz, and a bar of chocolate from Herr Lenhart. But that's not all. There were also the letters. I'd been looking forward to them so much! I'll do my best to fulfill your wishes. I'll become a real man, like Tata, and do something worthwhile in life. To prove that I'm serious, I can report a '1' for my Latin homework, and an 'excellent' in Geography. I'll keep my promises to you. I want to become just like Franz.

We had Schnitzel for lunch, and then a big Gugelhupf. In the afternoon, I invited Berta to come for coffee and Gugelhupf and pastries, and we had a good time. Berta brought me a box of notepaper and a very nice money box as well as some pastries.

Well, in all my twelve years I have never had such a lot of presents, and now I'm only waiting for a letter from Franz. It's 9.15 now and I'll have to stop.

Good night then, and love from your grateful son Rudi

20

Travelling

I inherited my father's childhood propensity for homesickness. I always dreaded leaving the safety of home and even now, as an adult, I am an anxious and ambivalent traveller. Not so my father. Although his school years were marked by a longing for home, in later life he travelled with the ease of one who knows how to pick up a suitcase and run.

When he arrived in England as a refugee in 1939, his suitcase let him down. Getting off the train at Bradford station, the case burst open, scattering his possessions over the platform. He told this as a funny story, but it must have seemed a poor welcome.

Throughout his working life, he travelled regularly to Northern Ireland, where he first worked for his employers and eventually set up a business of his own. The trips combined happily with the opportunity to see Franz and his family, who were then living in Belfast.

He packed meticulously for each journey in a small black attaché case. Whereas I am incapable of travelling anywhere without excessive amounts of baggage, guarding against every possible eventuality and risk, my father's needs were minimal. Pyjamas, clean underwear and a shirt, shaving gear, toothbrush, a hairbrush and comb, and, of course, the essential Odol mouthwash, aftershave, or 4711 eau de cologne. On this basic equipment, he contrived to look immaculate.

At first, travelling to Belfast from Bradford meant a long drive to Heysham and an overnight boat across the choppy Irish Sea. Later, he flew from Yeadon, the tiny airport that served Leeds and Bradford, where in those early days there was little more than a hangar with a passenger waiting area equipped with old bus seats. When I was older,

I would drive him to the (then larger and modernised) airport, and meet him on his return – a regularly repeated pleasure of leavetaking and reunion.

For family holidays, once my sister and I were deemed old enough to appreciate more expensive travel, we went annually to German-speaking countries – Austria, Switzerland – but never to Germany. For many years, my father refused to go there, despite the fact that compensation money paid to him after the war sat in German marks in a bank account in Aachen and, as he often remarked, could have been used most efficiently in Germany. When he was elderly, he did visit his cousin, Heinrich Herrmann, near Nuremberg. But then, Heinrich, who had survived the war as the son of a converted Jewish father and a Catholic mother, had only left Czechoslovakia in the 1960s, and Nuremberg is not far from the border. The compensation money in Aachen was still there when my father died.

The refusal to travel to Germany was born from grief, not hatred. Throughout our childhood, my father did not allow my sister and me to use the word 'hate'. It came out so easily that this was a hard rule to obey – although it was not so much a rule as a request, and not so much disallowed as disapproved of. Children say it all the time: 'I hate lettuce', 'I hate so-and-so', 'I hate going to the dentist', 'I hate you'. But my father's sensitive reaction to the word made me hesitate, and I cannot use it even now without feeling uncomfortably conscious of its power.

21

Baking

*V*alerie is baking. Baking comforts her, but tonight it would be more comforting if it was not so late. It is gone eleven, and it will be one or even two in the morning before she is done, because the Striezel dough must have time to rise before she can plait, glaze and bake it. She is tired, but she likes the warmth of the kitchen after the chill of the unheated shop, the gentle aromas are soothing, and the flat is quiet and still.

Heinrich has not gone to bed. He is sitting at the table in the next room, the room they call the Grosse Zimmer. He has brought up his papers from the office downstairs and is working where it is warmer, calculating and checking the figures, thinking anxiously about the future. He has his pipe by him, and he reaches for it and his soft leather tobacco pouch. He teases out some tobacco – he has square but surprisingly delicate fingers – and presses it expertly into the bowl, packing it just loosely enough, just tightly enough to draw. He lights up, takes a long sucking breath, and sits back a little in his chair.

In the room next door, he can hear Valerie moving from cupboard to table and back again, and a soft thudding as she kneads the dough. She has rolled up her sleeves and tied a large white apron around her waist. Her hair, pinned up in a low bun, is slightly disordered, and after a long day in the shop, her feet are aching with tiredness. Tomorrow, she will parcel up the Striezel and despatch it to Franz, along with the other supplies he has requested.

The house seems deserted now that Rudi and Berta have returned to Prague, and the shop too feels silent and empty, with fewer customers and less stock on the shelves. The war has even removed their shop assistants, Ladislav and Rudolf. Ladislav, who joined up early, has long been a prisoner of war in Russia, from where he sends postcards pleading for news. And now Rudolf has left too, and it seems it will be a long time until he holds his scissors or tape measure again. Only Maria, the plump, blonde maid, is still with them, and earlier in the day it was she who prepared the almonds and raisins for the Striezel, chatting all the while to Grossvater Abraham and lending a patient ear to his reminiscences.

Valerie is thinking about Franz. In the bedroom, on the table beside her bed, is the box containing all the letters and postcards he has written to them, and the most recent letters lie on top. She has read and re-read them, searching in the pencil scrawl for more information than they contain, trying to read his mood, longing to know his real circumstances and the risks he may be facing.

Franz's last letters have distressed her. Beginning in early January, there has been an uncomfortable exchange of letters, and her mind is on the misunderstanding that has grown up between them. So it is not just her feet that are aching but her heart too, and even now she weeps a little into the dough and has to wipe her eyes with the back of a floury hand.

2 January 1917
Franz to Valerie and Heinrich

Liebste Eltern!

This morning I received two five-kilogram parcels and this evening, three little parcels. In addition, I still have half a previous parcel in my hut. Dearest parents, I beg you, could you please send less! There's no need to send a parcel to me every day. I've only opened one of the big parcels. There are such marvellous things inside: a delicious Striezel with raisins, white bread, chocolate, pastries which melt in your mouth, sardines

(I've already got three tins), and lots of other goodies. But it's a waste sending such a lot. Please don't think I am ungrateful, but I am annoyed when five parcels arrive on the same day, and I feel ashamed at having such an abundance of stuff. Please send things less often; it will give me greater joy and benefit. If I'm ordered back to my battery today, I'll need a cart to transport everything you have sent.

Please forgive this letter, but this is how it is. Keep well, as I am, and love and kisses from your son

Franz

8 January 1917
Valerie to Franz

Liebster Franzl

I'm sorry that we have achieved the exact opposite of what we intended – that is, to make you happy with our parcels and help you over homesickness and perhaps let you have a taste of things from home. As it is, I haven't been sending so much of late, and this week, at your request, there'll be no five-kilogram package. In the early days you used to write 'if only some parcels would come', and I immediately wanted to send anything I could get hold of. And when I didn't manage to find things to send, I reproached myself. Well, from now on there'll be fewer things, until you ask for more. But you must promise that you will write at once if you need something.

Greetings from everyone here. Please write as often as you can.

With fondest love
Your Mama

10 January 1917
Heinrich to Franz

Mein lieber Franz

Let Mama send you things. The time may come when we can't do
it any longer. If you have too much, give something to your
friends.

Take care. God protect you.

Tata

Despite Heinrich's advice, Franz continues to send contradictory
instructions. In letter after letter he asserts that the parcels he
receives are too many and too big . . . he wants fewer and
smaller . . . and yet please could his parents send him this or
that . . . and the last parcel was so welcome, such a treat . . . but
they must economise . . . they are spending too much . . . and so
on and so on. In fact, even if his instructions were clearer, they
would probably make little difference. For as long as he is away,
Valerie will continue to wrap her love in oilcloth, tie it twice with
string, and send it east; and no matter how busy, both she and
Heinrich will snatch moments in which to write, sometimes daily,
or at least two or three times a week, enquiring endlessly about his
welfare.

But their middle-aged anxiety and Franz's sudden and frightening
independence, the stress and exhaustion of life at home and the thrill,
fear and boredom of life at the front, and maybe above all, their love
and concern for each other, make communication and understanding
difficult, even in a family of letter-writers. New misunderstandings
begin to grow. Valerie, looking for things to provide for Franz besides
food, and conscious of his long hours of boredom, sends him a
selection of books. He is already, by his own admission, reading
Nietzsche and studying Czech in his spare time, so at first glance her
selection of reading material does not seem so inappropriate: Plutarch,

Weber, Schiller, Demosthenes and Plato. But she receives a vigorous rebuff.

2 March 1917
Franz to Valerie

Liebste Mammalittl

I can't understand you, sending us translations of the classics! Us – poor soldiers who are pursued by the greatest enemy, boredom. Us – who hunger after books like after Manna. That stuff is all well and good if one is in the mood, but look Mammalittl, what we need are novels, poetry, humorous writing, interesting scientific stuff. It's got to be interesting otherwise we'll use it like the kind of paper that sometimes comes with a red cross on it, or the paper that advertises laxatives. Please don't be angry, dear Mama, but how could you, who are so well read, send such books?

Love and kisses from your son Franz

7 March 1917
Valerie to Franz

Lieber Franzl!

I am sorry to have chosen so badly! The books I sent you were simply the ones that I could quickly find on your shelves here at home. I'll do better next time and hope by my industry and good behaviour to win back your approval. So please kindly forgive me.

Love and kisses from your contrite Mama

12 March 1917
Franz to Valerie

Liebste Mammalittl!

I have received your letter of 7th March. Please don't be angry if I expressed myself clumsily. I think I was in too good a mood and wrote too casually. I am very grateful for all you do for me and have dipped into Schiller, Plato and Plutarch. Tata is right that sometimes I write stupidly and like a silly boy. Please forgive me, and please don't write so ironically. I'd rather you told me off. Are you still angry? Please write soon.

Kisses from your silly son Franz

19 March 1917
Valerie to Franz

My dear silly boy

How can you think that I'm angry? I don't know what Tata wrote to you, but there's nothing to forgive. I don't know what you're supposed to have done. Maybe you just imagined it all. Dear Franzl, don't write such contrite letters, I can't stand it. Nobody is angry.

Keep well, and a thousand kisses from your Mama who loves you tenderly.

The Striezel is finished and is lying on the cooling rack, a shining brown plait. The kitchen is filled with the soothing smell of baking. Valerie takes off her apron and looks into the next door room, but Heinrich has tidied his papers into a neat pile and has gone to bed. She sits for a moment at the table and sees that he has been working on a tax demand. She knows he feels it is unfairly high, and feels weary at the thought of the arguments and negotiations that may lie ahead. Heinrich is not well disposed towards the tax inspector.

She goes to the bedroom, where Heinrich is already asleep. It is nearly two in the morning. She struggles out of her clothes and into a nightdress. Reaching round, she lets down her hair, and brushes and plaits it with the same deft movements that she plaited the Striezel dough. She slips into bed and listens to Heinrich's steady out breaths. But it is a long time before she sleeps.

22

Putte

*B*erta loved Prague. When she returned there after Christmas in January 1917 and had left Rudi, tearful, at his lodgings in the Schwarze Rose, she didn't go directly to her own lodgings but wandered alone through the city streets, and from sheer happiness, smiled at the people she passed. She was fifteen, nearly sixteen years old, and in a mood to take risks.

22 January 1917
Berta to Franz

Mein lieber Schwanzerl!

You know how in Prague one is always hard up? Well recently, when money worries really got on top of me, I resorted to a last desperate way out – giving lessons. I answered an advert asking for someone to give English lessons. Sure enough, as I'd hoped, I got a reply from some chemical laboratory, from a Herr Cerveny. I imagined some old gentleman wanting someone to teach his thirteen or fourteen year old daughter English, and I got myself ready – which meant I curled my hair into a magnificent knot, put on my best dress, and off I went. Well, what more is there to tell? He was a young man, and he'd already found someone else. For the lessons I mean. I've got over my disappointment and have given up answering advertisements. Instead I will have to rely on you being promoted to sergeant, and then you can let me have some of your huge army pay. Meanwhile, I want your word of honour that you won't tell a soul about this.

Write soon, and lots of kisses from your faithful sister Bertl.

5 February 1917
Berta to Franz

Lieber Schwanzerl

You are naïve! You ask what I do with my money? Good Lord, one's got commitments, hasn't one? I've got four starving children to support, I pay 40 Heller for 1 kilogram of potatoes, and you'll surely realise that one can't live on potatoes alone but occasionally one needs to go to the confectioner. Besides, occasionally one has got to give to a beggar, and if I give a beggar 1 Krone, he can't live on that either. Besides, I have an irresistible liking for sweets, picture postcards, brooches, artificial flowers, powder puffs, rollmops and books. That'll do I think, although I have a few other extravagant passions. Anyway, as I told you, I have given up answering adverts. I'll just have to see how I can get along in some other way. Don't worry about me. At present I possess 13.92 Kronen in cash and have no pressing debts. And just so that you'll have enough to live on for three days, I'm sending you 30,000 kisses today.

Bertl

But for all that she loves Prague, Berta is also lonely. She has few friends, and she misses Franz. She confides in him occasionally in her letters, half ironically and often mocking herself. She speaks of needing to talk to someone in whom she can feel complete confidence – but she knows that even if she were to find such a person, or was able to talk to Franz himself, she would probably (as she says) retreat into her shell like a snail. Instead, she writes him brief notes, sometimes joyful and even ecstatic ('You should always read Rilke aloud. It is glorious!') but more often teasing, taunting, loving and a little mysterious.

For her sixteenth birthday on 15 March 1917, she received eleven books, including Ibsen, Strindberg and Rabindranath Tagore. Valerie is concerned that she is becoming a bookworm, 'always wrapped up in her books', and in a letter to Franz refers to 'our Putte' (a family nickname for Berta) as a 'strange girl'.

Was she strange? She is certainly living through extremes of emotion, and in her occasional letters, she records experiences which sometimes seem to overwhelm her, whether these are within herself, or a response to a piece of music or literature ('Have just read a *wonderful* letter by Bjoernson. You can't imagine how magnificent it is. So magnificent one can no longer think any evil exists in the world'). At sixteen, she is acute, intellectually sophisticated, independent and  increasingly capable. For these reasons, she is also frequently frustrated, impatient and irritable. Life is too slow and too limited. One can easily imagine the appeal of Ibsen – and Valerie's difficulty in appreciating it.

It may be that Berta had little in common with her mother. There is nowhere any record of the kind of intimacy or mutuality that can exist between a mother and daughter in a family dominated by its men. But then, there is very little record of anything. The letters suggest that, if she allied with anyone, it was with Franz. But there may have been other letters, now lost. There may have been (surely there were?) as many letters from Valerie to Berta as there were to Franz and Rudi, speaking of their shared Podersam world, of the family, and, most of all, of her love for her one, beautiful daughter.

As it is, in the vast collection of family correspondence, not one single letter to Berta from either Valerie or Heinrich has been preserved.

18 May 1917
Berta to Franz

Mein liebster Franzl!

I suppose that truly great artists do not have to develop: they are great from the beginning and remain great. Others reach a peak and then regress. I think with you, everything was there from the beginning, but I am developing very gradually and I fear the peak because after that I will decline. Maybe I'll never even reach the peak. At times, this makes me despair and I just want to give up. At other times, I feel young and courageous and want to climb to the top as fast as I can.

I feel sad that people I didn't even know a year ago are closer to me than my parents, but it is because they understand me and talk to me in the right sort of way. These days, I don't want to tell our parents anything. I tried it once, but never again. I think a rift often opens up as one grows older. I expect you'll understand what I mean, although I can't express it very well. I hope you won't write home about what I've just told you . . .

A thousand kisses
Bertl

23

Home Leave

At the beginning of April 1917, Franz saw action for the first time. In February, his regiment had been moved north to a new position near a bridgehead on the River Stochod in Volhynia. On 5 April, he wrote a nonchalant letter to Heinrich and Valerie in which practical matters about the winter clothing he no longer needed and was therefore sending home are mixed with a description of the successful assault on the bridgehead. 'Our battery excelled itself,' he says with pride, and goes on to detail the number of Russians taken prisoner, the weapons and artillery captured, and the damage done in the Russian hinterland by their long-range guns. Afterwards, he asked his captain's permission to visit the captured positions. 'What I have seen is terrible. We're not thinking of the havoc we caused. There will be fewer boys writing home!'

Although he wrote only briefly to his parents, scribbling a quick note in blue pencil, he was deeply impressed by the destruction caused by the fighting, and he recorded in his diary what he saw in one of the villages:

The village of Stobychova is no more. Where the houses once stood, there are only the remains of corner posts, a tumbled down brick stove, broken chimneys. There are rags of cloth from what must once have been bright curtains or clothing. Here and there, there is the charred trunk of a tree. Only the main street still runs through the village untouched, with grass verges intact and, remarkably, not a single shell or grenade hole. But where there was once a beautiful avenue, the trees have been blasted by the guns and stretch only two or three shattered arms towards heaven. There are still bits of grenade stuck in the tree trunks from the encounters here a year ago; and there are a couple of storks' nests sitting askew in the branches.

At the other end of the village, I discovered, to my surprise, a Jewish cemetery. All the grave stones were coloured: a red lion in front of a brown tree, two yellow doves kissing, a blue seven-armed menorah, and below it the name, Israel Loew ben Jitzchok.

Franz has recently heard that he is to be promoted to the rank of sergeant. He is proving a good soldier – capable, intelligent and hardy – and at eighteen years old he is doing the same work as many older men. His letters home are warm but mostly dispassionate, and it is only occasionally that he permits himself to express hopes and fears beyond disgust at the lice and mosquitoes and a desire for a warm bath and a dry bed. Imagine him, then, in a desolate village in Russia, discovering the Jewish graveyard, walking among the coloured graves, reading the inscriptions, and thinking of home.

---

16 April 1917
Franz to Valerie

Liebste Mammalittl

I'm so afraid that should I come home on leave (about which please don't entertain any hope at present), I'd find you looking less well than I imagine, because Bertl and Rudl say you're always baking and doing things for me. I do enjoy all your home-made things, but please don't work so hard. Spend some time in the Garten, and pick some tulips for the vase which stands on the table in the Grosse Zimmer on Saturdays. Ah, the Grosse Zimmer! That used to be something wonderful. I can picture it now. The lamp is shining, but not too brightly. Tata is reading *Jugend* and Rudl is bringing him his slippers. I'm in the far corner of the large sofa, and it creaks as it always does the moment I stir. Or maybe I'm sitting at the table, playing with my knife and fork and teasing Putte. Then at last Maria pushes the door open with her elbow and carries in a large bowl of . . . I mustn't ask what's in it. And behind her follows red-cheeked Mammalittl, asking where Rudl can be, because as usual, he is playing on the balcony with Robert.

I haven't yet received the parcel with the Gugelhupf cake . . .

———————— ↄ   ↄ _____

At home, Heinrich and Valerie are struggling to manage their anxiety. Indeed, they are struggling to manage. There are food shortages, fuel shortages, shortages of almost every commodity. Grossvater Abraham is deprived of beer, and there is a queue at Rosenzweig's, the tobacconist's on Ringstrasse, that stretches right back past the Kohners' shop door. It is almost impossible to obtain stock for the shop and much of what they had has been requisitioned. Heinrich takes a trip to Vienna in the hope of buying merchandise there, but he returns empty-handed. They continue to send parcels to Franz at the front – food, books, clothing, money, oats for Maxl, and almost anything else that Franz requests – aspirin, boot polish, an aluminium spoon, a hard rubber, leather gloves, his sergeant's insignia, a battery, two dozen nails, felt inner soles for his boots, Feldpost postcards, soap and a pocket mirror. Valerie, undeterred by his plea to work less hard, continues to bake for him, begging and bartering ingredients from friends and neighbours. But they are beginning to feel the deprivations of wartime, and Franz himself, writing to thank them for some delicious apples they have sent, says that he savoured them a little less when he rode past a notice saying, 'Soldiers, don't ask for food to be sent to you at the front. What is sent to you, those at home go without!'

It is now almost a year since Franz left home, and his parents' fears for him are increasing daily. They hope against hope that he will be given leave. Valerie is reluctant to go for her annual holiday in Bad

Gastein in case he should come home; and so great is their longing, they watch out for every train in case Franz should arrive unexpectedly. 'Tata is convinced you'll surprise us,' Valerie writes, 'but it's hard for me to believe anything so wonderful.' The possibility of a reunion dominates their letters. Valerie and Heinrich speak of it constantly, and after Franz receives not one but two medals, Rudi becomes especially enthusiastic about the prospect of showing his decorated brother off to his friends. As for Berta, she expresses her longing in her usual way.

23 April 1917
Berta to Franz

Lieber Franz

I think you may be coming home on leave soon. Do you think I'm looking forward to that? Not a bit. It will just mean I get less to eat because you'll be stuffing yourself all day long, and I'll have to clean your boots and polish your medals.

It's funny how one can be so full of macabre humour. I really ought not to write to you at all since I've nothing sensible to say and it's only that I want to make someone happy.

I am waiting for the promised letter from you. But please, take your time. I can wait till next Easter . . .

B

As spring turns to early summer, Heinrich and Valerie find comfort in the *Garten*. New plants, exceptionally, are not in short supply. Earlier in the year, Heinrich had ordered new roses, shrubs, conifers and fruit trees, and he has spent long hours with Wenta, the gardener, positioning and planting them. In the warmth of mid-May, the *Garten* is blooming, and even Wenta, a well-known grumbler, has been heard to say that, compared with the *Garten*, Paradise would be an arsehole.

15 May 1917
Valerie to Franz

Liebster Franzele!

One would need to be a poet to describe all the beauties of the
Garten. All the new shrubs and fruit trees are in bloom and give off
a wonderful scent. On the grass in front of the summerhouse,
there are two magnolias, both covered with magnificent blossom.
The violets have been glorious, and there are azaleas, pinks, Alpine
roses, and pansies in every colour. In the evenings, Tata and I
often go to visit Herr Hess, the market gardener, to buy a plant,
and then we go to the Garten and place it exactly where it will
give us most pleasure. In the morning, Wenta wonders where it
has come from. So the Garten is our joy, and when you come
home, you will be able to admire it all. But first you will have to
win the peace. Until then, one can't really enjoy anything.

Your loving Mama

June comes, but Franz does not. He writes repeatedly to say that there
is too much happening, too much for him to do, and he cannot get
leave just yet. It all 'depends on the Russians'. Disappointed and
depressed, Heinrich often closes the shop early. The weather is hot
and dry, and he spends his evenings filling his watering can at the
garden pump and carrying water to his thirsty plants.

His thoughts are all of Franz – so much so that he finds it hard to
give his attention to anything else. In the shop, there are plenty of
customers, but little or nothing to sell to them, and the effort seems
hardly worthwhile. At the beginning of July, Rudi comes home from
school, delighted to be back in Podersam and bursting with the
news that he is top of his class. His report has *sehr gut* against every
subject. Heinrich is pleased, of course – but not perhaps as pleased
as Rudi had hoped. And when Berta passes a university examination that qualifies her as a teacher of English (a project that has been

dear to her heart), Heinrich merely comments that he supposes it can do no harm.

Then, at the beginning of August, Franz arrives.

There is no record of his home leave. There is no letter heralding his coming, and no description to tell me whether he was, in the end, expected or a surprise. I do not know whether, after a year's absence, he simply arrived at Podersam station, walked down the hill, across Ringplatz, into Ringstrasse, and in at the shop door. But how else could his arrival have been? And did Valerie look round, hearing the shop door open, and suddenly see him there? Did Heinrich, deep in conversation with a customer, glance casually over the customer's shoulder and set eyes on his uniformed son? Did Valerie weep? Did Rudi come running? Did Berta, concealing her joy, say, 'Back so soon?'

For a fortnight, the letters stop. The family were together, and their reunion is marked by utter silence. It is only when they cannot speak to each other that I hear their voices.

24

The Attic

*M*y father was a very tidy man: he waged ceaseless war on a chaotic and disordered world. The papers, files and letters on his desk were always neatly sorted into piles and the piles arranged in geometric patterns. His violin music was tidily stacked in a cupboard, categorised and labelled. His shirts were folded and placed in the appropriate compartment of his wardrobe. If I left my own things around the house for longer than he could tolerate, he would gather my bits and pieces together into an orderly pile and leave it ostentatiously to await my attention. After a family meal, before beginning the washing up, we first had to arrange and stack the dirty dishes, ready for washing in the proper sequence. This was my father's initiative, not my mother's, and I suspect it was a tradition handed down from his own childhood since we spoke of it in German. We began our meals by saying 'Mahlzeit' (the equivalent of 'bon appétit') and ended with 'Zusammenstellen'.

In the areas of the house where my father held sway – namely, the garage and the attic – the contents were regularly tidied, arranged and rearranged. Both places were badly overcrowded because my father rarely threw anything away. The car had to be driven into the garage rather carefully as there was little parking space left, and in the attic there was hardly room to move. This made trips into the attic both hazardous and exciting. Access was through a trapdoor over the stairwell, and there was nothing as convenient as a loft ladder. My father would bring in the long wooden ladder he used for pruning the climbing roses and set it up on the landing. One then had to climb up through the open hatch and step round and off the ladder into the crowded, unlit attic. It was this last manoeuvre that always scared me.

Up in the attic we stored the usual collection of family detritus, to which were added objects my father had brought from the old country and the remnants of a once-loved wardrobe designed for a different lifestyle. His old ski boots, unused for twenty or thirty years, were so large and heavy that I could slip my feet into them with my shoes still on, and then could hardly walk. An ancient pair of tweed plus fours were the cause of much hilarity (from my sister and myself) and gentle derision (from my mother) but remained on standby: after all, the cloth was good and the style might come back. There was also a 1920s white tie outfit, complete with stiff-fronted shirts, separate wing collars with gold studs, a white piqué waistcoat, and soft white kid gloves.

My favourite object was a wardrobe trunk, a massive affair that must have accompanied my father on a great many trips as a young man, because around his initials imprinted on the side were stickers from a variety of European destinations: Vienna, the Riviera, Zell am See . . . This trunk had to be opened while standing upright on its short side, and it folded out in two halves, making a small wardrobe. It was lined with blue patterned cloth and on one side was hanging space for suits with special flat wooden coat hangers on an extendable metal rail; on the other were drawers of different depths to hold shirts, underwear and shoes. It was called, as its label announced, a 'Wata-boy' – an appropriate description for my father in his earlier, romantic years.

It seemed as though almost everything my father treasured had its own special container. His hairbrush nestled in a leather case; another round leather bag with a drawstring held detachable shirt collars. His tie pins were cushioned in a tiny, triangular box with a fancy catch. His amber cigar holder was kept in a little box shaped like a miniature trumpet case. The silver knives, forks and spoons with his initials, ROK, engraved on them had to be slipped back into their soft cloth wrappings after every use. Everything he possessed was held safe, and he held my mother, my sister and myself safest of all.

25

Hans

*I*n the Kohners' shop, the talk is all of the war – and the prospect of peace. In this small community, everyone knows who has a husband, son or grandson at the front, whether German or Czech, Gentile or Jew, and anxious enquiries are made, provisions shared, news and views exchanged. They all long for peace, and in the churches and the synagogue they pray for it – and, of course, for victory. Only their fears are, for the most part, suppressed. It is better not to voice what terrifies them all.

But in early September, there is news that cannot be suppressed. Hans, the nineteen-year-old son of Heinrich's sister Anna, is killed in action in Italy. For Heinrich and Valerie, it is a cruel reminder of the reality of what they most dread.

4 September 1917
Heinrich to Franz

Mein lieber Franzl

Can you imagine our shock and sorrow? On Saturday we got a postcard from Anna saying, 'since August 21st, I no longer have my Hans.' Mama and I immediately travelled over to Tachau to see her and unfortunately it was confirmed that he was hit in the chest by a grenade on Monte Santo on August 21st and he died instantly. The news came from the 1st and 2nd lieutenants. Please, Franzl, take great care.

Tata

Anna herself also wrote to Franz. 'Do look after yourself, dear Franz, for a tragedy like this is a terrible thing. One can bear almost anything but this. Take care of yourself.'

In his diary, Franz wrote, 'I don't want to die. Oh my dear world, not to die! I want to live through many another hot summer's day and be young.'

26

The Patriarch

*J*t is as though the family are holding their breath. The autumn comes, and day-to-day life resumes, but below the surface, there is a sense that ordinary, everyday events are irrelevant, a sub-plot, not quite the main theme. Valerie writes to Franz: they have harvested the cucumbers and pears (a heavy crop this year); they have celebrated Rosh Hashanah, Yom Kippur, and Sukkot; Tante Emma has come to visit; they have been grateful for a delivery of coal. But between the lines, unspoken questions sing out. Are you well, Franz? Are you safe? Are you still there?

Since Hans's death, disaster feels close and threatening. Even a day without a letter or postcard from Volhynia suggests a terrible possibility. There is a new undercurrent of pessimistic feeling. Heinrich and Valerie do not now write a single letter to Franz (and they write almost daily) that does not plead with him to keep safe; and even Berta expresses a new, more straightforward and more urgent kind of affection.

Lieber Franz

It is 10.30 p.m. and I have climbed out of bed to write you a letter. You know what you are? You are one of those people whose mere presence does one good. I love you very much.

Your Bertl

Berta is sixteen years old and has left school. Regretfully, she has had to exchange Prague for Podersam. She is going to live at home and it has been arranged that each week she will travel on the train to Saaz for violin lessons with Herr Lutz, English conversation with Fraülein Koch, and French with Fraülein Pollak. At home she will learn to cook, and she hopes to learn Czech and study art history. 'Good plan, isn't it?' she writes to Franz – although it is impossible to detect her tone.

One thing is certain: Podersam is not where Berta wants to be. She seizes every opportunity and every excuse to visit Prague – to shop, to do errands, to go to concerts and operas, and to wander the streets. Rudi, on the other hand, has wanted to be nowhere but Podersam all through the long school year. And this summer, his first summer holiday after his first triumphant year at the grammar school, Podersam has offered new delights. His beloved geese have been joined by three rabbits, three hens and a turkey, and this menagerie has been entrusted to his care. One of the rabbits has enlivened things further by producing a large family. On Sundays, Heinrich has taken him shooting, and on his first outing he bagged a fat squirrel, which he proudly presented to Wenta, the gardener, and which Wenta was pleased to eat. To crown these pleasures, there was the excitement of Franz's return. So in September, Rudi returns to Prague as unwillingly as ever, and from there he too writes to Franz more openly and confidingly than before. 'I'm homesick,' he says, 'and I'm not even ashamed of it. That's how it is. You know that, Franz.'

Valerie and Heinrich's great fear is that Franz's division will be moved south to the Italian front. That is where the greatest danger is and from where the worst news comes. Their fervent hope is that he will be given leave to study for his *Matura*. Like other schoolboys, he left school and enlisted before taking this final examination, and he can now apply for leave in order to take it. If his application is successful, it would mean not a week or a fortnight but at least a month at home. Both Valerie and Heinrich, as well as Franz himself, ponder frequently in their letters on the possibility or impossibility of such a piece of good fortune.

But the first news that comes from Franz after his return to his battery is not about Italy nor the *Matura* but about Maxl. Maxl, like other privately owned horses, has been sold to the state. He is still Franz's to ride, but no longer belongs to him. The deal, which was recommended by Captain Hossner who has sold his own horse in the same way, was concluded while Franz was on leave.

5 September 1917
Franz to Heinrich and Valerie

Meine Lieben

Yesterday I saw Maxl again. What a sight. It would have made you weep. He was haggard, trotting along with that cumbersome Government issue saddle on his back, a dirty bridle and collar on his sadly lowered head. His splendid muscles are shrunk and he's a picture of misery. He has three large unsightly brands, and the burnt skin is peeling off them. And the proud, nervy fellow now allows his head to be touched as he never did before and stands still wherever one leaves him. It's only if he spots a few blades of grass, or better, some fir trees, that he'll strain with all his might to get to them. And when he's out to pasture, so the stable boys say, he'll walk ahead of the other horses, followed by his two sweethearts, Weibi and Putzi. Sometimes he will bolt, and a hundred others will go tearing after him. Maybe that's when he senses what it was like in days gone by – how, in the courtyard, he'd gnash on the bit and paw the ground impatiently, and how we would trot through the summer countryside or, covered in froth, race along the banks of the Elbe. Those were the days Maxl, weren't they?

Love and kisses
Your Franz

12 September 1917
Rudi to Franz From Podersam

Liebster Franz!

Yesterday we had three letters from you, and today two postcards.
When I read about Maxl, I immediately sent him something. It's
not much, but better than nothing. Give it to him and tell him to
think of me. But only when you and he are alone, because
otherwise the other horses will want something too.

So you don't believe I shot a squirrel? But Tata, Berta and
Wenta bear witness! Wenta himself ate the squirrel. So do you
believe me now? I also shot a fieldfare. They're doing a lot of
damage. Shot in the head. Wenta ate it.

Love from Rudi

12 September 1917
Valerie to Franz

Mein lieber Franzi!

It gave us great joy to receive your letters, and also the photos of
your leave. We like the one in the garden, with Putte in the
hammock and Rudl with his mouth organ.

We're sorry for Maxl. The poor creature must be suffering badly.
To console him a little and give him a foretaste of better days to
come, we've sent him three helpings of oats.

Yesterday I sat in the garden all afternoon. Tata had gone to
Waltsch. I had to give the children a good talking to because they
were arguing. Today, Tata and Rudl went to Herr Makas to shoot
hares and Berterl went to play duets with Rosa. I picked cucumbers
in the garden. We've got masses of them. Nobody is eating
cucumber salad because there's a lot of dysentery about and all the
cucumbers are being pickled. We're going to pick the pears from

two of the trees but we'll leave the one by the pump. We've also been gathering apples. You'd love it all. The Garten is almost more beautiful now than it was in the summer.

Your faithful Mama
PS Do you remember little Fink who used to feed Rudl's rabbits and often came to see us? He died of dysentery today.

It seems the only good news is news about the *Garten*. In Podersam, there is not just dysentery but whooping cough too, and more lives are claimed besides little Fink's. Then, at the beginning of October, just as the days are drawing in, the gas plant is struck by lightning and the town is deprived of light. Valerie ends many of her letters saying it is too dark for her to write.

Letters from Heinrich become less frequent. He says he has not enough time to write, he is so busy in the shop, and in any case, he hasn't the inclination. His world is changing and he does not like the change. He senses disintegration and suspects defeat – the Empire's, the Emperor's, and perhaps his own. Austro-Hungary had nurtured and liberated him; it had provided the ground in which he could grow, and he had been ready and eager to take the opportunity. He was grateful, and his gratitude expressed itself as loyalty and patriotic identification with all things imperial. He admired, trusted, the imperial patriarchy, and he had created for himself and his family his own small empire, and had felt proud. But now the war – the unexpectedly lengthy war – is causing him to see things differently.

He is fifty-five years old and feeling tired. His business is feeling the pressures of the wartime economy – and the pressures of the wartime economy do not seem purposeful if the war is not being won. What he had previously thought of as a lifetime of determined labour and deserved achievement now seems to have been a sentence of servitude, not only for himself but for Valerie too. Others have built bigger and better businesses, have escaped the provinces and moved to Prague, and have flourished there. He becomes self-critical, and for the first time, he refers to Podersam in less than glowing terms: this 'hole', he calls it.

17 September 1917
Heinrich to Franz

Mein lieber Büb

Today, Monday, is the first day of the Jewish New Year 5678. On Wednesday, I am going to Prague with Rudi and Bertl, and Bertl will return with me on Thursday. So we're shutting the shop for four days. This week I'll also have to go to Bilin, to take the merchandise that was requisitioned last September. So that's another few thousand Kronen down the drain. I used to get upset over losses like that but nowadays I'm hardly bothered, especially not about money. It's of no value anyway. All my thoughts, my prayers, my wishes are only for my boy to come home safely, and that soon there may be peace. I urge you to do all you can to get permission to take leave for your Matura. Then I will have you here for a few weeks.

The shop is getting emptier and emptier. People would buy anything at any price, if only we had goods to sell. But we've got to be very economical with our stock and I don't sell to just anyone, only to people who give me something in return.

I'm sending you two Striezel today, and another two tomorrow.

Keep well, be good
Love from Tata

5 October 1917
Heinrich to Franz

Mein lieber Jungl!

I'm writing so little partly because I simply haven't got the time but also because I often don't feel like it. People are like madmen. They want to buy everything, but I have less and less to sell. My best merchandise is all requisitioned, and I'm sorry about it because I'm convinced the goods don't reach their proper destination. But who cares? Even if one loses 10,000 Kronen, it wouldn't matter if only you were back home.

Much love
Tata

20 October 1917
Heinrich to Franz

Mein lieber Franz

I have just heard that Herr Lenhart has bought a nice house at the corner of Čhelakovský Park. He's made a lot of money. Me, I'm just a bungler.

You'll be cross with your Tata because he's not writing to you enough, but I really can't manage it, I'm so overworked, and so washed out I can't concentrate on anything. You've had times like that and I'm writing this because you understand me. I tell you, Franz, I am very worried. I just can't visualise the future, it can't turn out well. On top of that, there's the anxiety about you, my boy. It wears me out and nothing gives me joy any more. Yet I keep looking forward to you coming home for a few days. Then I'd be cheerful.

I'm too soft, that's what's wrong with me.
Your Tata

26 October 1917
Franz to Heinrich

Mein liebster Tata!

With all this worry and work, you deprive yourself of your peace
and pleasures and ruin your health, and those things are all a
hundred times more valuable than money others use to buy
themselves houses. Why do you have to toil like this? You've done
enough and there's no longer any need for all this hard grind.

The artist of life is the one who knows how to make life
beautiful and desirable. So put your worries aside. Stop comparing
yourself with others. Why call yourself a bungler just because you
can't afford to buy a house in Chelakovsky Park?

You may be thinking it's all very well for your boy to talk like
this when I haven't been through anything like your experience.
Maybe you're right. But it would still be a good thing, for your
sake and Mammalittl's, if you could re-arrange your life in the way
I suggest so that you get a bit more fun out of your days. Can't
you give the shop a miss from time to time?

Don't be angry with me for writing what you may think are
foolish things. In any case, I know you will do as you please. But
my wish and my joy would be for you to find more pleasure in life
and forget about other people's misery and troubles. You have
enough of your own to bear.

Fondest love
Your son Franz

So Franz writes to Heinrich as Heinrich once wrote to Franz, and
Heinrich replies, 'You understand me. It's a long time since I enjoyed a
letter as much.'

27

A Jewish Brothel

A cold November night in a small town in Volhynia. A brothel that is not a brothel but the house of a rabbi.

The house of a rabbi who wears long side locks and a kaftan, who is thin and poor, and who has a wife and two daughters.

An eighteen-year-old soldier, who is staying in the town for a few weeks, attending a course at the artillery school.

A family gathered at a table, illuminated in a small circle of light. Sharing their food with the soldier.

Money changing hands.

The soldier and one of the daughters retiring into the shadows of the next-door room.

She told him she was called Blümele – the Hebrew name of his sister and grandmother. And he didn't sleep with her that night but lay beside her instead, talking of her life and his, his Jewishness and hers, and their acceptance of their different lots. '*Unser Herrgott hat einen grossen Tiergarten,*' she said. God keeps a big zoo.

28

Becoming a Man

*F*ranz wrote a letter home in which he described, but misrepresented, his meeting with Blümele at the house of the rabbi, and Valerie (a good mother) allowed herself to be deluded. 'Don't look too deep into the eyes of your Blümele,' she wrote. 'I know there will be all kinds of assaults on your heart, but I hope you will fend them off.'

She knows he is a man now, and old beyond his years, but she cannot quite reconcile herself to the loss of the boy he was. How can she? He left home as a boy, and the man he is now has not yet returned. Franz himself remembers home through boyish eyes, and their tender conspiracy comforts them both. Sitting at the desk in the back room of the shop one night, she runs out of things to write to him about. 'So I'll say good night, taking you on my lap and covering you with kisses. Then I'll tuck you in, pat the eiderdown a few times, and kissing you again, I am and will remain your loving Mama.'

But while Valerie is sometimes saddened by Franz's new adulthood, Heinrich welcomes the possibility of a grown son's companionship. The future he now fears losing is a future in which the two of them are side by side, when his present difficulties in business and his feelings of failure will be overcome by Franz's energy and resilience. 'You are der Grosser, the Big One,' he says proudly. 'You are the one who sets the example, and therefore you must be a real, whole man. You can and will be such a one, for it is on you that all our good fortune depends, and what I dream of lies in your heart.'

Rudi, too, is in the process of becoming a man. His bar mitzvah is planned for 16 March 1918, immediately following his thirteenth birthday, and because this is term time, the ceremony is to take place in Prague. He has been taking lessons with Rabbi Deutsch at the Jubiläumssynagoge, and, wartime trains permitting, Heinrich and Valerie will travel to Prague to be with him for the ceremony.

In the weeks beforehand, letters go to and fro between Prague and Podersam, and among the usual exchanges about home and school and Franz, there are some more formal and considered letters which seem to carry the emotional weight of the times.

28 February 1918
Valerie to Rudi

Mein lieber Bübl!

It is nearly 3rd March, our little boy's birthday! On that day, you'll start a new stage of your life, because your thirteenth birthday is supposed to mark the start of adolescence. Well, I shan't make a long speech, I'm no good at that anyway, but from the bottom of my heart I wish you good health, and may you grow up to be a decent, good man and a useful member of society, and give us, as you've always done, nothing but joy. There are always difficult things in life, no one is spared them. Try to get over them with patience and perseverance, be as pleasant as you can be, try not to be fearful, and you'll find your worries will soon be overcome. So, Ruderl, chin up, be cheerful! You are and always will be our dear little boy, whether you're thirteen or thirty.

With all my love
Your faithful Mama

3 March 1918
Rudi to Heinrich and Valerie

Liebste Eltern!

Now I am thirteen and I am entering a more serious period of my life. But I'll remain a child in many ways and my love and gratitude to you will always remain the same, even when I can stand on my own two feet. I'll try always to give you joy, and I will mind your advice and admonitions because I know they come from the bottom of your heart.

I have had a good birthday. It has been splendid spring weather and I went to a football match and then for a walk with six friends. It was great fun. Yesterday I got my new suit. It fits magnificently and is very large. My first proper waistcoat! Please send me clean linen and a white shirt with a white collar before my bar mitzvah.

Thank you for your lovely letters which filled me with joy. To you, dear Mama, dear Tata, I remain, with loving kisses,

your ever grateful son
R

Berta, too, writes to Rudi for his birthday, clearly feeling her responsibilities as an older sister. She will be seventeen years old in a fortnight's time, and from these heady heights, she condescends to write a loving but admonitory letter.

1 March 1918
Berta to Rudi

Liebster Rudel

You're celebrating your second birthday in Prague and now you are a man. So now you can't be homesick any more and must try to celebrate your birthday on your own in your own way. There probably won't be any birthday presents, you'll get them at your Bar Mitzvah, but instead you'll be getting letters from us all and in Prague everybody will congratulate you. Believe me, on the 3rd, we'll be thinking of you all day long. After all, you are our youngest.

On each birthday, you and I have always vowed that we won't argue any more. I'll do it again this year. We won't have any more rows, and each will do as we think best. But being four years older than you, I've got more experience and if I try to help you over one or two obstacles, you'll just have to trust me.

So, dear Rudelpudel, have a nice birthday, don't make any good resolutions, have fun instead.

Greetings to all from me, be good, and don't disgrace me.
Lots of kisses from your Bertl-Schwester

---

3 March 1918
Rudi to Berta

Liebste Berta

Now we'll support each other as brother and sister and we won't argue any more. Now I'm older, I understand you didn't always have anything bad in mind. On the contrary, you wanted to help me. I just misunderstood. So from now on it won't be as before. Together, the three of us will succeed in repaying our parents for all they've done for us and we will give them nothing but joy.

Many kisses
Your brother

---

24 March 1918
Rudi to Franz From Podersam

Liebster Franz!

I had a very nice bar mitzvah, and I wasn't at all afraid. The Haftorah was very long but I didn't make a single mistake. And so many lovely presents! Mama and Tata gave me a suit with my first waistcoat, a hat, opera glasses, 500 Kronen for my savings bank, stamps, and a book – *Ben-Hur*. On top of all that, I got cakes and pastries that dear Mama made specially for me. Herr Lenhart gave me a gold pencil, Berta visiting cards. When you come, I'll show you them all and tell you all about it. Did you have such a nice Bar Mitzvah? I can't remember.

The nicest present for me was that Tata and Mama were in Prague.

Now I am rated a man in the temple, but in real life I'll try to remain a child as long as I can, because you are only young once.

Keep well, and love from your brother
Rudi

But for all that the family congratulate Rudi on becoming a man, they feel, as he does, that he remains a child. Unlike him, though, they consider he should now behave in less child-like ways – overcome his homesickness, worry less, find more friends, have more fun and work less hard. Heinrich feels his youngest child needs toughening up, and Valerie, denying that she is mollycoddling him, complains gently that he is 'all soul'. Franz, recalling with astonishing suaveté his own time as a schoolboy in Prague, suggests to his father that he should write to Rudi informing him about the facts of life, which he might otherwise discover from more 'sordid' sources. Maybe, Franz says, Rudi is ignorant of these essential details and enlightenment would come most acceptably from an older brother.

This letter of enlightenment might have been written, ('Do as you think fit,' Heinrich says. 'I entrust the boy to you'), but if so, it has not survived. In other letters, Franz, like Berta, is generous with his advice, but not on sexual matters. An exchange takes place between them on the subject of literary criticism. Rudi writes to Franz about a book he has just read – G. Freytag's *Soll und Haben*. It is very beautiful, says Rudi, and 'the Jew is excellently portrayed'. Franz responds: 'You weren't expressing your own conviction when you said the Jew is excellently portrayed. You just wanted to impress me. The sentence reeks of German prep, or you picked it up from somewhere else. And it's obvious from your letter how difficult it was to pen it because all the rest of the letter is written normally, and that word '*charakterisiert*' [portrayed] stands out in clumsy Latin script. Enjoy pictures and books, Rudelpudel, but don't talk about them unless you feel inside that you really must. Beware of criticising and analysing your feelings. Live and have feelings but keep them to yourself. Just look at city people and how blasé they are. They talk so much about art that it's no more than a habit, and as a result, their views are dull and trite. Just say what you cannot keep back . . .'

Rudi, seemingly unoffended by this lecture and taking it as no more than his due, meekly replies, 'When I see what I wrote to you about *Soll und Haben*, I'm ashamed. You know, I did want to be clever, but I made a mess of it. Some of the boys in my class talk like that and being with them all the time, I'm infected. In future, I shan't think I'm cleverer than others and I'll certainly not write or talk 'blasé'. I'll just say things as they come.'

29

All It Is Is War

*H*einrich's and Valerie's wish had been fulfilled. In December
1917, Franz had been granted leave, had sat the *Matura*
examination, and passed. It was said that a soldier in uniform never
failed, no matter how ill-prepared.

He had been at home for five 'beautiful, beautiful' weeks – five
weeks when Valerie had all three children around her, when
Heinrich no longer called anxiously at the post office in the
hope of mail from the front, and when the house echoed each
day to the sound of violin trios. Then, in early January, he had
left.

11 January 1918
Berta to Franz

Liebster Franz

It is 6.30 and you've been gone six hours. In the last few
days before you left, I had the feeling that it wasn't just
home that made it hard for you to part. You seemed
preoccupied with some sort of nasty, depressing thought, and
it seemed as though you wanted to cling to every minute. But
I'd rather not write about that. One can't anyway, one can
only feel it.

The days are so empty again now. On Sunday Rudi is leaving
and I'll be on my own again. At lunch, we'll sit round the table
depressed and silent, and in the evening, Mama will sit next to the

stove and sew, and I'll be studying and writing to you, just like in the past. It will be as though the five weeks had never been. Your violin is asleep in the cupboard again. I think it misses you.

Keep well, Franzl.
Your sister

---

15 January 1918
Rudi (in Prague) to Valerie and Heinrich

Liebste Eltern!

It's 7.15 in the morning and I miss you so much I've got to write to you. Dear Tata is probably washing now and the lamp is standing on the chest and dear Mama is combing her hair and maybe thinking of me. I think of you, Mama, all the time, and in the evening I look up at the stars and think of you. I've never before found it so hard to settle down again. At night, when I go to bed, I always stretch my arms out, wanting you to give me a kiss. But there's no one here. Tante Ida told me I cried out last night, 'Franz! Franz! Mama!' And when she asked, 'What's up?' I answered her in my dream, 'Mama, are you sleeping here?'

I feel a lot easier now and I'll go to school. Please write soon, and come soon. See you before long.

Lots and lots of kisses
Your R

---

15 January 1918
Valerie and Heinrich to Franz

Mein lieber Franz!

Those were wonderful days, weren't they, my dear little boy. We were more cheerful and carefree than we have been for ages. Let them stay in your mind for a long time, and don't be downhearted.

Your ever loving Mama

———————

Heinrich adds:

It's as quiet as the grave here since you two boys left. Well, we'll have to get used to it again. Just you keep your spirits up and look forward to your next homecoming.

Take great care and keep well.

Your Tata

———————

A month later, Franz's battery was sent to Italy. Heinrich and Valerie heard the news on Heinrich's 56th birthday on 8 February 1918, when a postcard arrived from Franz.

'Now,' Valerie wrote to Rudi, 'the real worries begin.'

Franz's long train journey south through a snow-covered Europe began in the night at the railway station in Přerov, Moravia. The entire battery was loaded onto a train, the officers' carriage in front, carriages for the men behind, then the horses and guns. Slowly, over the next two weeks, changing trains and finding billets en route, they travelled in a wide circle round Vienna to Kufstein, over the Alps to Trento, and so to the Italian front. A thirteen-hour march took them up steep forest roads into the mountains, where they established their position within range of the Italian guns. British planes circled above them, undisturbed by inadequate anti-aircraft guns. The snow was waist-deep and trenches had to be dug so that the men could move from hut to hut and to and from their observation post. From this vantage point, on a clear day, they could see the towers of Venice and the sea.

Franz, promoted now to second lieutenant, was made *Protzenoffizier* and in this new role was responsible for behind-the-lines administration, finance and supplies. He travelled several times to Trento, Merano and Bolsano, coming down the snowy mountain slopes into the spring sunshine of the valleys below to purchase food by the wagonload for the men. At the same time he enjoyed himself on his own account and ate a good meal at a hotel, bought shoe leather and an Italian suit, books of poetry, and Virginia cigars for Heinrich. He picked a snowdrop on the lower, southern slopes and enclosed it in a letter home; and in return, Heinrich sent violets from the *Garten*, which arrived crushed but still smelling faintly of spring and home.

---

6 April 1918
Franz to Valerie and Heinrich

Meine Lieben!

I have only received eleven parcels from you out of the thirty-one you say you have sent. Please don't send any more parcels by post. It is unreliable and they do not reach me because of the difficulty of getting parcels and supplies up into the mountains when it is snowing. Instead, wait until I can tell you the names of people going on leave. Each week someone is going and can bring a parcel back.

You know, things like news of an advance in France really leave me cold. Advance, retreat, shooting, not shooting, speeches, re-arming . . . it's all the same and feels quite alien. None of it has anything to do with peace. All it is is war. Maybe there will be peace one day, maybe not. I don't know. None of us know. For me, there's only one thing that matters: home, and all the joys that means. Music, books, my little room, dancing, a girl . . . I don't know. Yes, and by the way, we'll be alive!

Much love from your loving Franz

8 April 1918
Valerie to Franz

Liebster Franzl!

There has been no mail for several days and as always it makes us anxious. Dear Tata does not like going to the post office if he can't bring back a letter from you.

It's been raining here, which is lucky because at least there's a chance of something growing. Everybody hopes so, because even here we're feeling the great shortages. The horses can't do their work any more because they only get straw to eat. On Thursday, when I went with Rudl to put him on the train in Michelob, we only just made it in time, the horses were so slow.

All is as usual here. We're all well. Occasionally we work in the Garten but otherwise do nothing except wait for mail from you.

Your loving Mama

9 April 1918
Franz to Valerie and Heinrich

Meine Lieben!

I am now no longer Protzenoffizier but back with Lieutenant Prusa at the observation post. I am positioned 1600 metres above sea level. We have put together two decent huts and the observation post is superb. There is mist all around us, sometimes snow, sometimes rain, but when the wind breaks up the clouds, the Italian plain below gleams bright and green through the gateway in the rocks. It's like the curtain going up at the theatre and the view is the most wonderful imaginable. The massive rocks jut out over the river where it breaks through the mountain wall. Beyond, and far below, the plain stretches out to infinity, with roads, parks and little white houses. Down there a train, trailing a plume of steam, runs away from the war. It looks so small, and we watch it for a long time, stopping at stations and moving on, and every time it starts up again, it blows a big puff of steam into the sky. We can even see people in the villages nearest to us – it isn't far, only 20 to 40 kilometres from here to the plains, and the spring air is crystal clear, and we have a powerful telescope.

Franz

15 April 1918
Valerie to Franz

Liebster Franzl

I'd just begun to feel relieved about you being lucky enough to do Protzenoffizier duty, when the fun was over. Well, the good Lord knows what He wants and it'll all be for the best, especially if you are with Lieutenant Prusa. He'll see to it that our little second lieutenant does not go without anything and that nothing happens to him. Have you stayed in your nice place in the mountains?

We had a lovely day yesterday. In the morning, there was a letter for Tata when he went to collect the mail. He was beside himself with joy. Then in the afternoon Tante Ida came from Saaz with a parcel from you. A soldier had handed it to Onkel Karl at the station. All the contents were okay. So as I said, a golden Sunday, and Tata was in such a good mood he would have given away the shirt from his back.

I'm so tired today that I shan't even fill the last page of this letter. My arms and legs are not up to carrying water in the Garten, but you ought to see it, it's lovely. All the shrubs are green now, there are blossoming cherries, and the buds on the apple and pear trees are about to burst. I'd like to be a poet to describe it to you.

So that's it for today. Love and kisses, also on Tata's behalf.

Your loving Mama

16 April 1918
Franz to Heinrich and Valerie

Liebste Eltern!

Here we have eternal fog, and occasionally snow and rain. But when the wind parts the clouds in the gap between the rocks, the plain below shines up at us bright and green.

In a couple of days, I'll be off again to the gun position while someone else joins Lieutenant Prusa here at the observation post. Lots of unpleasant things are happening here but I don't want to write about them.

The only thing left is to look forward to leave, and in the meantime, try to cope with oneself.

Your loving son

9 May 1918
Franz to Heinrich and Valerie

Meine Lieben!

I am sitting in the evening sunshine underneath a sturdy fir tree in
the centre of the gun emplacement. The telephone boys have put
up a table with two benches and rigged up some canvas over it.
The last plane has flown home, making a hell of a noise, and the
enemy has stopped shelling the mountain in front of us. Only the
mortars behind us fire every quarter of an hour and you hear a
howl and a rumbling in the far distance. Somewhere in our
position the duty officer is roaring orders, but otherwise, if my pen
wasn't scratching so loudly, it would be dead quiet.

Many kisses from your thankful son
Franz

Franz is seated, second from left

30

Sewing Lessons

*W*hile Franz swung between enthusiasm for his new position in the mountains and cynicism and fearful depression over the seemingly endless war, Berta was unequivocally enthusiastic about the prospect of a month alone in Prague. Life in Podersam frustrated her, and although she loved her parents deeply, her love for them fettered her, so that unlike her brothers, who for different reasons longed for home, she longed to make her escape.

She could not refrain from showing her parents how much she looked forward to some time away, and while Valerie tried to understand, Heinrich did not. He could not sympathise with her. Her cultural interests, her intellectual ambitions, and, maybe above all, her longing for excitement and fun, were of little importance to him. A girl belonged at home, and whatever feelings he himself harboured about the provincialism of Podersam, he was not prepared to allow them as an excuse for Berta's behaviour. Besides, his eyes were too firmly fixed on Franz, his anxieties too consuming, his pride too precariously invested in his eldest son for him to be able to give much attention to his daughter's predicament – even if he had wished to. As a result, a quarrel sprang up between Berta and her father, and while Heinrich wrote letters of praise and gratitude to Franz ('You are a splendid boy. I am very pleased and satisfied'), he refused to communicate with Berta and for a time, keeping her in suspense, he would not even explain his dissatisfaction and displeasure.

19 April 1918
Berta to Heinrich and Valerie

Liebste Eltern

It's been raining ever since I arrived in Prague and there's little chance of it improving. So I'm rather limited in what I can do. I started sewing yesterday and my blouse is making great progress. I think it might be finished in three weeks or so, but who would think how much work there is in a blouse? It's very pretty. Pity I haven't got the same material for a skirt; it would make a nice outfit. I also need a few accessories. Please send them with the other shoes and the red silk blouse, also the ointment for my eyes. It's in the drawer under the mirror in the big room.

I'm attending an English reading group with four other girls. They're all facing exams and are worrying themselves sick. They're older than me and I feel very important when I'm able to correct them and when someone mentions that I passed my exam last year. I also have French lessons with Fräulein Holzner three times a week, but there's no hope of swimming lessons so far. Pity because I'd like to learn to swim.

Tomorrow I'm going to buy myself a hat. The weather has been too bad so far for a new one because once I've got it I won't take it off. I've met Rudl a few times. He's very busy and playing in an orchestra. Otherwise, I've just about done all the things I had to do but will put off a few until the weather's better. I haven't got any waterproof shoes. Could you please send the black ones?

This evening I'm going to the Burmester concert at the Rudolphinum. It will give me a chance to wear my grey shoes.

Well now, how are you getting on without me? Surely not very well! How far have you got with the jobs in the house and the Garten? I'm glad I escaped in time! Write soon!

A thousand kisses
Your Bertl

---

21 April 1918
Berta to Valerie and Heinrich

Liebste Eltern

I've bought my hat. It's very beautiful, mauve-grey with a veil and pink flowers. Simply wonderful . . . but it cost 150 Kronen! There just wasn't any other I liked. I even dreamt about what you'd say, so thank goodness dreams don't come true.

The weather isn't so bad any more, just a bit cold. I've settled in very well, just like last year. We haven't got much bread because we can't get any from town, and meat is very hard to get too. The other night the maid stood in the queue from 1 a.m. until 9 a.m.! Otherwise everything's fine. Rudl is playing in a concert and I'm going to go. I had a letter from Franz.

Write soon.
Your Bertl

---

26 April 1918
Berta to Valerie and Heinrich

Liebste Eltern

This week I got a lot in the post – two parcels, a letter from you Mama, but I'm waiting in vain for one from Tata. I hope you'll have time next week to drop me a few lines. The parcel with the meat was very welcome of course, and the bread too. Now you won't have to send anything for a long time. If I run out of bread, I'll let you know. I noted what it said on the cake – and gobbled it up!

Everybody is thrilled with my blouse. It's really very pretty. Many thanks for sending the accessories. The blouse is coming on slowly, but I have already set in the sleeves. I wore my new hat for the first time today, and the leather jacket. Very posh!

I see from your letter Mama that you're not in the best of moods, maybe because of your cold. Or are you missing my invigorating company? It seems so. It would be nice if I could gather Tata's mood from a letter from him, but I think I'll have to wait a long time for that.

I'm with Rudl almost every day. Today at lunchtime we were on the Graben and he counted how many people were greeting me and got very excited. Yesterday I went to the Phil. It wasn't as good as last time but Fräulein Holzner grabbed me and walked me up and down and introduced me to umpteen people. I'm sure everybody thought I was a big noise because I'm so familiar with her and they probably envied me.

We've great plans for the theatre. Moissi [a famous actor] is coming, and we'll go to the National Theatre.

One of the other girls passed her English exam with distinction this week. Next year, when I'm old enough, I'd like to sit the State exam.

Will I get a letter from Tata next week? And one from Mama!!!

Write soon.

Lots of love
Your Bertl

4 May 1918
Berta to Heinrich and Valerie

Liebste Eltern

I haven't had any news from you for a whole week and am very worried, but I'm hoping a letter will arrive tomorrow. Herr Egnell, who arrived on Thursday, says that you, Tata, have a cold. Is it very bad? I hope not, for I'm certainly expecting you here next week.

I'm taking violin lessons again, though only once a week. Fräulein Spitzner organises nice concerts which Keussler also attends and so I couldn't resist the temptation to resume lessons so I could join the orchestra. We're to play under his baton in a church concert. I hope you're not cross about me taking lessons?

At last, this afternoon, a letter from you but again I looked in vain for a few lines from Tata. I'll really get indignant about it soon! I won't come home till Tata writes!

Could Tata bring my violin? At the moment I have to borrow one from Fräulein Spitzner.

I spoke to Herr Egnell at the station and told him I'd be on the Graben for lunch, but I was careful not to go because I get enough of him in Podersam and I simply can't be polite and friendly when I feel like being the opposite.

The weather is still lovely and I went rowing for the first time today. I'm going again tomorrow with Franz Glaser. The men here are almost all chaps on study leave and you see uniforms everywhere.

Will I get a letter from you Tata some time????

And will you bring my violin???

Thousands of kisses
Your Bertl

2 May 1918
Heinrich to Franz

Mein lieber Junge

I have had a cold and a fever but I'm well again now. Mama always worries when I'm not well, but she gets over it.

I've punished Bertl by not writing a single line to her while she's been in Prague and she's upset over it. Well, you see, to leave home for a time and enjoy a bit of air in Prague is one thing, but to be so keen about it that it's as if the peace of the world depended on it, and to have not the slightest regard for your parents, that upset me a lot. And then I think, if you don't care about me, then I don't care about you. Instead of being sorry for us having to put up with the mess here at home because Waversich is fitting the new stove, she rejoices in not having to be here. Well, she's made her bed, let her lie on it. A girl belongs in the house, in the home, and one soon gets fed up with a girl who is only 'educated'. It doesn't make any difference if she's attractive either, because that soon fades.

Well, dear boy, in the Garten everything is in bloom. The trees are laden with blossom and it's a glorious sight. It's a pity you can't see it. May you too flourish and prosper.

Love
Tata

In the second week of May, Heinrich visited Berta in Prague. Had she guessed by then that she had sinned? Or had she perhaps known all along, her letters more provocative than guileless? Did he speak to her sternly, maybe even reminding her of her good fortune and her reasons for gratitude? Did she defend herself or, like Rudi, merely accept and apologise, possibly weeping a little and softening Heinrich's heart? Whatever passed between them, their differences were resolved and Heinrich returned to Podersam satisfied.

10 May 1918
Berta to Heinrich

Liebster Tata

I don't want to write a long letter because I can't say in so many words how I feel. All I want to tell you is that I love you very,

very much, even if I can't always say and show it. But believe me,
I do. It did hurt me a lot that you were angry with me. But now
all's well again.

Your Bertl

31

The Problems of Defenestration

J can only remember my father reprimanding me once. I must have been quite young, and I have no memory of my crime, but I can recall sitting on the stairs, tearful and rebellious, and my father coming up the stairs towards me, very angry. He slapped my bare legs and shouted, 'I'm going to throw you out of the window.' Then he went back down the stairs, leaving me to mull over this puzzling threat.

How exactly would he do it, I wondered? The windows of our house were not large. Surely I wouldn't fit through even the most generous of them? Or did he intend to throw me *at* the window and break the glass? The panes were still not large enough. Surely he would not attempt it from an upstairs window? If he did, the landing window, which gave onto the roof of a porch immediately below, would be preferable: I could climb back in or make my way safely to the ground. On the ground floor, the kitchen window would be best. I could stand on the draining board and he would only have to push.

Once out, where would I go? Would I have to set up camp in the garage until permitted to return? Or in the woodshed where, incidentally, an imaginary friend of mine named Dabba already resided and would, no doubt, give me shelter. Maybe I wouldn't *want* to return.

All these possibilities ran through my head. In the end, I counted myself lucky that the threat, for reasons I did not understand, was not implemented. It certainly never occurred to me that he did not mean it and the words had simply come tumbling out in a moment of parental frustration.

My father was not capable of violence – not even verbal violence. When faced with conflict, in his personal life at least, he always sought a compromise. As a teenager it annoyed me, for it sometimes made him appear weak, although he argued that it was in fact a strength. He was also chronically indecisive. Choosing a new car, a holiday destination, a piece of furniture, was agony. More weighty personal decisions, such as moving house, were impossible. And when my mother, in later years, became unwell, he cared for her by the simple expedient of giving in to her every wish.

The many hundreds of letters that reveal him as a boy and young adult cannot tell me whether it was his character or his experience that led him in later life to examine so minutely every step he took. But his indecisiveness smelt of someone who has learnt that the smallest acts can have unimaginable consequences, and who is thereafter locked in permanent conflict with an uncontrollable world.

32

The Anniversary

The grenade was not thrown but was buried in the snow. Franz stepped on it and it exploded. The date was 11 May 1918, two years to the day since he had enlisted.

He was thrown into the air, screaming. His right foot, protected by the thick leather sole of his boot, was badly bruised but not broken. Instead, splinters of metal passed through the thinner leather of the side of his left boot, making deep, dirty wounds. Splinters also entered his thigh, scrotum and right forearm.

They carried him across country to a field dressing station where medical staff were working at a bench in the open air. They bandaged him roughly, and as he lay there in shock, he called for his mother. He was put onto a stretcher, strapped onto it across the chest and legs, and loaded into a canvas-covered lorry with other injured men.

He travelled painfully down the mountain. The road was in sight of the enemy and within range of their guns, so they travelled fast, rattling over the bumpy road, swerving to avoid the craters made by shells. The strap over Franz's legs broke and his wounded foot was jolted up and down, while the man in the stretcher above bled profusely onto him. He called out, but the noise of the engine – or the need to get out of enemy range – meant he was not heard.

Down in the valley the spring sunshine was warm and the cherry and almond trees were in blossom. Franz's stretcher was laid on the grass outside the small field hospital and he waited while a bed was found. Finally, lying between clean sheets, freshly shaved, a soft breeze blowing through an open window, he thought: I am lucky.

13 May 1918
Franz to Heinrich and Valerie,
from the field hospital in Primolano

Liebste Eltern!

On the second anniversary of my military service, I have had an incredible stroke of luck. Yes, really, luck. As you will have seen from the stamp, I am in hospital and en route to the hinterland. I expect to be in Trento tomorrow to be seen by the famous Professor Chiari; in about two days or so I should be in Innsbruck; and then, if I can manage, back to Prague. I'll wire you from wherever I end up and hope to see you there.

Now, to put an end to any anxiety, I'll tell you the full truth. I don't want you to be worried. I simply chanced on an Italian grenade and it exploded. I stepped on it with my right foot but it didn't tear the hobnailed boot. My right foot is badly bruised, and I have three or four big flesh wounds as well as a few splinters on my right thigh and right lower arm. Yesterday my temperature was 38.3, today 37.5 and 37.8. I am already down in the valley where it's nice and warm. So don't worry. Excuse the scribble – I'm writing in bed. Later, I hope I'll get leave. Hallelujah!

Keep well.

Love from your grateful son
Franz

After three days in the field hospital, Franz was put on a train and travelled in a goods wagon over the Brenner pass, looking out of a small window at the magnificent scenery. He spent a short time in a hospital in Innsbruck, and the hospital sent an official note of Franz's injuries to his parents. They were only slightly reassured.

20 May 1918
Heinrich to Franz

Mein lieber güt Büb

Today we heard from the Innsbruck reserve hospital about what
has happened. Thank God it is not as serious as they feared. My
dear boy, I just mustn't think about what might have happened.
We would have been the most miserable people. Bübl, Bübl, I
am so sorry. My heart will not be calm. I don't feel like doing
anything at all. You can't imagine how much we had been
looking forward to you coming home on leave, how much we
love you,

Tata
Do you need any money?

From Innsbruck, Franz was moved north again, finally arriving at the
Rudolfinerhaus, a big military hospital in Vienna. There, Valerie,
journeying anxiously from Podersam, visited him.

24 May 1918
Valerie to Heinrich, from Vienna

Lieber Heinelieben

My journey here was uneventful. I arrived in the afternoon and
immediately went to the hospital to see Franz. I was passing the
garden of the Rudolfiner building when I heard his voice calling
'Mammalittl!' He was sitting near the fence in a wheelchair. Alas, I
couldn't get through the fence, but after much telephoning, I was
finally admitted, even though it was late.

I don't have to tell you how pleased Franz was, and me too,
because I found him in much better shape than I had feared. Of

149

course, there's no question of walking yet, heaven knows how long that will take, but the doctors are the experts and will surely restore our little boy's health. He likes it here and is hoping to be able to go to the theatre and to concerts before too long.

I've had a look at a couple of shops, Gerngross and Herzmansky, and there's nothing for sale. The most you can get is 2 metres of silk, and nothing wholesale or in large quantities. The prices are fabulous, unbelievable. Compared with them we're giving things away. I wish our dear customers could see things here!

I'm staying in the Palast Hotel which boasts a grand name but seems a dump. Still, one's got to be glad to find a room, because there's nowhere else.

Dearest Heinelieben, I've told you all there is to tell, so don't worry about Franzele. We must thank God it all turned out as it did. It could have been quite, quite different.

Farewell. A thousand kisses from your loving
Wallei

Valerie stayed with Franz in Vienna, caring for him and cheering him as best she could, sitting by his wheelchair in the hospital garden, putting up with his moods. He didn't want visitors and frequently turned them away, preferring to be alone with his mother. Nor would he eat meat. In his state of shock, he remembered too vividly the dead bodies he had seen, the slaughtering of horses, the rats in the dug-outs and trenches.

His wounds were painful. From time to time, the surgeons would try to extract the splinters which were causing the wounds to fester; occasionally, the splinters emerged of their own accord. Meanwhile, in bed, his damaged foot had to be held in a stirrup, with counter-weights to prevent it turning inwards and permanently disabling him.

26 May 1918
Heinrich, in Podersam,
to Franz and Valerie, in Vienna

Meine Lieben

I was calmed and comforted to receive your news. I think it will
be best if you stay in Vienna as long as possible, and Mama too
should stay for a week or a fortnight. If you let me know what
is wanted, I will send money and anything else you need. If you
see something you want in Vienna, do buy it. I'll send you a
cheque drawn on the Union Bank for 5,000 Kronen. Go to the
theatre, or wherever you wish. Do what I say, enjoy yourself,
and be happy that we still have our boy. I can't put into words
what would have become of us if things hadn't turned out this
way.

Tomorrow my little girl Berterl is coming so I shan't be on my
own and you don't have to worry about me.

And you, Franzi, be good and cheerful, and rejoice with Mama. I
am with you and join you in your joy. I see you, I think of you, I
see how Mama's eyes are shining and how pleased you are. I see it
all as plainly as if I were sitting next to you.

Keep well
Much love from your Tata and Heinrich

26 May 1918
Valerie to Heinrich, from Vienna

Mein liebster Heinelieben!

I have been with Franzi every day and I will find it hard to
leave him in two days' time. He shares a room with three
others, all lieutenants, one fifty-three years old. But they are all

able to walk whereas Franzl has to be wheeled into the garden.

I think Franzl has about twenty splinters in his left foot and the doctors have not removed any yet so he has a lot of pain. His foot is in a splint most of the time to prevent it from becoming bent. What would have happened if it hadn't been for that mountain boot doesn't bear thinking about.

There are a great many visitors who want to come and many who have been but Franzl doesn't want to see any more strangers.

At other times, Vienna would have enthralled me, but now it's just the same to me as if I were in Lubau.

That is all for now. I am going on a trip round the garden with Franzl.

A thousand kisses from your
Wallei

27 May 1918
Valerie to Heinrich, from Vienna

Liebster Heinelieben!

Tante Adele was here this morning and we went for a walk. She wants to go to the Burgtheater, but I'm sure she won't get seats. She'll stand, but nobody's going to persuade me to do that.

I'm glad to hear that people bring so many things for Franzl. Don't waste them because when I get back we'll have to think about sending things to people here in Vienna who've been so kind to me. Onkel Ignaz was here last night and took me to the Prater. He paid for everything, despite my protests.

I intended to return home on Wednesday but the boy won't let me go, so I'll stay till the end of the week. He'd be so happy if you were here too, but he doesn't want any other visitors so please don't send anyone.

They took out one splinter today.

Keep well and strong.
Much love and kisses from your Wallei

28 May 1918
Valerie to Heinrich, from Vienna

Mein liebster Heinelieben!

You will be pleased to hear that they have taken out another splinter and
Franzl has no fever or pain. Tomorrow it'll be a week since I've been
here. I meant to leave but Franzl wants me to stay a few more days.

I am running short of clothes to wear and the weather has
turned foul. Perhaps you could send me some things?

I know you don't mind spending money, dearest, but I do. It
just disappears and you get nothing for it except poor food and a
few trips on the tram. And if amongst all the rubbish in the shops
one does find something one likes, the price soon puts you off. It's
unbelievable. Only the fact that Franzl gets so much pleasure out
of me being here makes me forget everything else. Even if I stay a
few more days, it won't be long enough for him.

Franzl needs a watch. Have you got one for him at home, just a
very simple one?

I'm still amazed at how quickly I've suddenly found myself in
Vienna. I never thought it would be this way, but I thank God
every day that it turned out as it did. You, dearest, have our girl
with you now, so that must make things a bit easier. Just keep
well, don't worry. I embrace and kiss you.

With all my love
Wallei

33

Bilin

*V*alerie stayed with Franz in Vienna until the end of May, and through June he continued to convalesce at the Rudolfinerhaus. He could now walk with the help of crutches.

In July, he was transferred to a small hospital housing twenty officers in the spa town of Bilin. The move was managed by Heinrich, who was now determined to do all he could to keep his son out of the war for as long as his injuries could justify. He begged a favour of his friend Dr Schroeder, who in turn spoke to Dr Vogel, the doctor of the spa. In Bilin, Franz had a better chance of being granted extended leave. Had he been sent to Prague, the notorious Dr Halbhuber would, without doubt, have recommended an early return to the front.

As the weeks wore on, Franz received news of his battery in letters from Lieutenant Prusa. They were under almost constant fire, one gun had been destroyed by a full hit, two more guns had been put out of action, five men had been killed and ten wounded. 'Yes,' Prusa wrote, 'we're having quite a war.'

The spa at Bilin specialised in cold-water treatments and used them to treat Franz for shock. Each morning at 5 a.m. he was taken to the hospital basement, placed by two large masseurs in a bath of cold water, and scrubbed until his skin was lobster-pink. Then he was placed in a still colder bath, and another after that, before being revived by a vigorous slapping and a communal breakfast.

It was a small price to pay for safety.

Valerie is standing on the far right. The exact location is not known but may well be in Bilin.

Bilin offered more than safety, however. The spa was only one and a half hours by train from Podersam, and three quarters of an hour from Saaz, and in Saaz there still lived Annie Wiener, the daughter of the schochet of the synagogue. Two years had passed since Franz had lodged with the Wiener family, and he cannot have seen Annie more than once or twice in that time – if he had seen her at all. But now Annie returns, kindly and available.

One evening, Franz took the train from Bilin to Saaz, arriving in Saaz as dusk was falling. He was dressed in full uniform, wearing his spurs, sabre and medals, including the newly awarded *Militaerverdienstkreuz mit der Kriegsdekoration und den Schwerten*. Annie met him at the station and helped him walk up the hill to the ground-floor flat the family now occupied in Bogengasse. She went in while he waited outside. She opened the window of her room, and he climbed in – not an easy feat, given his injuries, but thankfully the window was low. And there, lying naked in her bed, he waited for her, while the family ate their evening meal and finally dispersed to their rooms.

In the grey mist of the morning, he silently left and, with Annie's shoulder to lean on, made his way back to the station and the Bilin Kurhaus.

34

What Happened to Maxl

It is the summer holidays. Rudi is at home in Podersam and Franz is in Bilin. Rudi and Valerie go to visit him. They walk from the station to the little hospital, an elegant building set in an extensive park.

It is late July, and when they reach the hospital, they find Franz sitting outside, a walking stick by his side. Valerie has brought a Striezel, and they each have a slice, the three of them sitting there in the sunshine.

Rudi talks of school, and swimming lessons, and the new dog they have at home. His eyes slide towards, then away from, Franz's right foot. He wants to ask, 'Did it hurt?' Instead, he asks another question that has been on his mind. 'What happened to Maxl?'

'He died,' Franz replies. 'Most of the horses died.'

Tired, irritable and impatient, he adds: 'Maxl was made into goulash.'

35

The Wheelbarrow

Riding on my father's shoulders was precarious and thrilling. I must still have been small at the time, maybe not older than five. He would grasp me by the waist and swing me up over his head and onto his shoulders. I felt dangerously high up. There was nothing to hold on to, and his wiry frame wasn't solid enough to make me feel safe. I would put my hands around his head, leaning forward, trying to steady myself. His forehead felt smooth and very hard, and his hair smelt faintly sweet.

Riding in the wheelbarrow was another treat. It usually happened on a Sunday when, weather permitting, my father would spend almost all day working in the garden, coming inside only for the Sunday lunch that my mother spent much of the morning cooking. We would have roast beef or lamb, and a pudding, and to the outsider's eye there would probably have been little to show that this was not a conventional English household. Join us on the right day, however, and you would be served not roast potatoes but a strange concoction named as noodles, a mixture of flour and egg, rolled into sausage shapes and roasted in dripping in the oven. These were an invention of my mother's. My father had described to her the Czech *knedlicky*, or in German, *Knödel*, that he had loved as a child, and, unable to follow his account of how his mother had cooked them, she created her own alternative.

My father had a green wooden wheelbarrow, and through the course of a day's gardening he would fill it with a mountain of weeds and clippings. At the end of the day, he would take the wheelbarrow across and up the road outside our house to a piece of unused land where the weeds could be tipped. Sometimes there was enough room for me to ride on top of the debris; sometimes I had to walk. But either way, the journey back, when I could travel in the empty wheelbarrow, was a great excitement. As he rounded the corner towards our house, he would put on a reckless turn of speed that had me rocking and jolting in the barrow so much that, looking back, it's surprising I didn't fall out. I would scream, he would shout, and it was better than any fairground ride.

Any kind of game with my father provoked the same mixed feelings of thrill and risk, protection and exposure, love and distance. I never, not for one moment, felt rejected, but contradictory impulses seemed always at work within him – to love and yet not to commit, to commit and yet to let go, to let go but still to cling. He would talk about what did not matter and one knew that he was speaking of what did matter; he worked hard and valued the security he achieved, but a sense of true security eluded him. Strong and stoical, he was at the same time vulnerable, anxious and fragile.

When I was in my first year at the local grammar school, I tripped one day as I was running in the school grounds, and broke my leg. I was taken to hospital in an ambulance, and a teacher phoned my parents. It was lunchtime, and my father, as it happened, had called in at home for a quick lunch, so the phone call caught both my parents there. They came at once to the hospital and found me on a trolley in the accident and emergency department, waiting for the effects of my school lunch to wear off before I could be given an anaesthetic and the leg could be set. My mother sat by my side and talked to comfort and distract me. My father, utterly distraught at the sight of his daughter damaged and in pain, could not bear to stay with me.

That was how it was with him. His pride in my sister and me, his hectic enjoyment of life, his happiness when we were together, were real. But just below the surface, and sometimes ill-concealed, there was sorrow. I knew it, I think, from my earliest consciousness, and I grew up side by side with the extremities of love and grief.

36

Deutschtum and Jewishness

━━━━━━━━━━ ❦❦❦ ━━━━━━━━━━

*T*he war came to an end, and Franz never re-joined his
battery.

By the autumn of 1918, he was once again in Prague, lodging with
Frau Rabbiner and Dr Ernst Rychnovsky, studying chemistry and
physics at Charles University. Rudi was delighted. He had missed
Berta's presence in Prague. Now he had Franz to keep him company.

One day, Franz and Rudi are walking together across Wenceslaus
Square. Rudi is swinging his school bag, Franz is carrying his violin
under his arm, and they are talking, as they always talk, in German. A
group of Czech soldiers, returned from fighting in Russia, overhear
them and, picking the older brother, punch Franz in the face. He is
knocked down, gets to his feet, looks around, appeals for help. Rudi
runs to him, horrified. Passers-by avert their eyes and ignore him.
Swearing and hurling insults, the Czech soldiers move away. Franz
borrows Rudi's handkerchief and wipes his face.

This is Prague in the period immediately after the First World War
and the formation of a new Czech state. Austro-Hungary – the empire
for which Franz had fought – is no more. And while the constitution
of the new Czechoslovakia promises religious and political liberty to
all, many Czech nationalists would prefer it otherwise.

In Podersam, where the majority of people regard themselves as
German, the situation is still more confused. It may be a German
town, but it is the Czech minority that now holds power. This is felt to
be poor compensation for the town's contribution to the war effort,
which, when the final count has been made, includes the deaths of
eighty-eight men. 'The town has suffered greatly,' states an entry in

the town chronicle. 'Is this to be our reward?' And then, assertively: 'We want to remain German whatever happens.'

But following the incident in Wenceslaus Square, Franz is not so sure that he wishes to remain German. The experience turns him away from *Deutschtum* or German-ness. Wrestling in his diary with questions of national identity, he considers the alternative idea of Jewishness:

> I envy those who know without doubt that their nationality is Jewish. I am not sure that I can call it my nationality – this spirit within me, handed down through the centuries, from my forefathers, making me think and feel and act so differently to those amongst whom I live that they instinctively see me as a stranger. I've been born into a race that is also a religion and which, externally at least, keeps itself pure through its isolation. But does that mean I can speak about being a 'national Jew'?

A few years later, in 1921, still uncertain but increasingly feeling the appeal of Jewish nationalism, Franz attended the Zionist congress in Karlsbad and wrote enthusiastically in his diary about his admiration for figures such as Chaim Weizmann, Levin and Martin Buber. 'Now I have in my heart models of strength and courage. I know my doubts and am too honest (or cowardly) to ignore them, but at least I now know that if I do take this road, I must not set my sights any lower than the Jewishness I saw in Karlsbad.'

Rudi, at the age of thirteen, is less troubled by these issues and unquestioningly enters 'German' against 'Nationality' on a form he has to complete at school. 'Why?' asks Franz. 'No one else wrote down Jewish,' Rudi answers, 'and I speak German.'

37

Adolf Girschick

The facts about Adolf Girschick are sparse.

He was tall. He had smooth, flattened hair, parted in the middle. He wore glasses. He lived in Saaz and worked as an agent for an insurance company. He spoke fluent English and published a German translation of the letters of Keats to Fanny Brawne. He was a Doctor of Philosophy and a Freemason. He played the cello.

In the summer of 1919, he was twenty-eight years old and Berta Kohner was nineteen. He proposed to her, she accepted him, and a year later they were married.

These facts are unexceptional. But unfortunately, what mattered about Adolf Girschick as far as his future father-in-law was concerned was not what he was, but what he was not. He was not Jewish.

In his diary, writing just after the engagement, Franz speaks of a gap between the two families that 'should have been considered, for Tata's sake'. 'It worries me, but now it has happened, Bertl must be supported.' And he must have done his best, because in the only surviving letter in which Berta herself refers to her engagement, she thanks Franz for writing to Dolf: 'Dolf thanks you sincerely for your letter. He was truly pleased, and I even more so. You are the only one who sees him as a human being, not just a new relation.'

The marriage took place in Podersam, on 1 October 1920, at the registry office opposite the Kohners' shop on Ringstrasse. The ceremony was brief. By 10 a.m. it was over, and the guests assembled in the Kohners' house. A table was laden with pastries baked by Valerie, her sister Adele, and Heinrich's sisters Emma and Anna. There were many speeches. As tradition required, a cup and a plate were smashed for good luck.

Later, when the couple had taken the train to Prague and the guests had all left, Heinrich drank a glass of wine and wept over his daughter's marriage.

Dolf is hardly present in the family archive. Very few remnants of his life have survived, and those that have are remarkable mainly for their reticence. His translation of Keats' letters, published in Munich in 1924, contains no autobiographical information, and the translator's foreword gives away no clues. His initialled leather case, in which he carried his Masonic apron, does not speak loudly of his life. A few photos show him well groomed and urbane but without expression. A few extant letters, mostly written some years later, tell us little about the man Berta married.

A formal photo of Berta and Dolf, taken in Prague in 1921, perhaps in place of a wedding picture, shows Dolf's slightly arrogant face unsmiling above a three-piece suit. Berta, in a soft blouse, smiles and is beautiful. Does her expression tell us of happiness at last? Does her pose, leaning slightly backwards and towards her husband, show a new security?

It is all speculation. Berta's smile is a fact, and so too are Heinrich's tears. But the reasons for them both are an unknown story.

38

The Balcony: 27 August 1922

J t is a summer Sunday and Heinrich, Valerie, Franz and Rudi have just eaten lunch on the first-floor balcony at the back of the house. It is hot, but the balcony is comfortably shaded, and the afternoon is lazy and calm. Everyone is replete. The meal has finished with a compôte of plums and a home-baked cake. Heinrich is smoking his usual Kaiser-mixture tobacco. On the table, there is a large vase of flowers, gathered that morning in the *Garten*, and their scent mingles with the smell of the food and the hot air on the wood of the balcony rail. Muted midday noises float up from the yard of the Hotel Sonne, cut across by the buzzing of a fly or the comfortable creak of a rattan chair.

It is Franz who takes the photo. Rudi has gone indoors, and Valerie and Heinrich, content and a little somnolent after the meal, are reading. They do not move or look up when Franz brings out his camera. Later, when he has developed the picture, he inscribes across the bottom 'Podersam, 27 Aug 22' and pastes it into his diary, writing beneath it, 'A summer Sunday on our balcony. One day, much, much later, when we remember all this, we'll say we were very happy.'

It is this photo, more than any other, which brings me to the brink of the lost world that is my family's past and was my grandparents' present. Looking, as it must to an outsider's eye, much like any other old family photo, it is hard for me to explain exactly why this picture seems to pulse with life and feeling while others, cherished as they are, lie comparatively inert.

It may be, in part, the date scrawled across the bottom, for it is the date which means this is not just 'one day in the early 1920s' (which I might have guessed), nor 'a typical Sunday' (though it might have been), but *that* day, *that* moment, one brightly illuminated instant along the long, dark road of the past. In modern photos, where the camera or computer records automatically the date and even the time of a picture's taking, this kind of attribution is commonplace and easy. But old photos, inherited and unexplained, do not normally allow us to know the moment they are taken, unless they record more momentous events. In this case, the precise dating of such an unremarkable occasion as a Sunday lunch dizzies me with its significance. *This happened.*

It may be, too, the prescience of Franz's diary note. It is usually only with hindsight that we recognise the precious fragility of one ordinary day. Perhaps, for Franz, it is the fallout from the war – a continuing sense that things could have been far otherwise, and gratitude that they are not – that prompts him to write as he does. For me, looking back, his comment cannot fail to strike me, knowing as I do what lies ahead, and I feel glad that there was (one might almost say 'at least') this acknowledged happiness on that one shining day in 1922.

But more than any other reason, I think what makes me value this photo so highly is that it affirms all I have ever been told and all I have ever been taught to believe about my family. It holds within it all my father's nostalgic stories, his love and admiration for his parents, his sense of community, and that small, safe world of Podersam. It speaks of peace and contentment, of domesticity and small events, of the familiar and the known. This family meal took place twenty-eight years before my birth, yet I feel I could have been there. I could have drawn out a chair and sat down unnoticed, and I would have felt quite at home.

39

Die Goldige

---

*B*erta and Dolf's first and, as it turned out, their only child, a daughter, was born at 11.30 p.m. on Friday, 8 September 1922, almost a year after their marriage. The baby was a girl, and they named her Elsbeth Maria Valerie Girschick. Maria was Dolf's mother's name; and Valerie was honoured second.

Years later, the eleven-year-old Elsbeth was to record in her diary her discovery that she had once had a brother: 'I once had a brother. But he died. Isn't that sad?' The death of this baby, which must, surely, have caused great sorrow, goes otherwise unrecorded in the family journals and letters. Franz did, however, write in his diary about Elsbeth's birth, and although he sounds disingenuous, or downright naive, he was clearly moved:

'An incredible event. A baby is born, knows how to eat, turns to a spoon, feels pleasant and unpleasant sensations, has ears – so wonderful, tender and finely shaped . . . How does all this happen? It would be no more mysterious if someone was to tell me the stork brought her. I hope you tiny little mite will grow into a big, healthy person, and will one day love me.'

Franz visited Berta in Saaz soon after the baby's arrival and describes his sister as 'beautiful, tough and strong', lying back against a white pillow with her hair in plaits. He writes effusively about his mother, too, sitting by Berta's bed and feeding the baby. 'You were so lovely, dearest Mammalittl. Never before did you have such lovely red lips and such dark shining eyes.'

Heinrich, although alienated and distressed by Berta's marriage, was charmed by the birth of his first grandchild and adored her from the start. In a photograph taken on Elsbeth's first birthday in 1923, Heinrich sits proudly with the baby on his knee. On the back of the photo, a few lines in his own hand read, 'Here I sit with my grandchild on my lap, and my new trousers are all wet. Twenty years ago it was the grandchild's mother who did that, and I laughed then as I do now.'

Heinrich called her *die Goldige*, the Golden One, and indulged her as he had never indulged his own children. A saying grew up in the family: '*Die Goldige kann alles machen*' – the Golden One can do anything. He even allowed her to pick flowers in the *Garten*, a privilege afforded to no one else. It was the beginning of a close relationship that lasted to the end of Heinrich's life.

But how did the world appear to Berta as she lay back on her pillows and watched her mother at her bedside feeding her newborn baby? She was twenty-one years old; she had been married for a year. She had escaped the confines of Podersam for the slightly (though only slightly) wider horizons of Saaz, and she was comfortably provided for. She had acquired new roles in life, those of wife and mother, and she had a place in Saaz society.

Did the physical immediacy of childbirth, and the sense of having now altered the course of her life so significantly, satisfy her, at least for a time? Did her new situation put an end – at least for a while – to the restlessness that infects her early letters? Or were marriage and motherhood steps taken partly out of desperation and partly as a capitulation to the unwanted but inevitable?

The photos taken in the years after Elsbeth's birth show Berta well dressed and self-assured, looking older than her years, and they give no hint of anything unconventional or amiss. Yet in a letter written two years after Elsbeth's birth (one of the very few of Berta's letters from this period that have survived) there is sadness and uncertainty, and she writes regretfully about the broken bond with her family.

3 December 1924
Berta to Franz

Liebster Franz

When I want to tell you something, I always find I've lost my tongue. I express myself clumsily and can't put things well. I think it comes from talking too much.

I married young. Perhaps I hadn't thought everything through properly. At times I'm disappointed. What has made me truly happy and given me self-assurance are the experiences and impressions that I've shared with you. In the past, everything was so strong and certain, but then I got married and everything was different. All the time I've had to say to myself, 'You belong to those who are like Franz.'

It's ages since we talked to each other. At times I long for it with all my heart and I need it just to prove that I am still a human being and not a mask.

I wish I had the eloquence to write about the way I feel, but I haven't, so I must trust in the spark that leaps from me to you and in the sign on our foreheads which ensures there will always be a connection between us.

Elsbeth makes me very happy. I'm too young to be a parent, and even if I were older, I'd never have the self-confidence to bring her up. But I shall grow up beside her, and be young, and that is the best I can do for her.

Do come and see us soon!
Your faithful sister.

Berta married a man her father did not want her to marry. Yet it is Franz, not her father, who seems to represent the community she feels she has lost. She must be aware of Franz's growing sense of Jewishness and his exploration of Zionist ideals. But it is more likely that she is missing, not Jewishness but her Jewish family, not commonly held beliefs but the intimacy of the established group. Her letter speaks of her loneliness, and a struggle for identity that, despite the differences between them, is not unlike Franz's own.

40

Palestine

*F*ranz, having abandoned physics and chemistry and then toyed with other subjects in an agony of indecision about the direction his life should take, finally graduated with a law degree in 1922. He joined a Prague law firm, then moved to the Bohemian town of Brüx, a busy, dirty, industrialised town dominated by its open-cast coal mining. He was employed as an articled clerk in the office of a German Jew, Dr Moritz Bandler, and in his diaries he is alternately depressed and excited, bored and stimulated, by the realities of life in the legal profession in the provinces of Czechoslovakia. He sometimes thinks of returning to Prague and a more cosmopolitan life – or of emigrating to Palestine and a new world.

Rudi too is surveying what the world has to offer. In 1924, he left school and in September, aged nineteen, travelled to England to study textiles at Bradford Technical College. Like Franz in Brüx, he observes his new surroundings with a mixture of fascination and dismay. 1920s Bradford presents a black, angular landscape of mills and warehouses spiked with tall mill chimneys. Back-to-back housing, ranged along cobbled streets, spreads over the hills leading out from the centre of the town. Rudi writes to Franz: 'Bradford, Leeds, Halifax, Huddersfield are actually one huge city of a million people, a vast area as industrialised as the Ruhr. In comparison, Brüx is a friendly summer resort.'

By studying textiles, Rudi was equipping himself to develop – maybe even to take over – the family business, but it is unclear whether this is even part of his intention. For the moment, he seems simply to have an enthusiasm for 'business'. Taking life as seriously as ever, he is full of enterprising schemes and plans. Alongside his studies at the technical college, he takes on the agency for a glassware manufacturer, hoping this will lead to other business opportunities both in England and elsewhere. He works self-consciously on his English and finds occasional employment giving lectures on Czechoslovakia and Central Europe. He earns money playing the violin at concerts and dances, and leads a small orchestra. And in lengthy letters home, he worries about the possibility of being called up to do military service, which would, of course, disrupt his studies and business plans alike.

Rudi, front row, far left, with the Bradford Technical College Band

Joining the family business is not, at present, a very tempting prospect. Post-war business is slow, and Heinrich, hounded mercilessly by a nationalistic Czech tax inspector, is receiving tax demands he cannot meet. He has to enlist Franz's help with his affairs, and now, in his early sixties, he admits he is beginning to feel his age. After a day at home in Podersam, Franz writes in his diary:

This is the second Sunday we have spent doing accounts and pondering over tax matters. We're drowning in figures. It is clear that

Tata can no longer cope with these eternal business and tax worries.
He's giving up and willingly lets the waves break over his head.

For all their energy and their dreams, neither Franz nor Rudi can
quite take their eyes off home. The world may be full of opportunity,
but a deep sense of responsibility restrains them. Shortly before
Franz's twenty-seventh birthday, Rudi writes an emotional letter.

23 December 1925
Rudi to Franz

Liebster Franz

I know how much the tax affair has been preoccupying you and
you've really put yourself out to help Mama and Tata through this
difficult time. Now that things have calmed down a little, you must
allow yourself a bit of time to recover. Your birthday is next week,
and now you're such an old man, it's difficult to think what to wish
you – especially since we both know we wouldn't wish each other
anything but the best. So, looking on your birthday as the end of a
period, as a businessman might, I can tell you I'm very happy we
manage to achieve what we talk about so often in our letters. What
you have done for Ta and Ma in the past few months, and for our
home and family, makes me deeply grateful to you. And more than
that, I feel the deep bond between the two of us in relation to our
parents. You can be sure that if I had been in your place, I would
have made just the same effort to keep Ta and Ma in good health.
I'm so glad that on your birthday I can share this with you. Even if
we are getting older and are far apart, we are always close to each
other as brothers and friends. Think of this on your birthday.
My most heartfelt wishes for your happy future.

With love and kisses from your faithful brother
Rudi

In 1926, Franz visited Palestine. Victor Gruenwald, a friend and fellow lawyer who shared and encouraged Franz's Zionist ideals, had already taken the decision to emigrate. In doing so, he had turned his back on a share in his uncle's prosperous law practice, and had left his widowed mother behind in Czechoslovakia. Franz was impressed and disconcerted. Should he – could he – take the same step?

In the letters that the family wrote to him while he was away, the lure of the new country and the gravitational pull towards the old sing in counterpoint. Rudi is thinking of the business opportunities Palestine may offer, but his immediate concerns are focused on home. Valerie jokes about going to Palestine herself, if only she were young and fit enough. And Heinrich, who is in the spa town of Gräfenberg being treated for prostate trouble, urges Franz on, yet fails to conceal his fear that the promised land will deprive him of his eldest son.

---

6 July 1926

Rudi (in Bradford, England) to Franz (in Palestine)

Lieber Franz

I have received the letter you wrote on the day of your departure for Palestine. I hope the journey will be a rich experience for you. It is of interest to me, too, and I hope you will be able to bring me back some information, particularly concerning the textile industry there and possibilities for import into Palestine, including the import of glassware. I am very busy in this line, and during the holidays, I am hoping to organise it on a larger scale, but we had better talk first face to face.

I've completed this year's studies successfully and have decided to continue them in the autumn, maybe at my own expense.

For weeks I've been uneasy about Tata's state of mind, but let's hope he is making a good recovery in Gräfenberg and when you come back, we will all have a happy reunion. I'll help in the business of course and do what I can, and I do hope the days are not far off when Tata can get rid of his business worries. My impression though is that our business needn't give more trouble than others do but that it is, or has become, Tata's unfortunate pessimistic attitude which shows up more in a retail business than it would in a larger enterprise. That's why advice isn't much use. I have of course only limited knowledge of the situation at home and may be getting it wrong. Anyway, I shouldn't write such things to you in Palestine, which is supposed to be a holiday, although these lines may also remind you that for the time being there are reasons for you to come back. I myself would very much like to see that new world, but that is something that still lies ahead.

Send my greetings to Gruenwald.

With love and kisses from your brother Rudi
Au revoir in Brüx or Podersam.

9 July 1926
Valerie (in Podersam) to Franz (in Palestine)

Liebster Franz

I would love to write you a long letter but have very little time so I can only send you this note. I got a lovely long letter from Tata from Gräfenberg. He says he's feeling better. I hope to God it is so! I'd be very glad if Rudl were here because since you left, even though you only came home occasionally, I realise how lonely I am. Yesterday Frau Hohaus was here all day and kept me from getting on with things. It was such a nuisance. It's raining every day and I'm finding it hard to cope with the intolerable heat. Give my regards to your friend Gruenwald and tell him that if I was still young and fit, I too would go to Palestine.

Stay healthy and strong, my lovely Büb.
With many fond kisses from your Mama

15 July 1926
Heinrich (in Gräfenberg) to Franz (in Palestine)

Mein lieber Grosse

If anyone had said to me thirty years ago that I'd be writing a letter
to my boy in Palestine, let alone from Gräfenberg, I'd have laughed.
That's what I'm doing now, and I'll laugh even more once you're
back home. I'm greatly looking forward to hearing your account of
your journey, your impressions of the place, what you feel about it,
and what you have achieved there. I have been wondering what
has been passing through your mind. There is someone who has
come all the way from Tel Aviv to take the cure here in
Gräfenberg. His luggage is covered with labels and I would say he
is clearly not the kind of person you would want as a travelling
companion.

I wonder what your friend Dr Gruenwald will be saying to you. I
would love to be there to listen to your discussions. You will
probably come back even more suntanned than you did from Italy.
I imagine it's very hot over there, so just you take care not to fall
ill and to come home healthy and happy. As for me, I can tell you
that I am well, have good company, have put on two kilograms,
am cheerful and hope to make a very good recovery. I expect Rudi
will be home by now, and when you come too it will be your turn
to tell your story. That will be the best way to help me complete
my convalescence!

Mama keeps writing how all her anxieties vanish when she
knows you're coming home. Dr Gruenwald will surely tell you,
'Franz, stay at home for the time being. You can do more for Israel
there than here.' But if your heart and your ideals draw you there,
we shan't stand in your way. Everything will be as it is destined.

All love from your father.

Franz continued to think of emigration for many years, but when, in the end, emigration was forced upon him, it was not to Palestine but to Northern Ireland. Rudi travelled in Europe, but in the 1930s he returned to Podersam and home. Out of all the family, it was only Valerie's younger brother Karl, the seed merchant from Saaz, who moved to Palestine. And as a child I remember my father receiving a photo sent by Onkel Karl, showing him proudly standing before a large cactus with his wife. A cactus was something I had never before connected with my family, and even now, looking at that picture, it strikes a strange note.

41

Breakfast in the Garten

*V*alerie and Heinrich now awake each morning alone in the house. Lying in bed, watching the growing light at the window through half-closed eyes, Valerie thinks not of herself but of what the day might hold for her children and young grandchild.

Heinrich lowers his feet over the side of the high bed and eases himself upright. It is five o'clock, and a beautiful summer's morning. He washes, shaves and dresses. He goes to the kitchen, where his small wicker breakfast basket hangs on the hook behind the door. He puts bread, a piece of cheese, a small pot of rosehip jam, a ripe pear, into his basket and calls to Sekt, the terrier, who follows him downstairs. He lets himself out onto the street.

He walks briskly to the end of Ringstrasse, left along Saazerstrasse, left again onto the path beside Friedrich Loewy's barn. He meets no one. Only Sekt accompanies him, tail up and body alert, stopping occasionally to sniff or lift his leg.

He lets himself into the *Garten* through a wooden door in the high brick wall. He walks more slowly now, surveying his territory, pausing to smell a rose and admire the newly planted rockery. Ahead is the summerhouse where he will eat his breakfast. He brings out and lays the little table, fetches fresh water, arranges cushions and a small vase of flowers, unpacks his basket and takes out his pipe. The sparrows fly down from the trees, waiting to be fed. On the hill behind him, the church clock strikes the half hour.

He drinks his first cup of tea with relish. The *Garten* is peaceful. Only the faint noises of the waking town reach him over the brick wall. With his second cup, he lights his pipe and settles back in his chair. Scented tobacco smoke rises in a bluish cloud. This is his time for dreaming, and this morning he is dreaming of his childhood.

He remembers a fat little boy, boisterous and unruly, at school in the village of Piwana in the district of Skytal. He remembers that one day, his teacher, Herr Track, gave him some liver sausage to eat. Herr Track had just killed his pig, and his wife had made the sausage. It tasted so good! But his father, Abraham, heard about the liver sausage and explained to Heinrich that he should not eat it. He said, 'If you eat that sausage again, a horn will grow out of your forehead.' 'I will put it right for you this time,' he said, and smoothed Heinrich's forehead with his thumb, 'but don't eat it again.' But Heinrich thought, if my teacher eats liver sausage, it must be all right. After all, isn't Herr Track wiser than Vater? So the next time Herr Track offered him some liver sausage, he ate it again. It still tasted so good! And he didn't grow a horn.

When he was nine years old, he was sent to the grammar school in Pilsen. He travelled sixty miles to take the entrance examination, sleeping curled up in the straw in the back of a cart. His father said, 'Now you can make something of your life!' But he had only been at the grammar school for three years when Abraham broke the news that he must leave. 'Your Onkel Mann in Nachod wants an apprentice. He wants you, Heine. You will go to him straight away.' And so ended all Heinrich's dreams. So much for becoming a doctor of medicine.

Abraham put it to him plainly. 'Look, you cost me almost twenty Gulden a month at the grammar school. I can't earn enough to pay so much. With Onkel Mann, I won't have to pay anything.' And when Heinrich began to cry (he was only twelve years old), Abraham gave him a loaf of Elbogner Pumpernickel. It must have cheered him up because he agreed to go to his Onkel Mann, his mother's brother, in Nachod.

The trip to Nachod was quite an event. It meant travelling from one side of Bohemia to the other, and the journey took a whole day and a night. Nachod didn't even have a railway station: the train only went as far as Skalitz.

Abraham and Heinrich travelled from Pilsen to Prague on the mixed train, which carried freight as well as passengers. In Prague, they carried their luggage from the main station to the north-west station to catch the train for Skalitz. In Skalitz they got out and took a coach to Nachod, and arrived in Nachod after midnight. The coach stopped outside the hotel. 'Would you like a room?' they were asked. 'No,' Abraham said, 'it's not worth it at this hour.' And he made Heinrich a bed on the billiard table.

The next morning, Heinrich was introduced to his uncle and aunt. He thought they were very grand. His aunt was so well dressed he thought she was an empress.

When his father left him, he howled. Abraham told him to be good and obedient, and set out on the long journey home. Heinrich wasn't allowed home for four years. How could he have gone home anyway? Where would he have got the money?

He had to work in the house, clean the boots, fetch the coal, sweep the floors, light and tend the fire, and go to market with his aunt, carrying a basket on each arm. He slept with his cousin Julius in a tiny, cold room. It was swarming with bugs and the two boys painted the walls with the insect corpses. In winter they couldn't wash because the water in the basin was frozen. In summer, they bathed in the River Mettau.

After four years, Heinrich was free. He was sixteen years old and regarded himself as a man of business. He bought his first suit, boots and a hat, and took presents home for everyone. His mother cried when he arrived. She hadn't seen him since he was twelve. And he had to be introduced to his little sister Anna because she had been born while he was away.

Heinrich sits outside his summer-house, smokes his pipe and dreams. He listens and looks towards the garden gate to see if Valerie is coming. 'I'm an old fool,' he tells Sekt, the dog, 'to love her so much.'

The church clock strikes again. Is she coming?

He pictures his wife as he first knew her. He remembers her pink, glowing cheeks when he kissed her at the ball in Poder-sam. He remembers how excited and impatient he was on the way

to Libotschan to meet her. He remembers waiting for her in Saaz, and seeing that she was pleased to see him too. Those were happy days.

He refills his pipe. The clock is already striking eight and still she is not coming. He is looking, listening, and thinking only of her.

She will come. She must come.

She is here.

42

You Are My Father

'*B*eing with Tata gives me strength and joy,' Franz wrote in his diary. 'I think I am only truly happy at home.'

But Franz now has an established career and his practical independence is secure. For him, being at home no longer means living at home; supporting his parents – although it may deny him Palestine – does not mean surrender. In 1927 he becomes a fully qualified lawyer and formally announces the opening of his practice in Brüx.

Rudi seizes the opportunity for a humorous letter, typewritten in English, boasting of his own recently acquired qualifications:

29 July 1927
Rudi to Franz

'We have been instructed by our Director, Mr R. O. Kohner, Member of the Textile Institute, Diploma Graduate of Bradford Technical College, twice Silver Medallist and winner of the first prizes London City and Guilds Institute, 1926 and 1927, Royal Society of Arts Graduate, to inform you that he has taken due notice of the opening of your new offices and beginning of your activity as barrister at law and that after careful consideration we have agreed to patronize your firm with all legal affairs arising in the future and hope to be satisfied by your services.

Mr R. O. Kohner thinks it desirable to refer to this matter in a private interview and therefore extends a hearty invitation to you to spend this weekend with him at his country seat at Podersam. He will also be pleased if you will bring along your handball and fiddle so as to exercise your honourable body and brain, if any.

I am, dear Sir, your obedient servant

For and on behalf of R. O. Kohner, Managing Director

For Rudi, more than six years younger than Franz and with decisions about his career ahead of him, the draw towards Podersam and home raises questions that are larger and more exigent. As he nears the end of his studies in Bradford, he begins to consider more seriously the possibility of becoming involved in the family business. 'When I reflect on my future,' he writes to Franz, 'I am not averse to taking over our business. But it all has to be carefully weighed up. Perhaps I would feel more decided about it now had not Tata, in the very years when I was most suggestible, constantly advised against it. What is your view of the value of the business and its prospects? I've been well trained for it. By the end of this year, I'll have a good technical, commercial and general education, as well as knowledge of languages and some useful experience.'

Postponing the decision, in 1928 Rudi accepted a job as English representative for Oscar Dathe and Co., a German company manufacturing machinery for the weaving industry. He travelled between England, Germany and Czechoslovakia, taking in other destinations en route. His passport for this period is liberally decorated with

stamps and visas, and contemporary photos show him debonair and smiling, often with a fashionably dressed woman on his arm, posing against an English landscape or strolling down the pavement of some sunny European resort.

Then, in 1929, writing from England, Rudi sends a lengthy, considered letter to Heinrich that arrives shortly before the latter's sixty-seventh birthday.

February 1929
Rudi (in Bradford, England)
to Heinrich (in Podersam)

Mein liebster Tata

This letter will reach you at about the time when all your relations are reminding you that it's once again your birthday. And you may think that it's the first time in your life that you've received a birthday letter like this from your youngest.

To me, birthdays are not just about getting older. In fact, ten years ago you may have been mentally older than you are today. But in one sense it is true that we are all getting older, and for that reason I am faced with a problem: my future career. It's strange that the two of us have never discussed this matter seriously, and I must admit I've always been glad to postpone any serious discussion because I wanted to get a taste of other things first. When business and related matters were discussed at home, it was always under pressure and because of particular circumstances – because either you or Mama were ill, anxious or depressed – and at those times I always said to myself that the decisions taken were only temporary. But now, thank God, you are well and active, and everything is normal, and that is why I would like you and me, in complete peace and a rational, business-like manner, to discuss what we ought to or shall do for the future.

Actually, I have only got the choice between two careers – either to come home, or to continue what I started about a year ago. It doesn't matter which of the two I'd prefer. Both have pros and cons, and whichever one I opt for, I'll put my whole self into it.

You know that I am doing quite well at present, although you don't know all the little advantages and disadvantages of my current occupation as well as you know those of your own business. We've never finally decided that I should not return home, and I know that many of the improvements you have made recently in the business have been made with me in mind. But if I am to return, and take on a real role in the business, I will first need to know my working conditions, pay, scope of activity and so on, before I make up my mind.

Why shouldn't you and I go over these matters, just as you would if you were thinking of employing a manager? You must realise that as a young man I need a job that gives me a chance to prove myself. So I now need you to write to me about how I could continue and expand your work, whether there is any capital and how much, how long you would intend to help and instruct me, what my duties would be. You would have to tell me how much I would earn per month, and in short, whether I would be taking up an important post. In addition, there are of course personal considerations, for after all, you are my father and it is your business. There are essential, practical aspects to talk about, such as where I would live at home, and how much independence I would have. I'm sure you realise how important these matters are. As always, I was very pleased with your letter of 30 January, but certain things you said in that letter have made me write like this, because one can't forever discuss things casually and superficially.

You know very well that I am not firmly rooted at Oscar Dathe's and it may be that as his business expands, he will have less use for an English representative. It may be that in the future, I could reduce the amount of work I do for Dathe and combine it with work at home. An arrangement like that could be quite practicable for the next few years, for you certainly wouldn't want to give up work completely. But these are just ideas which have no firm foundation without a proper discussion between us. That's why I'd like us to talk it over calmly in several letters. In the summer, I'll be going to Germany again and I'll talk with Dathe, but before that, I'd like you and me to have reached a decision. We can't put it off beyond this summer. That's why I'm raising it with you now, because such things take time, and I am hoping that you will be able to discuss it all with me thoroughly and without sentimentality.

Dearest Tata, you mustn't say you have reached the end of your life. What you have done so far has certainly not been wasted effort. Your work is your life, and that has no end, because I, my brother and sister will continue it. I think that on your birthday you should not only look back with pride but also forward to the future. My gratitude to you is as great as ever. I am always aware that nearly everything I do and achieve is built on the foundations you have laid for me.

This long letter isn't really a birthday letter but only the first of many in which we'll discuss the things I mentioned today and I hope I am not causing you anxiety or upset. I'd like once more to wish you and Mamalittl all the very best. May the coming year bring you happiness, good health and contentment, and may the Lord protect you.

Rudi

No exchange of letters follows between father and son, discussing, in the ordered way that Rudi envisages, the future of the family business. Rudi's own, carefully composed letter has survived as a yellowed carbon copy. It is possible to picture him, seated at the typewriter in his Bradford lodgings, a grey February day outside the window, working laboriously at what he felt he wanted and needed to say, finally pulling the completed letter out of the machine, setting his own copy aside to be filed. But even as he signed the top copy and sealed it in its envelope, he surely knew he had little hope of achieving the 'reasonable' discussion he longed for, or of avoiding the sentimentality he feared. He knew, surely, in his heart, that he did not have a choice but would, in the end, take over the family business, not cleanly and decisively but simply as his father's son.

In 2001, on a visit to Podbořany town hall, I was shown plans for the extension of the Kohner shop that my father had lodged there some seventy years before.

My daughter and I had come to Podersam that year with other discoveries in mind. We had paced the streets, located shops and houses, and visited the Jewish cemetery; we had lunched, not very splendidly, at the Hotel Rose; we had talked with officials in the town hall and admired their collection of old photos of the town. The plans for the extension of the Kohner shop simply turned up by chance.

They bear my father's signature and are dated 1933. Two years later, the building work was carried out and Rudi opened a new carpet showroom. The business was once more thriving.

The extension that was built was modest in comparison with the plans. One architectural drawing shows a complicated three-storey structure that transforms the old family shop beyond recognition, eclipsing it beneath a stylish Thirties façade. Rudi may have struggled within the confines of Heinrich's proprietorial pride, but these plans smell of ambition and optimism. In the wider world, German nationalism was taking hold; and in the small-town world of Podersam, a different kind of expansionism was at work.

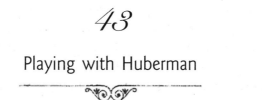

43

Playing with Huberman

*F*ranz drives from Brüx to Saaz for the concert, arriving in the late afternoon. He has just acquired a car, a Praga Piccolo Cabriolet which he calls *der Graue*, or the 'Grey One'. He parks it outside Onkel Karl Herrmann's new house – a suburban villa very different to the old family house in Schünitzplatz and testament to Karl's now-established status as a successful businessman and a leading member of the Saaz Jewish community.

It is Saturday, 29 October 1932. The concert will take place at 8 p.m. in the *Grosser Schützenhaus-Saal* in Saaz. Bronislaw Huberman, the celebrated violinist, has come to Saaz to play. Berta is to lead the orchestra, and Dolf will occupy his usual place in the cello section.

Onkel Karl is married now, and has two small children, the youngest just a few months old. So Else, his wife, has said she will not come to the concert but that he, Karl, should go. The opportunity to hear Huberman is not to be missed.

Valerie and Heinrich will also attend and they have come to Saaz by train from Podersam. When Franz walks in, they are sitting with Karl and Else, drinking coffee and eating cake.

Rudi cannot be with them: he is on a business trip to England. But Elsbeth is there, a gawky ten-year-old, a favourite with them all. She has spent the day at Karl and Else's house because Berta and Dolf have been rehearsing. This evening she will be allowed to come to the concert.

Sitting together before the concert, Franz and Karl discuss Franz's current project – the building of a Jewish hostel, a *Sportheim* for young Jews in the Erzgebirge mountains not far from Karlsbad. For more than a year now, Franz and his friend Robert Heller have been working to raise money and support for this ambitious scheme, and now the 'Heim' is near to its opening. The chalet-style building, with its tall, steeply raked wooden roof, is almost complete, and young Jews will gather and live there together at weekends and in their holidays, walking and ski-ing in the mountains. Karl is an enthusiastic supporter of the project and has contributed money and visited the building site. Now he wants to know the latest news.

So Karl and Franz talk together in one corner of the room, and Else and Valerie pour the coffee and cut the cake, while Heinrich sits, his pipe in his hand, Elsbeth by his side, and looks at the sketch book she has brought to show him. It is an October evening, just growing dusk, with one lamp shining behind Heinrich's chair, and the quiet of autumn over the room.

What music was played at the concert that night? What did Huberman say when, at the end, he turned to grasp Berta by the hand? Did the family, seated close to the front of the hall, stand to applaud, and did Berta's eyes shine as she looked towards them and took her bow?

In the concert hall in Bradford, to which my father took me as a child, the uncomfortable seating in the stalls was removable. The chairs were linked together in long rows but were not screwed down to the floor. Standing at the start of a concert, as everyone did, for the national anthem, there was always the danger, greatly feared by my long-legged father, that the people occupying the row in front would push back against their chairs, increasing their legroom and decreasing ours. Our strategy was to hold tightly to the backs of the seats in front, preventing their backward movement, while furtively pushing back as much as possible against our own seats in the hope of gaining an advantage over the people behind us.

The manoeuvre meant that any concert I attended with my father opened on a note of hilarity – which was in keeping with my father's general attitude towards music and the arts. He enjoyed straightfor-

wardly anything and everything there was to enjoy about a performance and was utterly without pomposity. He was capable, within the
space of moments, of foolish laughter and passionate tears, and had
the emotional honesty to give vent to both without discrimination.
Had he been present at the Huberman concert in Saaz, he would, I
think, have stood to cheer the famous violinist and he would, without
doubt, have applauded his sister with heartfelt admiration and
pleasure.

44

Quiet and Tender

The word 'snapshot' hardly applies to most early photographs. They are formal and composed even when taken outside the studio. But gradually, from the earliest photos of the Kohner family through the first twenty years of the twentieth century, the pictorial record becomes more relaxed and more real until, by the 1920s and 30s, the photos take on a life of their own that cannot be so very far removed from the life they represent.

Although now carefully ordered and mounted in albums, they are still an incoherent collection. They come in every size, shade and shape. There are sequences of pictures obviously taken with the same camera and on the same occasion; and there are a few pairs and trios of photos commemorating some special event. But even using these clues, the order I have attempted to impose is an illusion, and at best the photos can only be described as a miscellany, mostly undated, preserved for reasons I can no longer know, their precise significance obscured.

It doesn't matter. I will never know why this particular photo was taken . . . or this . . . or this. I will never know which ski-ing trip this was, which of Franz's girlfriends is standing beside him, or whether the garden in which Elsbeth is playing is the garden of Dolf and

Berta's house in Saaz. I long to know these things, because my curiosity is insatiable. But they don't matter. I treasure these photos for other reasons.

The *Garten* is the still centre, the place to which the family, now adult and dispersed, continue to return. There they come together at weekends for meals, for sunbathing and sleep, for conversation and games, and on every page of the album there are photos of the family in this beloved place.

Here is Heinrich, seated beneath a garden umbrella, stripped to his vest and with a handkerchief on his head. Sekt, the terrier, is in attendance, and in other photos alternately sleeps, begs, sits on Heinrich's lap, and looks inquiringly at the camera. Here, hardly comprehensible in black and white, is a rose bush in abundant flower. My father, with the aid of colour photography, took countless such photos of the roses in his 1960s English garden, each picture communicating the astonished pride a gardener feels at cultivating such natural glory. Here is Valerie (now Omama, by courtesy of Elsbeth's birth), always more formally dressed than Heinrich yet looking relaxed and smiling broadly, her teeth now obviously uneven, her ankles showing the thickening of age. Here is Berta, seated at the garden table with Valerie, Elsbeth perched between them, and the two older women, mother and daughter, leaning towards each other behind her back so they can exchange a word.

Here they all are, in photo after photo, in the *Garten*, on holiday, in the mountains, by a lake, on the streets of Podersam or Brüx or Saaz, and even, darkly, inside the house and shop. Photo after photo, living their lives.

Then suddenly there is one particular photo that bewitches, causes me to catch my breath, peer at it more closely and pause for thought.

Valerie is seated in a deckchair on the grass. A newspaper is on her lap. Rudi, stripped to the waist and wearing shorts, is sitting on the ground, close beside her chair.

It is, as always, the ordinariness that startles me. The photo is not posed. The photographer, almost certainly Franz, has caught, as the best photographer might, a particular glance in Rudi's eyes as he leans towards his mother, a particular consciousness in Valerie's bearing as she looks down towards her newspaper, and has captured a moment which, had it been precisely the moment before or the moment after, might never have had the poignancy that this particular moment seems to have.

There is an equivalent photograph that, if I had wanted to make a comparison, I could have placed alongside this one in the album. Franz and Heinrich are pictured at the spa of Bad Wildungen. They

stand side by side, both in swimming trunks, roughly equal in height, both conscious of their physique. Franz, who is in his early thirties, is in his prime. Whatever uncertainties his diaries may reveal, he announces to the world the proud conviction of his own success. And beside him, his father unhesitatingly claims his share of his son's achievements.

On the same page, the photo of Valerie and Rudi might almost go unnoticed. Yet there they sit, caught for a moment in casual but close communion, quiet and tender. And it is obvious that Rudi can never be anything but 'der Kleine', the Little One, and that no matter what responsibilities he shoulders, each morning Mammalittl will continue, maybe a little absent-mindedly, to butter his bread for him before he sits down at the family breakfast table.

45

Edithlein

At the Zionist Congress held in Prague in August 1933, Franz Kohner danced the Charleston with Edith Geduldiger.

Is it possible to fall in love while dancing the Charleston? Edith later claimed that when Franz danced deliberately off the beat and, disregarding the music, she followed his lead, he decided he would marry her.

They became engaged three months later and married on 27 March 1934. Franz was thirty-five years old, and Edith was twenty-two.

Through the early 1930s, Valerie had had frequent periods of illness, and in February 1934 she was confined to bed. She wrote longingly and affectionately to 'her dear little daughter':

8 February 1934
Valerie to Edith

Mein lieber Tochterlein

My new notepaper is proud of being initiated with a letter to you, although because of my pains, I can't write prettily. Yes, my dear girl, if I had had you sitting by my bedside, I would have been on my feet long ago. Your sweet chatter would have made me forget all about my pains. Instead, I have to put up with going to the hospital every day and having diathermic treatment, which doesn't seem to have done any good whatsoever so far.

But Edithlein, you aren't well either. What's the matter with your teeth? Are you suffering with them? Are you swollen up again, poor girl, as you were before? I'm so sorry, and if there was anything I could do to make you better, I would happily do it. But I think Franzl is better at that. He's got his own well tested way, hasn't he, Edithlein? I know he's with you today, and it would have been nice if he could have brought you over to Podersam for Sunday, and then we could have had a good long talk together.

Don't worry about what his favourite foods are and things like that. Whatever you prepare, he'll sense your hand in it, and he'll love it, and that will be the right thing to give him. I'm sure our boy will be well cared for by you, you are such a sweet, clever girl. May you be happy and contented and may your home be in his heart.

I know you will both also make your home a place for all those who love you – for your dear parents, and for us two old ones too. I thank the good Lord for letting me perhaps live to see it all.

Rudi sends his love, as does Tata, and lots of kisses from your faithful

Mama

Sekt has just jumped on my lap and sends his regards too.

————————— ᴎ ᴄ ᴎ _____

Like Valerie, Heinrich welcomed Edith with unreserved affection. When he went with Franz for a brief visit to the Heim in the Erzgebirge mountains, he wrote a short note to Edith, who had gone to Vienna with her father:

——————— ᴎ ᴄ ᴎ _____

Edith

I'm here with Franz at the Heim. It's raining but inside it's bright because the lights are on. On our table are ten mushrooms that we found today. I believe Franz is thinking of you as much as I am, but he loves you more. We're listening to nice music, eating cheese and I am having a beer. And you are sitting with your Vatti and are probably eating Viennese Schnitzel in Vienna. I'd like Franz to eat well too, because his nerves need fat. I'm sure you'll have a good effect on him, Edithlein.

I think you'll soon be going to bed. Sleep well, greetings from Franz, and lots of kisses from your Tata.

————————— ᴎ ᴄ ᴎ _____

Through the months before the marriage, moved by his son's relation-ship, Heinrich writes many pencilled notes, sentimental verses and reflections, thinking of his own long marriage and hoping for his son's future happiness. He may not have shared all that he wrote with Franz:

Will Edith be what Franz hopes she will be? Will she be content with what he has to offer? Will the child he was become a man? We have always been poor and modest; our wealth was our love. Hand in hand we built a world for our children, a garden filled with flowers. They knew nothing of our toil and sorrow. We did it all for them alone. We started the struggle with life and not every day was blessed with sunshine. But we never reproached our parents for not having provided us with more and we worked gladly, hard, with understanding and love. Will the two who are now starting life always remember that married life means many sacrifices which one must make joyfully and lovingly, that it is not all roses all the way and that illusions often fly away.

The wedding itself draws near. In Edith's home town of Trautenau, the new young Orthodox rabbi will not provide the kind of ceremony that Franz and Edith want. To marry in Podersam, the groom's home town, would be unconventional and unacceptable to Edith's parents. So it is decided that the wedding will be a civil one and will take place in Prague, in the town hall in the Old Town Square. A week before, Berta writes a short note to Franz in Brüx:

---

20 March 1934

Berta (in Saaz) to Franz (in Brüx)

Mein lieber grosser Bruder

A week from now you will be married. I don't know why I am howling. A little while ago, I found a poem which you gave me on the eve of my wedding. It's something about cakes and wedding bells and so on. That was a long time ago, and I can't compose a poem, but I just want to tell you again how fond I am of you and how much I wish you every happiness. You're marrying such a lovely, good woman. Be good to her and stay good to us, and make a better job of it than I. All the very, very best, Franzi!

Your sister

---

26 March 1934
Valerie (in Podersam) to Franz
(at the Hotel Zlata Husa in Prague)

Mein lieber Büb

How often have I had to let you go with a very heavy heart –
when you were a very little boy, and later too. My heart was so
often heavy and sad, and I shed many a tear over you. Today, too,
my heart is heavy, but it is something quite different, for today
there is also joy. I know this farewell is the beginning of a new life
for you. You are marrying a good, sweet woman who will help you
bear more easily the burdens which no one is spared, and who will
love you as she does now and as you love her. She too is giving
up her carefree youth to be with you. Be not only her husband and
lover. You must also take the place of her father and mother so
that she knows that her true home is with you alone.

Oh my dear Franzele, if only I weren't laid up here in Podersam,
I'd be with you both and I shouldn't be writing such a silly letter.
But you wanted it, I promised it, and one has to keep one's word.
In my thoughts I shall always be with you, and so we shall always
be together, till we meet again in happiness. Amen.

Your Mama

So the family gathered without Valerie in Prague and Franz and Edith
were married simply, without the Jewish rituals they might otherwise
have chosen. Yet Franz still whispered, for Edith's ears alone, the
Hebrew words from the Jewish service, '*harei at mekudeshet li ba-tabaat
zu*,' as he placed the ring on her finger. 'With this ring, you are made
holy to me.'

And at the time and even through the honeymoon in France and
Italy, the family continued to write to the couple and to record their
happiness and concern for them, each locked into their own responses
to this long-awaited family event. And Rudi, increasingly conscious

that Mama and Tata will now be his responsibility, speaks out with a different voice and writes for Franz an untranslatable, part incomprehensible, multilingual letter of out-and-out fun.

———————— ∿ ‿ ————————

31 March 1934
Rudi (in Podersam) to Franz
(on his honeymoon on the Riviera)

Sehr verschätztes Ehepareček

C'est aujourdhuie ce que nous avons le premier jour de notre Pesach festival et je suis quite sure, že Mr le Ober a servi pour votre café au lait les mazos. Oh, Monsieur, j'ai vu une petite annonce que vous ěteskupplé avec une mademoisele de Trutnov, zvané Edith, c'est la měme made (in Czechoslovakia) quelle a été a Poderbořany, n'est-ce pas? Elle es une girl tres jolie savonarola pajouli es qu habiamo transmesso dans le harbour de marriage, mais non my little boy, no rosche ponim face, pourquoi prěceti a cannes, if you are not canned. Tomorrow werde ich machen une little excursion a le chateau des juifs a Stolzenhain, ou ils ont 60 cm de sněhu mais le chateao est tout a fait ausverkauft, therefore weiss ich nicht mit wem je serai dans le postel. Mais c'est tout a fait egal, nicht Wibei Dir, etsch, piave po?

Our scholettopf upstairs ist schon etwas besser, immermal steht sie auf, elle ne voudrait pas take une topf plempl pour moi parceque je suis le seule über welchen sie noch ein Dispositionsrecht aus üben kann. Dans la zahrade nous avons des violets at croquis et le soleil scheint den ganzen Toch daruf, but they're all indanthren. Le Geschäft ist tres miserable et nous n'avons pas de mesumen de payer les rechnungs. Mais, trotzdessen nous stavirons et après il y aura une little insolvence arrangé par messieurs les docteurs Bandler Kohner at Most et tout sera en máslo. Les meisses avec Schubert est très jolie mais maintenant nous avons 3 Tage Pessach Frieden. Eh bien, mes chères pigeons, restez vous bien a la Riviera parceque il sera la dernière okkasion de vivre en Sus and Brus et après vous aurez 70 annees des tachlis, meissis, dětí, broischis, et acceptez de moi les Rüsselkissis tres enfonces.

Rudi

46

Vote for SHF

*M*arried life for Franz could have been very different. For several years before his chance meeting with Edith, he had been deeply involved with another woman who was not Jewish. He wanted to marry her but constantly hesitated, expressing his uncertainties not only in private in his diary but also openly to his father who, in return, wrote frequent letters of advice. Heinrich's views about Berta's marriage ten years before are never mentioned or alluded to in this correspondence, and although he expresses concern, he promises to support Franz in the marriage he wishes to make. In the end, it is Franz himself who decides that he wants 'a wife who will light the Sabbath candles'.

So Franz and Edith create a life together, first in the flat where Franz was already living, then moving to a new and larger flat on the hill overlooking the town of Brüx. In March 1936, their first child, Dinah, is born; and their second, Ruth, follows a year later.

Heinrich and Valerie remain closely in touch with them. Although Brüx is only short distance from Podersam by car and visiting is not difficult, they still write frequent letters, telling of their own lives and dispensing advice freely to the young family. Only very occasionally do Franz and Edith seem to suffer from a sense of intrusion. Mama and Tata have simply expanded the scope of their affections. They draw Edith into their loving circle because she has undertaken to love Franz, and that is the ticket that opens the doors of their hearts. She is independent, educated and intelligent, but she is dancing to Franz's beat.

In Podersam, Heinrich continues to preside over the shop. On summer mornings, he still walks to the *Garten* and picks a rose for his buttonhole. Later, he stands at the shop door. The street is busy, passers-by greet him, and he talks and teases and flirts. Inside, Valerie organises the day, gives instructions to the shop assistants, rules up the account book for the day's sales; and in the office at the back, Rudi is on the telephone, dealing with suppliers, reviewing the stock, working on the plans for the extension.

Rudi chafes under the difficulties of the régime. He turns to Franz for the understanding he feels he does not get from his parents, but there are arguments between them, and Rudi must repeatedly try to explain his frustrations and sense of isolation. He writes late at night, seated at his typewriter, keeps a carbon copy, and receives similarly typed letters from Franz.

5 October 1934
Rudi to Franz

Lieber Franz

You know full well it wasn't an easy choice for me to come to Podersam, but there were circumstances, not to mention our love for our parents, that induced both you and me not to do what we would have chosen at that time had we been able to be independent. And now I am here, and for the time being any sudden change is out of the question. So I have to force myself to put up with everything, and I endeavour to do it in a way that causes least conflict and anxiety to myself and others.

You have always been free to do what you wanted. Try and visualise everything you have been through over the years and then transpose it all to Podersam. Would you have managed to live here in the way you wanted? You come home visiting, which is always nice, but you always remain a visitor. The rest of the time you are free and can do what you like and nobody interferes. I am thirty now, and have no freedom. I'm not only tied to the business but also living with Tata and Mama, and living with one's parents is not the same as living with a wife. Here I have to be part child, part son, part man, part bridegroom, part boss, part apprentice. Sometimes I have to be resolute (when, for example, Tata isn't well or is sleepy), and at other times very humble and obedient when he does things in the way *he* wants to do them. I can't talk about anything because that upsets Mama especially, and I just have to do whatever is necessary. When Tata throws a parcel onto the floor in the store, it's me who has to pick it up because I don't want Mama to stumble over it. When he decides to water the yard, I have to do it as well to stop him over-exerting himself. And meanwhile I have to stow away my own ideas, for I've got to be glad, as everyone is, that Tata is active and energetic in the shop. Because otherwise it would be the end of him. And in general, he won't tolerate opposition.

I don't want any praise, and anyway, I get it extremely rarely. Maybe that is why I seem to praise myself. I do know that Tata and Mama realise the business could no longer run without me, but I don't want them to feel they have to admit that to me. What I am managing here, often in the face of great resistance, isn't bad. I'm still ambitious and it hurts if one has to curb one's ambitions too often. Small wonder that at times I get things wrong.

You or Bertl always come home to enjoy yourselves, but I am here, and I have to deal with everything. You know that as far as material things go, I have nothing, except the prospect of owning something some day. I could help myself to what I want, but it would mean much more to be given it, for it would signify that I'm appreciated. Business is slack and I am trying to save, taking very little out of it and not allowing myself too much. In these circumstances, I can't be carefree in the way you advise, and in any case, it's quite impossible in Podersam and in the situation I've described. Yet I do think your fears that I'm 'going to the dogs', or 'haven't really got the knack', are unfounded. Beneath that hard crust of mine, it's all there – cheerfulness, intelligence, energy, knowledge, adaptability. Some animals hibernate and feed on the fat they've laid by during the summer . . .

Please tear up this letter.

Rudi

Franz finds it hard to understand. He asks Rudi not to blame his situation on either Podersam or Heinrich. He feels the answers lie within Rudi himself, and there is little acknowledgement of the constraints he is suffering or the bitterness that sings out from the lines of this and later letters.

1935 (no date)
Franz (from Brüx) to Rudi (in Podersam)

Liebster Rudi

It's true you live a restricted sort of life, and that you're lonely and torn by doubts, but I see the beginnings of this back in your childhood, and I ask myself which part of your attitude is the consequence of the unsatisfactory situation in which you find yourself and to what extent the situation is the result of your character and make up.

Do you really know what you want? Do you believe in anything? Sometimes, in a crisis, one has to think about that, even if one doesn't want to talk about it.

What can be seen objectively is reducible to two basic issues: (1) to marry or not, and (2) Podersam or not. You are now in Podersam, unmarried. You know the business you are to take over, but not the woman you are to marry. But you can't stay alone in Podersam unless you want to become a complete loner – to which you strongly incline – quite apart from the fact that Ta and Ma will never get out of the shop as long as you stay single. I hope you do want to marry, because in that case you will find someone, and when you get to that stage, you needn't worry any more. Love and kindness will secure a moderately nice wife even in Podersam, and you needn't worry about money. Ta has said repeatedly that she needn't have any money. The business will surely support two families and needs no capital investment. So no concessions are needed from you.

You are in a *very happy* position – which is not something I can say for myself. If anything should happen to me, if I catch the flu, for example, and there are consequences, I'm *finished*. I have had to curtail my ambitions and ideals in any case. One can't sit on two stools without it making your bottom ache. Any chair *you* sit on will be well upholstered and big enough for two.

You rightly criticise me for the way I react to difficulties – violently, angrily, pessimistically. True, but I thought they were real obstacles, matters of principle. And there have been instances too when my nerves have given way, for which I can claim a little excuse because of the war. I don't see those problems in you and I tell you openly, I don't like the way you always put Tata in the centre of the battlefield. Maybe it's difficult in day-to-day life to get on with such an individualistic personality, but fifty per cent of the difficulties lie within you. You constantly make him your excuse by including his ideas about the future in your own views and turning your struggle with yourself into a struggle with him. Whatever the external circumstances, you must co-operate with him, you depend on his material arrangements, you must do your duty. But inwardly, you can loosen up, free yourself, and that will enable you to make the right decision about which woman you'll choose and where you'll go from there. I myself think you will stay in Podersam, but whether that's the right thing to do is another matter. And you will marry when things have settled down a bit more.

If you remain as difficult as you are now, you'll either make a bad choice or be unhappily married. But if you give a bit and are generous, then marriage won't be a business deal but will be what you desire. So – good luck.

Franz

The news from Germany is not mentioned. It is not often within the family's focus. Although it is impossible to imagine that, aware and informed as they are, they are not discussing the disturbing political developments in the world outside, neither Rudi's depression nor Franz's advice seem connected to any wider anxiety. They are living in their own moment.

In Germany, the *Sudetendeutsche Partei* (SdP), headed by Konrad Henlein, is now closely aligned with Hitler and Nazism and, from 1935, this party is actively campaigning for the return of Czechoslovakia's historically most German areas, the Sudetenland to German ownership. As a town within the Sudetenland, Podersam would thus become part of Germany. The Kohners are German, but they are also Jewish, and the racial laws announced at the Nazi party rally in Nuremberg in 1935 can have left members of the Podersam Jewish community in little doubt about the implications of German possession of their area.

In Podersam itself, political activity is increasing and there are signs of growing German separatism. It is Valerie, more watchful and thoughtful for her family and less self-absorbed, who occasionally notes what she observes. In 1935, she writes:

'Everything here is rotten, it doesn't bear description, the whole atmosphere, this hostility, you feel it all over.'

'Tomorrow is 1st May and the SHF [the *Sudeten Heimat-Front*, a previous name for the pro-Nazi party that became the SdP] are planning a big do. Six bands are going to play, and during the night, posters were slapped onto all the houses saying 'Vote for SHF!' In our case, they stuck them on as high as the first floor. I feel sorry for Rudl, who has to spend his life here in the future.

And yet for now, they do believe they will spend their future lives in this town, and they continue to work and invest in their business, take holidays, seek treatments for their various ills, worry over the children and grandchildren, curse the constraints of age. They hold tenaciously to the gifts that life continues to bring them.

12 February 1937
Heinrich (in Podersam) to Edith (in Brüx),
immediately after his seventy-fifth birthday

Meine liebste Edith

Your verbal congratulations were so cordial and deeply felt that even the nicest letter could not have expressed them so well and I felt how fond you are of me. And now you and my darling little Dinah have written me a lovely letter and this morning I have also received the nice tea cosy. I really don't deserve so much warmth and kindness. I am so touched and don't know how to thank you for everything. If I tell you that I love you very much and have come to honour and cherish you even more, let this be my thanks. If from time to time I suffer a little illness and am not as high spirited, it's my age. But your and Franz's love and loyalty is better than any medicine; they cheer me and I regain the will to live. I am convinced that, since I have the will, I shall be with you all for quite a while. You must not worry. The dear Lord has been good to me so far and will hear my prayers in future too. He will protect you all and will grant me many years to be spent with all of you in joy and happiness. Keep well and cheerful. Once again, my sincerest thanks and much love

Tata

47

The Telephone

*B*erta has taken a lover.

Franz suspected long ago that Berta has not been faithful to Dolf and once mentioned it, disapprovingly, in his diary. 'Terrible, if it's true.' Now it is Elsbeth, aged fourteen, who writes indirectly but knowingly in her diary about her mother's most recent affair.

Elsbeth has been keeping a diary since she was ten years old. The entries are scrappy and varied, but she persists, and as she grows older, she writes more frequently – about herself and her parents, her relationships with her friends (and with boys in particular), her teachers and achievements at school, her passionate love for music. Her writing is always frank, fun, full of verve, rarely self-conscious. She adds drawings and little jokes, sometimes criticising and mocking herself, sometimes painfully revelatory.

On 25 January 1937, she is at home around lunchtime. She has a cold, and at first she thinks she won't bother with her diary. But then she writes:

> Maybe I will write after all. Herr Trama just telephoned. I'm pretty sure it's him because Mutti always speaks quite differently when it's him. She's just said that he is not to wait for her. Maybe it's someone else but I don't think so! It's strange that she always picks up the phone when Herr Trama rings, probably so that Vati doesn't answer the phone. In the past such a thing would have upset me, but not now. And there's nothing I can do about it because if I were to make any remark about it she immediately says I'm cheeky and is cross with me. Auf Wiedersehen!

Is this old news? Have the family known, almost from the start, that Berta's marriage could never satisfy her? And what satisfaction does she seek? Is it sexual? Is it romantic? Or is it friendship that Berta has sought and failed to find? Is it something that is lacking in Dolf, or something that she would find lacking in any man, a lack that her own father has taught her and her mother has never felt?

In January 1937, Berta is thirty-six years old. Letters and photographs tell me only of her sophistication – the sophistication and refinement of a busy, middle-class, cultured woman living in a busy, middle-class and cultured town. Her marriage functions, at least in some outward sense. She has a bright, successful daughter. Is the news of her deception not only old news but in truth, no news at all?

Dearest Berta, loved by them all, and more than loved, admired. Admired, certainly, by Herr Trama, who nonetheless eventually abandoned her – or was, perhaps, abandoned.

48

Der Tag

The Munich Agreement, made in September 1938 between Germany, the United Kingdom, France and Italy, allowed Hitler to occupy Sudeten German territory in Czechoslovakia.

The Agreement was signed on 29 September, but from long before this date it was known that the German invasion of the Sudetenland would take place, and that in Podersam, Saaz and Brüx, as in other towns, a day would come when the German army would drive in – and the Jewish families must drive out. Exactly when this day – '*der Tag*' – would be was unknown.

Elsbeth recorded the turmoil of the September days in her diary.

14 September 1938

Dear, dear God, when I recall last night I know that I'll never forget it as long as I live – that is if I live that long. We went to bed, as it were 'peacefully', and in the midst of my dreams, about 2.30, there was a ring at the front door. I remember hearing, half asleep, Mutti going to the window and talking to someone, and then she went downstairs. Friends are outside in their car with all their things. They're driving off somewhere secure and say we ought to get our belongings together and go away too. Then they drive off. We all get dressed in a terrible state of agitation, packing money, passport, Vati goes to the shop, tries to order a car, but none to be got, all have been mobilised. Mutti and I are packing. Then there's a ring at the door. Uncle Franz is there. He too is driving off into the Czech area, with wife and children and their things. Little Dinah came in to have a pee and laughs. Heaven knows whether I'll ever see her again. I simply can't write any more, I simply can't.

18 September 1938

I never thought I'd come to Ledeč so quickly. Mutti brought me here by car with all my things. I've been here since the 14th and it makes me sad when I think of my parents still being in Saaz. What's the use of me being safer here? If something were to happen to Mutti and Vati, I don't want to live any longer either. I'd rather have stayed at home. Maybe Mutti will come here. What these days of uncertainty are like I don't have to describe to you, dear diary, for if I survive the war, I'll never forget this time. That one night when we thought we must leave changed me. In a way, it steeled me, as they say so nicely in novels. But I do want to live. I've got all my life ahead of me. And all because of these German swine. And there is me being German myself and I used even to be proud of it. But now one no longer knows where one belongs. And out there the sun is shining, autumn sun. Bright autumn – my favourite season!

21 September 1938

Today they announced on the radio that our German areas are being ceded to Hitler. My homeland gone . . . that's it, the end . . .

22 September 1938

I am sitting in the Ringplatz, unsuspecting. Suddenly Vati and Mutti arrive, they've run away, all they have is the clothes they're wearing. The swastika flags are out.

The German army marched into Podersam on 10 October. They were greeted by enthusiastic crowds in the town square, proffering flowers, waving flags, raising their arms in Nazi salutes. The soldiers proceeded down Ringstrasse, past the Kohners' shop. Two English officers accompanied them as international observers of the occupation, and at the town hall one of them made a formal entry in the town council record book, 'wishing all good fortune to Podersam'.

The day before, Rudi had left the shop for the last time. In the photograph that records the invasion (taken, presumably, by an official or press photographer), the blinds are drawn down over the shop windows. Rudi and Franz had already helped Heinrich and Valerie to move to Prague. It was, Franz wrote of Heinrich, like moving a king into exile.

And so by October the family are living in Prague, crowded into a flat with their hastily retrieved belongings. Only Edith has decided to go elsewhere and has taken the children, Dinah and Ruth, to stay with her own relatives on their farm in Bela. Franz stays in Prague, Rudi joins them; Berta, Dolf and Elsbeth are also there. And now they must all decide what to do.

49

The Welcome

I did not know that the invasion of Podersam had been recorded. The photograph turned up unexpectedly in a book about the town – a history produced in 2001 by the town itself. The picture is grainy, poorly printed on over-glossy paper, faintly embarrassed by its historical importance. It is a photo I never expected to see, telling a story I never expected to be told.

An invading German army. An abandoned shop. Loss of property, home and homeland.

I was not ignorant – I knew what had happened. Over the years, I had learnt of it gradually through the letters, diaries and papers, submissions for foreign compensation claims, conversations with my father, historical and archival research. But none of what I had learnt made a story. I simply knew that the family had left Podersam before the German army arrived, and that subsequently the shop was taken over, the house occupied, the keys to the safe obtained, the contents taken. That knowledge had seemed sufficient. It was, I knew, what had happened to thousands of others across the Sudetenland, and perhaps this sense of common experience somehow dulls the piquancy of the individual history.

Now, though, I am suddenly filled with urgent questions. Who are these cheerful and excited people, welcoming the German soldiers into their town?

As a child, I had naively thought in terms of an enemy. It was the only way in which I could sufficiently explain to myself what became, for me, the stuff of nightmares. One day, I childishly imagined, unknown and hostile people had entered the safe territory which was my father's home. They had come unexpectedly, but with the clear and absolute intent of destruction. I grew up knowing such things could happen, and because of that knowledge, the security on which my childhood had been built was, it seemed to me, an illusion. I cried out in the night for comfort because I dreamed that this too could happen to me and the apparently safe world I inhabited.

Looking on this photograph, I looked on the enemy for the first time and began to realise that horror comes slowly and subtly and sometimes in disguise. These cheering people were my father's neighbours, acquaintances, customers, even friends. In previous weeks, some of these Podersam Germans had been exchanging greetings with my grandfather, buying a length of suiting fabric from the shop, commiserating with my grandmother about the pains in her back, checking on progress with their order for linoleum. Now, caught up in a larger event, they are welcoming into their town what must, for my father and grandparents, signify the end. But these one-time friends and neighbours do not look forward, they cannot know, and most have no malevolent intent. The Jewish families have had to leave the town, the synagogue will now be empty and unused, but who knows whether they may, perhaps, be able to come back? Who knows what is going to happen?

My father's account, such as it was, was nothing like the photograph, and the way he remembered it must have contributed to my childish understanding. In his mind, the man who walked out of the shop that October day was not my adult father but the little boy who had played in the *Garten* twenty years before and, leaving for school, felt homesick for his flock of geese. In his mind, the Podersam that was left behind was not the Podersam of 1938 but that small, safe place in which he had grown up and which, years later, replaced in his mind any other Podersam. The leavetaking was not a leavetaking, with all the practical necessities of planning and packing and transportation, but a flight, a dispossession, the crystallising moment of loss.

So the photograph of the different reality of that day is shocking, and I am forced to write a new story, imagined but closer to the truth. My new story must replace the childish nightmare, even though it does not deny it, and serve as a reminder that now, when the family's story has suddenly, and in full photographic view, collided with the events of the outside world, their lives continued and they remained themselves.

It is late summer, 1938. Heinrich spends much of his time in the *Garten*. Rudi travels frequently between Podersam and Prague, trying to secure a flat to rent and make arrangements for the future of the business. Valerie quietly continues to run the shop and the home.

In Podersam, the small Jewish community speak nervously among themselves. Their position is uncertain. Is there safety to be had in the Czech areas or not? For how long? Will they be able to return? What will happen to their property? The German occupation of Austria the previous March made Hitler's intentions clear, and even in Czechoslovakia, antisemitic measures are beginning. It is known that in Prague (though not in provincial Podersam), there are boycotts of Jewish shops. But the meaning for individual lives is uncertain.

Heinrich walks slowly through the late-flowering roses and the falling fruit. He sits, wrapped in a blanket, outside the wooden summerhouse. He writes on scraps of paper gathered from the shop, stuffing them into his pockets as he rises to leave, so that when Valerie folds his jacket at night, she discovers his daytime wanderings, and leaves the scraps of paper, uncertain, on the table beside the bed. She lies beside him through the night and wakes when he gets up to relieve himself because the prostate problem is still disturbing him. In the darkness, she runs her tongue around her sore mouth. Her last remaining teeth have had to be removed and she is having new dentures fitted.

Rudi is full of energy but fears it may be misdirected. He looks with despair at his parents' treasured possessions. He makes lists and inventories and begins the slow process of moving furniture and possessions by lorry to a rented flat in Prague. He has found one in

Lodecká Street, quite central, with sufficient room for them all to stay. But the furniture from three houses (Podersam, Saaz and Brüx) cannot be fitted in and much must now be packed and stored.

Berta proves an unexpected ally. She is practical and energetic, finding friends and contacts in Saaz who can provide packing cases and transport. She comes to be with Valerie, bringing Elsbeth with her, and the three of them work together at the sorting and packing.

By the end of September, Heinrich and Valerie are in Prague and Rudi is living alone in the house. The day before the scheduled invasion, he walks into the shop in the quiet of the morning. Stock is still on the shelves. It is tidy and organised. He must complete his arrangements with Hans Petschinka, a previous employee, who will now take over the business. The arrangements are illusory since this is no real takeover, but the two men will go through the motions and Rudi will not be impolite.

In the afternoon, it is Rudi's hands that pull down the blinds, and he leaves by the back door.

50

All of Us

$\mathcal{F}$ ranz writes from Prague to Edith in Bela. They have decided that for the sake of the children it is best for her to remain in the country on her grandmother's farm, and she is almost enjoying it. She loves her grandmother, Karolina (always known as Babička), and her aunts, Marketa and Zdenka. Other family members have gathered on the farm too, there is food to go round, country tasks fill the days, and the atmosphere is very different to the hectic and hysterical mood in Prague. Nevertheless, Edith feels remote and writes anxiously to Franz; and he for his part finds it hard to be separated from her, trying to make decisions that affect them both so nearly. His confused letters speak loudly of the desperate times and the impossible uncertainty into which the family have been plunged.

September 1938
Franz (in Prague) to Edith (in Bela)

Mein liebstes Maedl

If I were to tell you what I have been thinking about all day, and what I would like to have discussed with you, this sheet wouldn't be long enough. I'm writing this at Lodecká Street. Ta and Ma moved in today, we've just had a cosy supper, and sharing accommodation is starting well. Actually, I don't belong here, because I'm still staying at Lenhart's, but they don't want to let me go. Anyway, it's warm, and our marvellous Rudi is here, always serene with the odd friendly joke and never stopping in his quiet

activity. I too am doing things. Yesterday I was on the go for
twelve hours, and up again this morning at 4 a.m. I spent an hour
in Rieger Park this afternoon, but there were so many children there
with their parents, and at least two prams by every restaurant table,
so my outing didn't do my sensitive soul much good.

I spent the whole of yesterday dealing with registration and
drafted four explanatory notes which I dictated at Dr Reiner's then
re-wrote in the afternoon in your father's office. I'll hand them in
tomorrow. You have been registered, and also the children, with a
note stating 'at present in the country', without describing your
whereabouts. At the moment there is probably no danger of
anyone being deported, but the registrations have not yet been
completed and yesterday 160 people were taken to the Wilson
Station to be returned to their home areas. Then, after a whole
day's to-ing and fro-ing, an order was given in the evening for
everyone to be released, and so far there's no known case of
anyone being deported.

The question of residence is only the first of all the problems we
have to solve. There is (a) our choice about citizenship, (b) my
job, (c) liquidating our finances, (d) emigration and change of
occupation, (e) family. As to (a), I don't see any great advantage in
choosing Czechoslovakia. Citizenship here, even if it were possible,
would offer neither of us major possibilities for working or
emigrating. The Kronen isn't worth much, there'll be no foreign
currency. The laws will be largely adjusted to those of the German
Reich.

As to (b), the *Prager Tagblatt* reports today that even the men
who fought on the front in Germany and Austria will only be
allowed to practise as lawyers for another two months, and after
that there will only be Jewish legal consultants to advise Jews.
They will not be permitted to act in Court and they will have to
hand over part of their takings to support former Jewish solicitors.
No doubt this situation will also be introduced in the Sudetenland,
perhaps within the next six months. Here, practising as a lawyer is
for the time being absolutely impossible and according to Prager

Börsenkurier it will remain so. I'll send you the newspaper report. It is in no way antisemitic but clearly sees only one possibility for lawyers and doctors – namely, a change of occupation and to emigrate as quickly as possible.

Re (c), liquidating our finances, Dr Šlemr offered to help with liquidating my office in Brüx. We need to sell everything as soon as possible. The steel chairs have already attracted some would-be buyers, although no doubt the amount of furniture, cars etc on the market is going to grow. I intend to get rid of the car soon, perhaps in your area. I'd hardly get anything for it here.

Re (d), there is a tremendous rush to emigrate, even among the Czechs. There are few chances. The sooner one leaves, the better. The local Jewish Religious Community intends to organise 'occupational restructuring' courses. The best chances for emigration are for farmers, including cattle and sheep breeders, chicken farmers and bee keepers. I'll have a look at these prospects as soon as our legal position is more secure, and meanwhile, please keep writing to all the addresses you have and ask about each and every possibility of emigration. Bertl would like to go to England as a cook. Rudi says that anything he gets for the stock in the shop is at the disposal of us all, and that he will probably make his way to England thanks to his diploma and contacts. Dolf has had a disgraceful refusal from the English Foreign Ministry.

I still keep thinking that Ta and Ma will be best to spend their old age in Podersam. They might be able to make a living by leasing the business. Meanwhile everything is up in the air, one can't even look beyond tomorrow, and we just have to hope this uncertainty doesn't last too long. Write to me, every day if possible. I've got to be able to talk to my wife! Surely you'll find a few minutes for that? Good night, kiss the children for me, and my fondest kisses to you.

Franz

The confusion grows, and so too does the tension between Franz and Edith. He is lonely, he misses her strong support and loving presence. He misses the two children and the family life he has recently embraced. He has lost his occupation and his role, he must consider endless new and never-before-contemplated possibilities; he cannot see a clear way ahead, and his days are spent – as everyone's days are spent – in what seems like futile effort. His next letter, addressed to her by her pet name, is full of affection and complaint, written in a telescopic style that reveals his frantic mood.

October 1938

Franz (in Prague) to Edith (in Bela)

Liebstes Hasi-hasili

Received your recent letter this morning. Meanwhile difficult day passed and I've got to describe it to you because as we are apart you don't see certain things as they really are.

Morning: filling in questionnaires with Rudi to Batà and Anglobank. Bank holds 100,000 Kronen under our names in Brüx. Deposit cannot be withdrawn, we are 'aliens'. Apply for 2,000 Kronen to the National Bank: they say come back Friday. At Laenderbank, ditto. Finally I manage to get a promise that I'll get the bank book at lunch. BUB can't be done, will call again tomorrow.

Off to hotel, pick up mail. Your father is just leaving, your mother not there. Nagl writes the flat is vacated, he kept the lino as compensation for damage, am to send keys, the Housing Office demands them. Off to Lenhart, Alex Sattler waiting for me, has come from Brüx with information. My office has been sealed. Off to Neubrunn, Herr Weiss wants to see me urgently. Isn't there. Off to Dr Reiner. Urgent consultation. Off to police HQ, then to Robert next door. Consultation about emigration with an agricultural collective. Arrangements for meeting. Back to Reiner. Impossible to contact Gruental. Enquiries: where has Brüx District Authority moved to? Klimpl regarding Canada. Then to Café Paris, enquiring about change of occupation. Off to police HQ, over to Lenhart's flat to change shoes and underwear, off to shoemaker, to laundry, to Hotel Steiner. Then meet Rudi. Confer re bank books as above. In between, taxi, telephoning, meeting people. Some have bits of advice or an essential address for me. Back home, it's 5 p.m. Piepla accompanies me, twice émigré, sends his regards to you. Now I'm with Ta and Ma, absolutely exhausted, slump down on divan and sleep for half an hour.

So here I sit after this wearing battle. What am I to say to you in reply to your reprimands? Maybe tomorrow I'll travel to Rakovník, to Kladno, to Louny, looking for an office or court which isn't there. And when I ask Dr Beck he'll say again, 'Don't be angry with me, but today I've got to there, and there, and yes, I'll certainly phone you.' I'll go to ask about a possible change of occupation, and about emigrating, and the bank books, to the Regional Office to find Šlemr, to the US Consulate about registration to emigrate, to the Lawyers' Chamber, and from one place to another, up and downstairs, everywhere 'Good morning,' 'Good day,' nothing achieved, new difficulties, writing letters which never arrive, are not answered.

Now I sit with Ta and Ma. Ta constantly thinks of the children. He is very sad. But it's better than me lying alone in the room at Lenhart's where the street lamps shine in all night and the roar of the traffic never stops. Bertl has arrived, much brighter again, and once stoical Rudi arrives, it'll all be better. What I learn from him is to think only of the next day, as one doesn't know what the day after that will bring. But I am as I am, and the way I think is to work out in my mind what is going to happen. I can't kill my feelings. And yet you want me to change. How wrong an idea you have of the life I am leading. All one can do here is to join in, make mistakes, do things that get you nowhere, go home disappointed time and time again, help others, keep calm, comfort, don't talk about the past, keep hoping. Don't write in that way. It doesn't help me – or our girls. I've carefully examined your advice, but most of it is overtaken before I have even read it. You have no idea of the complexities I had to sort out yesterday. I did it, and no one else could have done it. Rudi has already written to England on my behalf, Bertl also did so for herself. All of us are writing many letters, every single day.

The end of your letter is comforting. I will do what I can. My children and you, my sweetest, shall live. You will never let yourself be crushed, I'm sure of that. Even though the hardest time is yet to come. Don't be depressed . . . It's asking too much when one sees so much and is in the thick of it all. But I shall fight, as long as you believe in me. Write a lot to me, and good things, my prudent, silly dear Mullilein.

Your Franz.

All of them, writing letters, travelling about the city, telephoning, queuing, filling in forms, answering questions, seeking information, meeting with anyone who can (but sometimes cannot) help them.

Only Valerie and Heinrich, in the flat at Lodecká Street, uncertain of their future, watch the children's efforts and do not join in. They live among the transported remnants of their home, and the remnants of their children's homes. In the tiny kitchen in the flat, Valerie patiently stretches the *Strudel* dough on the old nursery table brought from the Girschicks' house in Saaz. Elsbeth, often with nothing to do, sits by her side. The *Strudel* is familiar, a brave attempt to do what has always been done, and Valerie keeps steadily to her task, so that when Franz and Rudi return from their daily confrontations in the offices and streets, she will be able to care for them as she has always cared for them, and in the flat the old familiar smell of autumn apples will settle like a blanket over the sharp sensations of chaos, uncertainty and fear.

They are fearful for their children more than for themselves. Their own future seems irrelevant, and in any case, what is there to be done? Edith's parents, who are currently lodging in a hotel in Prague, are making organised efforts to emigrate and extract what benefit they can from their business. They are as busy as their children, and they urge Franz on to greater effort on his own account and for Edith and their grandchildren. But Heinrich has no sense of a future elsewhere. In the chilly mornings, after the others have left the flat, he dresses stiffly and goes out to walk the streets of a city he knows well. But it is the city of his youth and has no meaning to him now. He is seventy-six years old. He has already been thinking of endings. And Valerie, though younger, mimics him because she cannot, even now, when he sometimes seems to separate himself from her, see a life ahead that is not determined by Heinrich's wishes.

Franz, sitting with her and Berta as he finishes another hastily typewritten letter to Edith, urges them both to add a pencil note. He pulls the paper from the machine and hands it across the table to Valerie. It is early evening, growing dark, and the flat is quiet. Rudi has not yet returned. 'Add something,' he urges. 'She wants to hear from you.' And Berta shakes her head a little and Valerie is reluctant, because the old loving phrases are suddenly harder to articulate and meanings are altered and unclear.

Mein liebes Edithlein

What am I to say? We miss the children sorely but it is better for them to stay where they are. Here everything is so utterly sad that I can't even write about it. Fondest kisses to you and the children.

Mama

And finally Berta, still unwilling, writes, 'Many kisses to my girls. Tante Berta.'

51

Berta

$\mathcal{B}$erta has organised a school for Elsbeth in England, and having fluent English, has acquired employment for herself. Her future is looking relatively safe.

On the evening of 7 November, she leaves the flat in Lodecká Street and walks towards the river. She crosses the Charles Bridge and climbs the narrow streets of the old town below the castle. She books herself into a small hotel.

The next day, Rudi is called to the hotel. He finds a note beside her body.

I cannot go on. I haven't the courage to start a new life. I'm not capable, only tired and ill. I haven't been a good mother to my child. It's no art to be kind and tender towards such a lovely human being. She always treated me better than I her. What can I do for her? She's to be taken to England to friends who have better hearts than me. Some day she'll be happy without me.

May my mother forgive me. I don't deserve her having loved me. My husband has always been unhappy because of me. Now he is free. Do stay with the child. I am afraid, I am frightened, I am sick and bad. Forgive me!

I hope you won't find me too soon.

Putzerle, your beautiful eyes, don't cry for me. My angel, don't cry, forget me.

Cremate me or bury me secretly somewhere. I don't deserve any better.

It was not until December that Elsbeth made an entry in her diary:

4 December 1938

> Since 7 November . . . no more Mutti . . . since 7 October . . . no more homeland . . . no Mutti . . . never again . . . my Mummerl . . . never to see her again . . . !

And Valerie, after the cremation, wrote in her prayer book where, thirty-seven years before, she had joyously recorded Berta's birth.

> Our most dearly beloved child our Berterl parted from us in the accursed year of 1938. She died from loving too deeply and from a broken heart. She will live within me forever.

52

The Sound of Breaking Glass

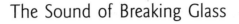

*I*n the days after Berta's death, it was quiet in the flat, but elsewhere was noise and violence. On the night of 9 November 1938, the assassination of Ernst von Rath, a German diplomat at the Embassy in Paris, prompted the Nazi vengeance of *Kristallnacht*, the burning of synagogues, the destruction of Jewish property, murders, assaults, deportations and humiliation. Germany's cities and towns were filled with the sound of breaking glass.

The news of the atrocities came to the family from far away, muted and subdued.

They thought of her through each day and each long Prague night and could not explain her despair. They knew and did not know her.

On the day of the cremation, Heinrich and Franz walked the streets together and talked of the past. Heinrich's eyes are fixed on death.

53

Bitter Sorrow

*I*n Prague, they have become part of a transplanted community. Family, friends, and other Jews from Podersam are scattered in lodgings about the city. Onkel Karl, his wife Else and their two children, Tante Ida and her husband Otto, Heinrich's brother Eduard and his wife Luisa. The Löbl family from Bahnhofstrasse, the Mühlsteins from Saazerstrasse, Rabbi Duschak himself with his wife Charlota and children . . . All are engaged in the same daily activities, the same speculative conversations. They bring news to each other, knowing their information is often unreliable or out of date but having nothing else they can use to plan their lives. Each has an idea, several ideas, recommendations, suggestions, places to go, places not to go, people to rely on, people to avoid, experiences of kindness and mortification. Exhaustion grips them all.

In January 1939, Franz visited Edith and the two children at the farm in Bela and Valerie wrote to him there. The future is almost as uncertain as it was when they first moved to Prague. Rudi and Dolf have some tangible possibilities of employment in England, and there is a plan to send Elsbeth to an English boarding school, although for now, she remains in Prague. But Franz and Edith are still searching for ways of emigrating, and despite Franz's efforts, no real prospects have emerged.

For the moment, Valerie does not seem much concerned with these practical matters She writes nostalgically, held, just for now, by the immediate past.

6 January 1939
Valerie (in Prague) to Franz (in Bela)

Mein lieber guter Büb

Your letter of 4 January arrived and gave me boundless joy. I keep re-reading it and it makes me feel as though I am watching you write it. I can see Ruth, such an energetic little thing, strutting about so that everybody has to pay attention to her. And Dinah bringing you a plate of bread to eat, taking so much care over carrying it. And then I visualise us all, just like in the old days, sitting together at the table under the lamp, and I see you, in your tenderness, almost smothering Tata with your hugs and kisses until in the end he has to tell you off, and I see you trying the same assault on me. I keep hearing your repeated 'Mammalittl', which always entered my ear and heart so sweetly . . . I could almost forget the bitter sorrow that has become our lot since those times and has torn us apart.

But I'll not moan and lament but continue to hope that our gracious Lord will return to you children all that an evil, undeserved fate has taken from you. From a distance, I shall then rejoice in your happiness. For I shall not, and cannot, rejoin you, dearest children . . . In any case, it would be irresponsible to heap more worries upon you, as you all have enough anxieties making your own way. It's bad enough that I am sitting here without any occupation or duties and am doing nothing but consuming what ought to have been yours some day. I'm reproaching myself a good deal without being able to change anything.

I don't need a gramophone. There was a time when I enthused about Rossini and Verdi, Mozart, Smetana and Dvořák, but now I have given all that up.

I'm learning languages, and although I still don't know our own country's language [Czech], I'm learning English. But it is very difficult and [the next sentence is written in English] 'I am an old woman and have an old head.' Well, what do you think of that?

231

I'm learning on my own, without a tutor, only Ida, who's better at it than me and tests me occasionally.

I embrace you all, my dearest ones, and remain with all my love your faithful

Ma

In April, the family moved from Lodecká Street to another flat. There was an accident. Heinrich fell, broke his hip and was admitted to hospital. In May, still in hospital, he died.

Valerie wrote in her prayer book:

My dear good husband left me on 9th May 1939 and I thank God that He took him to Him and spared him still more sorrow and disillusionment. He will live on in his boys.

Rudi, who by this time had succeeded in reaching England, returned to Prague for the funeral on 13 May. It must have been uncertain whether he would be able to leave again. On 15 March, German troops had marched into Prague and the German occupation of Czechoslovakia had been completed.

Shortly after Heinrich's funeral, Elsbeth followed Dolf to England. She was sent to Badminton School, near Bristol. In July, Rudi received a permit to return to England, and at the end of that month, Franz and Edith made their escape to Northern Ireland. Now the family were scattered and Valerie was left in Prague. On 1 September, Germany invaded Poland, and two days later, Britain entered the war against Germany.

54

Opapa

For most people, grandfathers exist in their childhood. They grow up with them, form a relationship with them, and then part from them. But I never knew my Opapa, and so it is only as an adult that, through reading his letters and writings, I have been able to form a relationship with him. And so it is as an adult that I watch him do what seems so against the spirit of his times – I watch him grow old, fade, think much on death, and die.

It was only a few years ago that I discovered that after the war, and for the first nine years of my life, a plain stone plaque bearing his name lay beside Berta's in the Volsany crematorium in Prague. It seemed odd that I had remained in ignorance of this while others – although there were precious few of them after the war – had occasionally visited and brought flowers to his grave.

Nearly fifty years later when I visited the crematorium in Prague and enquired about the plaque, it had long since been abandoned because the upkeep had not been paid. The administrators in the crematorium office were apologetic but they had no need to be. I had no particular desires or expectations, though I suspect that Heinrich might have done.

Had the plaque been there, I might have laid some flowers, although I would probably have had some difficulty, in twenty-first-century Prague, in finding anything like the simple bunches of snowdrops, violets and other spring flowers that Valerie and Elsbeth had laid lovingly on the grave in 1939.

In every picture of Heinrich he seems to stand a little apart, firm and distinct, unashamed, overbearing, a little naive. If a family has to have a patriarch, it is best to have a self-proclaimed, successful one, and Heinrich was well suited to the role. His sons believed in the myth he made, and passed it on well polished.

For Elsbeth, his first granddaughter, he always shone, and she, his *'Goldige'*, shone for him. The proximity of his death to her mother's seems to have comforted her. After his funeral, she wrote in her diary, 'Now he is with you, Mutti.'

55

Staying Beside Her

*V*alerie did not know what her future would hold.

Reading her letters, it is almost impossible to keep this important fact in view.

From the time of her children's departure from Prague in July 1939, she writes to them once, twice or even three times a week, and her letters continue, with little alteration in their content or tone, for the following three years. She writes about practical and financial matters, which constantly distract and worry her. She writes about relatives and friends who concern her and to whom she is frequently grateful for kindness and support. She writes movingly about her hopes and difficulties and fears and, as time passes, she tries to imagine her growing grandchildren and her changing family far away.

She writes in ink on tissue paper, her handwriting tiny and crabbed to fit the limited space. The thin sheets are now crumpled and fragile, often difficult to decipher, sometimes illegible. Much is crudely concealed. Names are in code or deliberately misspelt, sentences often incomplete or muddled; there are contradictions, questions and uncertainties. Anxiety about the whereabouts of an old pair of slippers and mention of having enjoyed a cucumber salad ('I would have loved to have sent you some') intertwine with perplexities about the fate of the house and *Garten*, Rudi's and Franz's employment, the disposal of valuables and possessions. The trivial and the significant rub shoulders, and who can say, anyway, what is truly significant in this world gone mad, where the only chance of holding onto stability is to create hope in the face of apparent hopelessness?

Valerie holds on to hope. She writes firmly and encouragingly of the need to believe in possibilities for the future, though more for her children than for herself. But my post-war knowledge is so overwhelming, so impossible to set aside, that I cannot hear her encouraging words for what they are. I think I know what is held in her heart.

In our post-Holocaust world, my grandmother is already cast in the role of victim. Living on in the flat in Prague, she is ignorant of the future, but we are so filled with knowledge, and our retrospective view is so entrenched, we lose sight of her lived experience, even in the face of her very words. She speaks of missing her children. It is a simple statement of loss. But what we hear and feel in what she says is not the sharp sensation of loss now (they had said goodbye at the railway station only days before) but the enormity of loss for ever (they will never meet again).

How can I read her letters as they really are? How can I set aside what I know (and wish I did not know) and stay beside her in the flat in wartime Prague, looking no further ahead than she herself can look, thinking only of what she tells me concerns her, and not of what I fear on her behalf? How can I hold to the person I have tried to get to know, who has eluded me all my life but now grows so close? I have listened to her words, looked at her pictures, travelled with her from girlhood, laughed, wept, worried and worked with her. With her, I have soothed and supported Heinrich through forty-two years of marriage, and I have loved three children through years of risk, uncertainty, disappointment, pain and pride. Valerie is now sixty-four years old, and to leave her side now would be a betrayal.

Staying by her, then, means reading these letters as the letters she wrote, discarding the layers of meaning that come with the dubious benefit of hindsight. It means resisting the future and knowing what is only for now, because the present experience is what matters and what is being lived. And if, in time, some prescience grows of what lies ahead, for Omama as for others, then this knowledge must be permitted to grow as it did grow, slowly and painfully, sometimes firmly rejected, sometimes admitted, taken up and possessed. And this is the story that my father could never tell me but which waited on its own telling, in the words of the woman whose story it is.

56

The Earth Goes Round and Round

*F*ranz and Edith found employment running a settlement farm
for Jewish refugees outside Belfast. They travelled to Northern Ireland via London, narrowly missing a meeting there with Rudi,
who had moved on to Bradford a day or so before.

In Prague, Valerie felt her isolation keenly and was made anxious
by the lack of news. In a rush of letters written in the days after her
family's departure, she writes about her concerns for their safety and
future – and about her own difficulties in dealing with business affairs
and practical matters that are now her sole responsibility.

29 July 1939
Valerie (in Prague) to Rudi
(in Bradford, England)

Mein lieber Büb

You'd think it would be easy to sit down and write a letter but
suddenly there's so much to do you can't begin to know. Franz left
on Tuesday and I'd be happy if I could hear he'd arrived safely,
met with you and moved on as quickly as possible. I had a
telegram from Bradford – was that from you? – saying that Franz
would lose his job if he didn't sign on by the end of the month. I
didn't know what to do and asked Hansi to wire Dolf and Belfast. I
hope he wasn't too late.

I must tell you about business. There's been a letter from the
Finance Department which states that after listing all sums not

238

accounted for by the previous accountants, we still owe more than 8,000 Kroner. I had to get a list of debtors. Luckily the list was here and I asked Edith Pollak to make copies. Then a letter came saying Jahn wants to buy our garden. He offers too little of course, and the other offer we have is smaller still, but Rolf recommends selling quickly, even if for very little.

There was also a letter from Josef Wagner about the shop and the house. After submitting the correct papers, and with the commissioners' approval, he'll hand over what suits him. He's moved into a room in the house and furnished it. He wants to buy furniture from me – a chair, table and chest, and other items too – and wants me to agree at once. It all amounts to the same in the end, even without agreement.

All of a sudden all sorts of things are piling up. Taschitz was here. When he emigrates, he wants his mother to come to lodge with me, but it would restrict my freedom, even though it would help with the rent. I would have to do all the cooking, and that puts me off.

Here I am writing such a lot about myself and I ought to refer to your letter. If only I knew that Belfast is as it should be – I'm so worried about the loss of Franz's job. I can't stop wondering whether you have met up with him and whether he will get there on time. It would be awful if he didn't.

See to it, my dear child, that you sort yourself out soon and get work. Don't worry about me. I'm not doing badly, but the anxieties wear me down. I've got visitors from morning till night. Yesterday I got home at 1 p.m. and tried to have a little rest and deal with the mail, but from 2 p.m. onwards the stream of visitors started and went on until 10 p.m. so I couldn't write a line. I had to telephone Hansi about the telegram and she sorted everything out and came round in the evening.

Give my regards to all your friends. I'll try to find out whether I can send a parcel and pack the old slippers. It's Sunday morning and I'll visit Tata and Bertl. Thank God they no longer have any worries.

It's nearly 8 a.m. and the sun is shining. Courage, my dear little boy, be strong, and things will brighten up for you and your brother. The Grosser too must be energetic and not allow himself to be so troubled by doubts. Keep well and strong. A thousand kisses and blessings.

Your loving and faithful Mama

30 July 1939
Valerie (in Prague) to Franz
and Rudi (in Belfast and Bradford)

Meine liebe Kinder

I am anxious for news from you all and to hear you have arrived. Here everything is so terribly empty and desolate, it makes me shudder. True, friends are caring for me, but it's not much help. You children were so sweet, so dear to me . . . What is going to happen now? Edith will have such a struggle, and you, my dear boy, what worries you will have. Be strong and courageous. I too am trying to be brave and am dealing with the various matters that now have to be settled. You should not have spared me so much in the past.

Your flowers on Tata's and Bertl's graves are blooming beautifully and I have added some white flowers too. After visiting them, I spent a while with Aninka and then went to have a bite to eat with Ida and Otto. It's all so senseless.

My dear, good children, don't despair. I am praying for your happiness.

Your Mama

1 August 1939
Valerie (in Prague) to
Rudi (in Bradford, England)

Mein lieber Büb

I've had a letter from each of you and am very happy that you have been so well received. It's a pity you couldn't wait another day in London and meet with Franz. He is having such a hard time, what with the two children and no money. He writes that Belfast is rather far away, but to start with they are safe, and the rest will sort itself out. As long as he doesn't lose heart. Do talk to him about it. It is such a comfort to me that you will stand by him, my dear little boy. It's not easy for you either but I've no doubt you'll make your way. Nor do I doubt that our Big One will, but it'll be a bit tougher. He mustn't let his nerves wear him down.

My dear boy, you mean well but how can I lead a quiet life, always worrying about you two and the situation here? Today the Petscheks were here, making notes of the names of everyone in the house, heaven knows why. The Kaschitzers want their mother to lodge here, but I don't know if I ought to, I'm afraid of agreeing. I'd rather rent a smaller flat if possible. What do you think? It's definitely too expensive here. I use up too much money.

I can't think of emigrating. I didn't really want to say this to you in a letter, my little one. You don't have to take it too tragically. We'll muddle through.

I had a photo from Dolf. He looks quite well but much older. Putzi [Elsbeth] is looking forward to the holidays but complains about the cold and says she's frozen even in bed.

Wishing you success in everything you do.
From your Mama, who loves you deeply.

Rudi's responses are determinedly optimistic. In his letters at least, he is not prepared to accept that his mother's emigration is now impossible. 'Never say never,' he counsels her. And using her new nickname '*Standuhr*' (grandfather clock), he writes to her, 'Keep well, dear *Standuhr*. The sun is shining today and soon it will shine for all of us. The earth is going round and round for you.'

57

A Birthday in Prague

On 15 October 1939 it is Valerie's sixty-fifth birthday. From Bradford, Rudi writes:

9 October 1939
Rudi (in Bradford, England)
to Valerie (in Prague)

Meine liebste Standuhr

It's your birthday and you surely must have sensed how I am thinking of you today more than ever. To mark the day, I've decorated your photo in my room with red poppies which I picked in a field yesterday. I do hope, dearest Standuhr, the clockwork is in order, you are well, and have no difficulties. God will protect you until we meet again in joy.

I hope you've had my previous letter, and maybe a second one from Edith's uncle. This week I got a postcard which you posted on 1 September and I'm sending it off to Franz. He of course sent me yours from Bela, so everything you write does the rounds. Dolf, who's posting this letter, will add his greetings. Franz has written me a letter, part of which I enclose, so you should have enough reading matter, and I can't begin to list all the greetings my friends are sending to you, especially the Jagger family.

I am well. Last week I had a bit of a cold but it passed quickly and not even the lumbago bothers me very much, almost less than in Prague. It's not cold yet, occasionally there's a little rain, but I lack neither food nor clothing. And when the authorities decide I can start a job, then I'll also have work.

On Friday I went to my friend William Brooks. We are playing duets together again, and you'd have loved it, I played so nicely. As a rule, I get up early and tidy up a bit. I like to have things in order. Then I light the stove, have a bath, and get ready to go. Various errands take me up to 11 a.m. and after that I go to study at the library and I've already learnt a lot. Back home at 1 p.m, listen to the news, then lunch, and similar things in the afternoon.

Mamalittl, do write to me about all your troubles and affairs. Please tell me how things stand. I suppose you see Libor occasionally. In my last letter, I mentioned that he should try to retrieve the smaller of the two sums deposited on 9 March. I hope all your arrangements and the insurance are in order.

I'd love to ask you what you cook, whether Andulka is with you, where you go for walks, who's visiting you, whether you read the 'Tag' . . . in short, what you and everyone are up to. I have no end of questions. Well, try to reply. We'll read it, all of us.

As to recipes, I've asked Putzi [Elsbeth] to lend me her cookery book. It's only a question of simple things. For example, Mama, we'd like to know how you prepare grated beetroot, baked cauliflower, and how you boil sprouts. I'd also like to have your prescription for headache powder, and how to make your own Franzbranntwein for gargling. I also wanted to ask you whether you have Tata's square watch, and a mother-of-pearl cuff link with his initials – I've got the other one here.

I am also writing to Putzi. She's got a good home, but unfortunately we all often think of her Mutti, and it makes our hearts ache. Otherwise I'm always in good spirits. Don't be misled if Franz says that Edith thinks I'm depressed. That's what she thinks. She'd like nothing better than to marry me off – but I shall wait to marry until the times change. Maybe one day I will be able to build you that villa I promised you!

Now, mein liebstes Mummerl, I've bombarded you with
questions and requests, so answer soon. Love to all and for you,
today, extra special, extra good kisses.

Your old, faithful
Klaner R

And on the day of the birthday itself, Rudi sat down at his typewriter
again and wrote to Elsbeth, allowing himself to think of Berta, his
dead sister, and trying, across the gap between his own thirty-four
years and Elsbeth's sixteen, to find some hope for an unimaginable
future.

15 October 1939
Rudi (in Bradford) to
Elsbeth (at school in Bristol)

Meine liebe Putzi

This is Oma's birthday. Yesterday I came home from a walk with a
bunch of red poppies which I placed beside her photo. May God
keep her for us for many a year. Don't you worry, she's so brave
that she's armed, I trust, against even worse things to come. You
must not give up hope. Try to look ahead. You and all of us must
struggle to make the future better than our enemies want it to be. I
know that it's hard to restrain oneself at times, and you need to
have a good cry, but then look around, see how beautiful the
weather is, go for a walk, and soon you'll feel better.

I've sent off at least forty job applications, but I'm not giving up.
Our families are still doing relatively well. Just imagine if we, like
the Poles, had been involved in the war. The end would have been
even more dreadful. When I'm in Keighley, rummaging round in
my store room, and when, like last week, I put some new golden
ribbons round the things for your dowry and repack the covers I
had washed for you because water had got into the trunk, then I

often think of your Mutti and you, and my heart aches. But then again I think I'm doing these things for a future in which I hope to see her in you, and that is a joyful thought which will also give you new heart. So carry on studying hard and cheerfully. You're well provided for. And when you've finished school, you'll turn to something practical and you'll get to the top. As for me, I'm studying hard with the same aim in mind.

So chin up, courage – that's the best thing you can do. I'll look forward to hearing from you soon.

Rudi

58

Hansi

I do not know who you are. Through years of correspondence, your name has not arisen, not even in these later years. Now, suddenly, at a time of crisis, you slip into the picture as easily and naturally as though you have always been there, and your name seems to stand for all I could hope. Someone warm, affectionate, ordinary, funny and sad. Someone, it seems, who loves my father.

In 1939, Hansi Pick, then in her early twenties, was living in Prague with her mother Anna, not far, it seems, from Omama. She is a friend of Rudi's, though how she has come to be so I do not know, and it seems that when Rudi left from the Masaryk Railway Station, Hansi was there to say goodbye. She is a teacher, working at a Jewish kindergarten in Prague, but I do not know whether this is new and temporary employment or whether she has always lived and worked here. What is clear is that she is fond of Omama and visits most days, caring for her, supporting her in practical ways and, it seems, growing close.

She has a married sister, Suse, and Suse and her husband have been lucky enough to make their escape to England, leaving Hansi and her mother behind. So, like Valerie, Hansi is separated from her family, glad for their sake that they are free but pessimistic now about her own future, no matter what possibilities are dangled in front of her.

She writes to Rudi in England; he writes back – although his letters to her have not survived. Valerie mentions Hansi frequently, and as the months and years pass, her affection, and dependence grow. But it is difficult to know whether this relationship is based on anything real or just a creation of the peculiar circumstances in which it is being nurtured, not just by Rudi and Hansi themselves but by Valerie too, who longs for some connection with her distant youngest son and is comforted by dreams of a loving, conventional future. 'Hansi is very sweet and tender to me, I wish she could soon become my daughter. Then we should all be together again. Can one even imagine such happiness?'

<hr>

15 August 1939
Hansi (in Prague) to
Rudi (in Bradford, England)

Lieber Rudi

To prove how much your kind letter pleased me, I'm replying at once. I got it the day before my sister left and you can imagine what a to do that caused. Afterwards, when Suse had gone, I was so exhausted I walked around for days as though in a dream. Now, thank God, we've had news from her, and we're glad she's over there. She's been through a great deal these last few weeks.

I learn from your dear mother that you're all right and I'm really glad for your sake that you've settled in so quickly. I always told you, and I'm sure with your diligence and efficiency you'll soon be a success.

There is hardly anything to report from here. We'd planned to go to Radošovice and take your mother along, but unfortunately it's no longer possible because I have to start this week in the Kindergarten and get ready for the start of term. I don't mind staying here, but my mother badly needs a rest and I feel sorry for her. And it's true I could do with a bit of time in the countryside. It's a pity people here haven't got time for beauty contests these days because I'd be sure to win as Queen of the Drearies.

There's a lot of nonsense being talked here. One tale I liked, which was also in the newspapers last month, was that the world would come to an end in July. Now it's mid August and it's still here. If it had ended, I'd have known how to console myself. Just imagine us meeting in heaven and me floating towards you as an angel. What a divine sight! My tender elfin shape in angel's clothing!

It's a holiday here today and Mama and I will visit your mother.

I hope you'll write again soon, I so look forward to your next letter. Put one for your mother in with it.

I close for today with all best wishes and remain

Your Hansi

PS Another thing. Are you sure English kisses are duty-free? But no need to enquire. If necessary, I'm happy to pay duty!

—————

17 October 1939
Hansi (in Prague) to
Rudi (in Bradford, England)

Lieber Rudi

Everything is okay here, just the same as before, so you need have no worries. Your mother went to stay with Edith's relations in Bela and I have had a letter from her saying how kind they are and how much she is enjoying herself. She has even been bottling plums! I've told her to stay as long as she can, she's not missing anything in Prague, but it's been raining for the last three days so I don't expect she'll stay. I'm missing my evening walks to her flat and find it strange when I'm home by seven.

You'll have heard from Suse that for a while my own affairs seemed to be making progress and for a time I had every reason to look forward to seeing you. It would have meant so very much to me. We keep making plans with your mother too, but it is all castles in the air.

Did you get my last letter? I sent you a lot of local kisses in exchange for your English ones. I hope to hear from you very soon, as the connection via Yugoslavia is very good. Please also write to your mother via me. She doesn't know I'm writing to you and I'd like to surprise her.

Goodbye for today. Please write immediately. You can imagine how happy your mother will be to hear from you, and so will I.

Your Hansi

26 November 1939
Hansi (in Prague) to
Rudi (in Bradford, England)

Lieber Rudi

We haven't had a letter from you and everyone is worried, especially your mother. Suse and Kaethe both write to us regularly and I don't tell your mother because I feel guilty having letters when she doesn't receive any. You simply *must* have time to write to your mother. Make sure you write every week.

I am still working at the Kindergarten and have at present fifty children to look after, so there is plenty of work. The Jewish Community is taking over the Kindergarten and I am now getting a proper teacher's contract and better pay. It's something I'd have felt proud of in the past but gradually these things seem to matter less and less and one gets to the point where one doesn't really care.

I am also giving and taking English and French lessons, and there's a course at school that I have to attend. It's interesting, but it's a pity it's on Sundays from 9 till 1. Then there's a course on Tuesday evenings from 6 to 8. The only advantage is that my mother can wait for me and we can go home and eat together.

We thought of moving because it was very cold here for a while and we thought we might take a smaller flat, but the weather has improved so maybe this winter we'll stay in the old flat and consider a move next autumn. Best of all I would like to be near Suse [in England]! They say it's lovely there.

I hope you don't mind the way I started this letter, but you know me, what weighs on my mind comes out of my mouth . . . or rather my letter. Take a leaf out of Putzi's [Elsbeth's] book. She writes more often than you. Don't be cross.

Your Hansi

6 December 1939
Hansi (in Prague) to
Rudi (in Bradford, England)

Lieber Rudi

It was a wonderful surprise, receiving your letter on 2 December, and I had one from Suse too. Your mother's eyes lit up when she saw the letter.

I miss Suse terribly. It is a pity that you can't visit her. Then two people who are close to me would be together. Maybe you're waiting until I get there? I'm afraid we'll both have turned grey long before that day arrives! Sadly, I'm not as optimistic as you, but how can I be, after all that's happened? And it isn't even the end yet. But if it please God, maybe you are right, perhaps you know more than I.

We have mothproofed and packed away all our summer clothes now. Such things don't really matter any more. The main thing is to keep healthy, all of us, until the day we meet again. You don't know how I am longing for that day. You know, I'm busy from morning till night, but time still creeps by at a snail's pace. At the moment, I'm very busy with preparations for Chanukah, and some of the children are being very naughty, but they are all lovely.

I'm sorry to write such a disorientated letter. I'm constantly being interrupted. The main news is to tell you that your mother is all right. I will be going to visit her again tonight. Your ears will be buzzing, because we talk about you all the time. I keep thinking, 'How much longer?' But then I remember your advice and try to be patient. Anyway, I have no choice but to be. If only the future were a little brighter.

I'm not a great correspondent, am I? But then remember, I'm only at a Kindergarten!

Write very soon, please.

Many regards, and I nearly forgot, little kisses from
Your Hansi

There is a photo taken in Valerie's flat in Prague, probably some time in 1940. Seated round a dining table are Valerie's brother Kamill, his wife Friederike, Hansi and her mother Anna. The photo is dark and the faces drawn and unsmiling, none looking at the camera and none at each other, so that one wonders why the picture was recorded in the first place and what each person is thinking as such a dismal moment is captured. On the table in front of them are two cake plates, scattered with crumbs: some treat has been consumed, but, it seems, without enjoyment.

Kamill, who is ill with tuberculosis and whose head in this picture is skull-like, had converted to Catholicism many years before, but he and Valerie remained close. Kamill, Friederike and their daughter Elizabeth have now moved to Prague, and they visit Valerie frequently. He is sixty-eight years old and will survive the war.

I look at Hansi in this picture. If the facts I have managed to assemble about her are correct, she is only twenty-three years old – very young in comparison with her companions. She is dark, with long hair tied back, a heart-shaped, slightly chiselled face, beautifully shaped eyebrows. She looks at nothing, is thoughtful, unwilling to take part. Above all, she looks to me as though she is waiting.

59

An Effort of Love and Will

*V*alerie sits at the table in her flat. She covers sheet after sheet of paper, and yet her news is scant. She sends her letters not knowing whether they will arrive. Those which do are passed between Franz and Rudi and they reply, but their letters are often delayed, and sometimes lost on the return journey, and she worries about periods of silence which sometimes last for many months.

She tells them little about her own limited existence, and the Prague she inhabits is not one they would recognise. The *Zentralamt für jüdisches Auswanderung* (the Central Office for Jewish Emigration), which reports directly to the Gestapo, now controls every aspect of Jews' lives in the city, and in October and November 1940 all Jews had to register with this office and with the Jewish Religious Community. Regulation after regulation is passed. Jews are allowed no clothing coupons; Jews have to surrender their valuables; clothes shops are closed to Jews; shopping hours are restricted; Jewish doctors and dentists can no longer practise; Jews cannot rent vacant apartments but only live with other Jews; Jews are forbidden to leave the city, to use public libraries, to use telephones, to go to the confectioners . . .

A photo taken around this time made its way to Franz and Rudi. Holding a handbag on her lap, Valerie is seated on a bench somewhere in Prague, frowning towards the camera. It seems as though the photographer has called her name, reminding her that a picture is being taken when she had, for a moment, forgotten. Despite that, she is not prepared to smile. There is no concession, no attempt to provide her children with a reassuring image. And I see in this photo not my grandmother but a saddened and mistreated elderly woman who has been forbidden to borrow a library book or go to the confectioners, and I do not feel close or drawn to her, only depressed and frightened by her plight.

And yet her letters are an effort of love and will that reach across the years. Seated at that table, in that flat, in that city, she speaks out to me, and I feel an unavoidable honesty in what she writes, just as her frown, and her plain, laced shoes, and the slight stoop of her shoulders are unavoidable and honest. So I believe what she tells me, and when she expresses pleasure, I know that she feels it, and when she expresses longing, I can feel the longing too. Above all, I can feel her mood of resignation, and her need to communicate that to her children – who do not wish to hear it because they feel they must be active and fight, and because they long for her to fight and struggle too.

17 August 1940
Valerie (in Prague) to
Franz (in Northern Ireland)

Liebster Franzl

I have been delighted by your recent letters, which have arrived after some long delays. I realise it must cost you a lot in postage. Maybe you could do as Rudi does who recently sent me a letter with seven enclosures. Put all your letters together and I will see they are distributed.

Dearest Franz, don't worry about my loneliness. There are so

many others in the same situation, and I'll cope. What can happen
to an old woman? The worst thing you could have done to
yourself and your family would have been to have acted differently.
You know nothing of what is going on here, and I can't explain it
to you. Just be glad that you're as far away as you are. What is
happiness? My dear Büb, happiness is what was, once upon a
time. We have to feed on the past, when we lived such a
beautiful, peaceful life. It's a good thing that no one can take away
our memories.

Even if your life seems empty just at present, be happy that you
have your dear wife and sweet children and that you all belong to
each other. It's for them that you must preserve your health and all
your strength. Some day you will be very happy again.

I hope Putzi [Elsbeth] is now with her father and happy. The
picture I had from him clearly shows how he has aged. I constantly
think of our Bertl and cannot get over her leaving her child whom
she loved so much, and leaving us all in the lurch. When I look at
her photo, I still think it's not true, just a bad dream.

Keep well and strong. I kiss dear Edith, the little ones, and you,
my handsome, good boy. I would like to give you the heart to
fight and persevere. I bless you from the bottom of my heart.

Oma

---

1 March 1941
Valerie (in Prague) to
Rudi (in Bradford)

Meine Lieben!

I'm especially fortunate, having received so many letters from you
in quick succession. I also heard from Felix, passing on darling
Edith's charming account of the children's lives. It is such a treat to
read and re-read this lovely description, and you two boys have
given me such a full account of everything, I feel I can fully share

the lives you are leading there. I'm really perfectly contented and thank God He has so far provided such good fortune for you. As long as I know that all you dear ones are well, can make a living, and live relatively carefree, I am happy and contented.

I like your photo, my little one. You look well, with that old mocking smile at the corners of your mouth. I'm glad to know that you have your work and can apply your skill and experience. I'm delighted too that your violin is back in favour. Ta would have been so pleased. He always urged you to keep up your music. How beautiful it was when we were all still together.

I'm not surprised that you've developed a talent for cooking. You always dabbled in it a bit. Now you just need to practise. I can't do much in the kitchen because of my old enemy, the back ache, but Hannah is looking after the cooking and Tante Ida comes nearly every day, despite the long trip from one end of town to the other. Hansi, the good girl, also visits, so I have many friends around me. Onkel Kamill also sends greetings.

My thoughts and prayers are constantly with you and today I'm thinking of you even more than usual, if that's possible. Maybe it will be as you say. What are a few years in life, and perhaps, perhaps, there will be a reunion one day. Der Grosse has sent a wonderful letter, really like himself, and just like your letter a true image of yourself and of Opapa. Now I really should put on the blue dress. It hasn't had an airing for three years. But it will have to wait because we still have ice and snow, and I won't go out because of the cold. I'm afraid of slipping, and Hansi will go to the post office instead.

Now, my dear boy, once more all love and good wishes, and loving kisses from your faithful Ma, who would go on talking to you if only she could. All my thanks for your care for me.

Your faithful Ma

15 March 1941
Valerie (in Prague) to
Rudi (in Bradford)

Mein liebes Kleinchen!

Your birthday has gone by, and I'm sure my good wishes, which were all I could send you, were late. I just hope you spent the day as happily as I hear your brother's was celebrated. I imagine Christmas was a specially joyful occasion too, with the Goldige there too. I can't picture her as grown up. To me, she'll always remain the little girl I saw romping round the house and garden, and as you say, she really has remained like that in many ways.

Today is also another birthday [Berta's], and it calls up such sad memories for us all. I took lots of flowers, and many greetings from you all to our dear one. Perhaps my prayer will merge with those offered by all who suffer, and maybe it will be granted. May God protect you, my dear ones, and give you strength, courage, good health, and everything that will contribute to your happiness.

I have received your letters. I cannot send you any noteworthy information, but there is no need for you to worry about the Standuhr. Her clockwork has to be repaired now and again, but it hasn't stopped. I have enough to live on and a warm room – which I hardly need anyway when the sun shines.

Hansi has just been here and sends her love. She would like to have wings – a wish that can't be fulfilled.

I can't write any more today . . .

With my love and a thousand kisses from
Your Oma

24 March 1941
Valerie (in Prague) to 'all my dear ones'

Although my thoughts are constantly with you, I am writing to be closer to you, and I hope you will receive this letter as all previous ones. I have received your recent letters and am anxious for further news.

In spirit, I celebrated Dinah's birthday with you. It must have been a great occasion, being together, and the same will happen when Ruth's birthday comes. Alas, I can't contribute anything except my most fervent good wishes for her future. May you see them both grow up into upright, free human beings. How I would love it if my grandchildren could stand in front of me and I could talk to them.

Really, your worries about me and my existence are unnecessary. I have all I need, my daily bread, warmth, and good people who care for me. Sadly, there is nothing one can do about the fact that one's heart does not get its share. It is fate, and all one can do is hold out, patiently, and trust in God. If God will grant me a few years more, I shall see it all come true. I can't tell you much more, there's nothing worth noting in my life.

A thousand kisses from your loving and faithful
Oma

She has made it her habit on a Friday evening to get out the children's letters and re-read them. By the autumn of 1941, there must have been a great many, for Rudi, Franz and Edith, and Elsbeth too, have been writing to her for two years. 'So I celebrate the Sabbath in my own way,' she explains. 'I see you all before me and life is again as it was, unthinkably far back. Was it really thus, and not just a lovely dream?'

I fetch a magnifying glass and peer at the photos of Omama which, some years later, Franz had placed in an envelope with her final correspondence, writing on the front 'Last letters'. They are the only pictures from this time that show her hands, though not close up, and I am using the magnifying glass to see what her hands were like and whether I might be able to picture them, smoothing out the folded sheets of her children's letters, turning the pages, and finally putting them carefully away, maybe in a special box like the one in which she once stored Franz's letters from the front. But although in one of these pictures she is even holding what looks like a letter, I cannot make out whether her fingers were long or short, whether her hands were lined and worn, or whether her nails were maybe ridged with age.

In October 1941, working through the Central Office for Jewish Emigration, the Germans began to organise the transport of Jews from Prague to concentration and extermination camps in Polish and Soviet territory in the east. From 1 October, the Jewish Religious Community in Prague was ordered to register about a thousand Jews each day, and the first transports left on 16 October. On that same day, Valerie sat down to write a rather different kind of letter to 'my dearest ones'. She hints at change to come, and her reference to moving to a new flat now carries a note of uncertainty.

---

16 October 1941
Valerie (in Prague) to 'my dearest ones'

Meine Allerliebsten

I received your telegram on my birthday and thank you very much. Recently, the quality of life here has deteriorated, but one has to thank God if one is half-way healthy, which is also what I wish for you with all my heart.

I may soon have to move to a new flat and will let you know my new address as soon as possible, but it may take a little longer than usual. I still hope to receive a few dear letters from you, and perhaps I shall be able to write to you once more. My golden, darling children, your dear letters, your stories of the children, their pictures, and every word from you, have always been a great comfort to me and the only joy I have really had. May God grant that they continue, as long as I live. I have never given up hope of seeing you again, and I shall not abandon it, even now that I am so old. Ta, our dear old Ta, was a clever man and retired in time, saving himself many a thing I must now go through. It would have been better to be with him.

Forgive my fantasies. I am lucky still to have you, and thus something to hope for. I shouldn't be writing today because the right mood eludes me, but I have just a little time and I need to make use of it. I'd like to tell you so many loving things, my darling children, if only my thoughts had not dried up so much. From the first days of your lives, you were my happiness, just as darling Edith has been since I first set eyes on her. I re-read all your kind, lovely letters about the golden days of old, and those of Berterl and Putzerl and Dolf, before putting them away. My heart ached so much when I did. Stay united, and stick together, then you'll be strong and no hardship will defeat you.

A thousand fond kisses to you all, and to my dear Kleiner and Grosser. I press you all to my heart and am into all eternity your fervently loving, ever faithful

Oma

60

The Messepalast

heresienstadt (in Czech, Terezin) lies in northern Bohemia about thirty-five miles north of Prague. It was an eighteenth-century fortress town named after the Austrian Empress Maria Theresa. In October 1941, the Germans established it as a Jewish ghetto. It would be, they claimed, a self-governing Jewish community. But the order signed by Reinhard Heydrich, Reichsprotektor of Bohemia and Moravia, on 2 October 1941, stated: 'The Jews from Bohemia and Moravia will be concentrated for evacuation . . . in one transit camp. From there the Jews will be taken to the East.'

Valerie was informed that she would be transported to Theresienstadt on 16 July 1942, on Transport Aar under the number 273. She received the news on 8 July and had a few rushed days of preparation before reporting to the *Messepalast*, the old Prague trade fair building. There she stayed for three or four days with the other nominated deportees before boarding a train. There were one thousand people in the Aar transport.

She had anticipated the deportation for many months and, when the news eventually came, was almost relieved – although she knew that the time spent at the *Messepalast*, a disused wooden building with poor plumbing and no heat, would be difficult to endure. Strict regulations governed the amount of luggage that could be taken, so, in the few days available to her, she had to hurriedly dispose of her now surplus belongings, pack what she wished (and was allowed) to take, and write letters to those she was leaving behind.

Her last letter is not written to Franz and Rudi but to Edith's relatives at the farm in Bela. During her time in Prague, and while regulations still permitted her, she had often visited Bela and become fond of the family there. They for their part had cared for her and supplied her with food from the farm.

12 July 1942
Valerie (in Prague) to
'my dear, good relatives'

Meine lieben guten Verwandten!

Yesterday it was impossible for me to acknowledge your wonderful parcel or thank you for your generosity. I thank you still more for your kind words, which went straight to my heart. I can feel your love and goodness in every line. If only I could do something for you too, but I feel powerless and empty-handed.

I got up at dawn today so that I could at least write you this letter. You can't imagine the goings on here. Visit upon visit from early morning to late at night, so one can't get any work done, and just as one thinks one has everything prepared, there's more to do, so that one doesn't know whether one is coming or going. Luckily, I had Hansi and her mother here. They are so efficient and helped with the packing and did everything they possibly could.

Today the big luggage – that is, the blankets and the larger suitcases – are being fetched. One is not allowed more than two pieces. My hand luggage is a little case, a food bag, a handbag and a shopping bag. I'm sure it's overweight, but it's impossible to stick to the limit. I only hope there won't be any trouble.

You can't believe how calm I am, and not at all nervous. Before this, I was terribly worked up – all that endless waiting, the fright every time the bell rang, the loneliness, and the trouble one had if one dared set foot outside. It had made me utterly miserable. Now I even look forward to the fact that I won't have to climb the stairs any more, something I could barely do of late, for I've become very weak and thin, and have been suffering from all sorts of complaints and pains. I just hope I'll survive the Messepalast, and then I will hope for a happy reunion with all of you, and better days with you and all our loved ones!

I must stop, though I could go on writing. From the bottom of my heart I wish you well, my dear ones. Stay calm, everything will turn out better than you fear. My hope is for a happy reunion, and for all to remain steadfast, healthy and strong. Heartfelt kisses to you all, and to all your loved ones. Wishing you all the very best, in deepest love, your devoted

Vally

Written as a postscript and on a separate piece of paper, Valerie added:

Perhaps I shall not see my golden children again. You know that my every thought has been of them and that I always prayed for their good fortune. I should be so happy if they could learn this from you. Tell them I do not cease to pray for them. All the best!

61

Theresienstadt

───────────⁓⊙⊙⁓───────────

A sixty-eight year old woman walks from the village of Bauscho-
witz, where the train stops, two miles to Theresienstadt. She
carries her carefully packed luggage – the little case, the food bag, the
handbag and the shopping bag. Others walk beside, behind and in
front of her.

She reaches Theresienstadt.

Now there are no letters, no documents, no information except
what research can piece together.

The overcrowding in the ghetto may mean that Valerie does not
know of acquaintances and family who are also there. But there are
many, and many who arrive shortly after her. Did she meet with
them? Did they talk and share stories?

The Podersam rabbi, Rabbi Ignatz Duschak, was there, with his
wife Charlota, and daughters. Gustav Hirsch, the Podersam Tempeldiener. Ida Hirsch, wife of a Podersam shop owner. Alois Kohn and
his wife Emilie, who lived on Saazerstrasse, round the corner from the
Kohners' shop. Adolf Kohn, from Spittalgasse. Wilhelmine Pollak,
wife of the Podersam vet, with her daughters Alice and Edita. Moritz
Popper. Hugo and Alice Mühlstein, who ran their leather business in
Saazerstrasse. Anna Stein, like Valerie one-time President of the
Podersam Jewish Women's Association.

And not only acquaintances. Valerie's brother-in-law Max, hus-
band of Heinrich's sister Anna, and her sister-in-law Luisa, wife of
Heinrich's brother Eduard, made the same two-mile walk from
Bohusovice to Theresienstadt.

In Theresienstadt at the same time as Valerie, there were at least twenty of her relatives. Heinrich's sisters, Emma and Julie, both in their seventies. Several of Valerie's cousins. And Viktor Kohner, Heinrich's nephew, the brother of Hans who had been killed in action in Italy in the First World War.

Valerie's sister Ida, and Ida's husband Otto, arrived in Theresienstadt on 20 July 1942. Valerie would have been there when they were put on board the train to Baranovici eight days later and sent to their deaths. Did she meet them? Did she say goodbye? Or did they pass each other unknowing in the crowds and confusion?

Valerie was deported from Theresienstadt to the death camp of Treblinka on 22 October 1942 on Transport Bx, number 1757.

Valerie's cousin Olga Krafft and her husband Rudolf, and Alfred Kraus, husband of Valerie's cousin Klara, travelled on the same transport. So too did Ignatz Duschak, the Podersam rabbi, his wife Charlota, and the Podersam Tempeldiener Gustav Hirsch.

In October 1942, there were ten gas chambers at Treblinka. Diesel engines pumped carbon monoxide through pipes into the chambers. By these means, between twelve and fifteen thousand people could be killed in a day.

In 1944, Franz and Rudi were still sending Red Cross food parcels to the Theresienstadt ghetto.

62

The Handbag

*E*ight years and one thousand miles divide my grandmother's
death from my birth.

I often think about those eight short years. In the lives of my own
children, eight years have been the blink of an eye. I might feel, 'I so
nearly knew her.'

But the miles are a different matter. The miles, and the terror.

In 1994, on a visit to Munich, I met Elizabeth, Kamill Herrmann's
daughter, Valerie's niece. Elizabeth was then in her early seventies,
but as a nineteen-year-old she had been with Valerie in Prague.
When Valerie packed her belongings before her departure to
Theresienstadt, she gave Elizabeth a handbag and a monogrammed
linen handkerchief. When I met her, Elizabeth offered these
treasures to me.

A handbag and a handkerchief connect me across time and
distance to Valerie Kohner, née Herrmann, Heinrich Kohner's wife,
Franz, Berta and Rudi's mother, my Omama.

I own many things that Valerie possessed. I have letters and photos
in abundance. I have bedlinen and tablecloths I know she must have
laundered. I have furniture she must have dusted and polished. I have
china and glass from which she ate and drank. I have her autograph
book with dried flowers pressed inside. My sister has her handwritten
recipe book. But none of these objects talk as the handbag talks.
These objects sing a lullaby. For me, they speak of peace. The
handbag is the horror.

It happens to be an ugly thing, black leather with a mock-snakeskin interior, but I didn't notice that at first. On receiving it, my first feeling was profound gratitude, my second was joy. It felt good to hold in my hands something so directly linked with my grandmother's final days. I wanted to walk with her, comfort her, observe and learn from her courage, and the handbag seemed to allow me to do that. I handled it. I tried walking with it in one hand, putting it over my arm, holding it on my lap, opening and closing the clasp, taking out the little snakeskin purse which is attached by a chain inside, looking at my face in the cosmetic mirror, trying to see not my own but my grandmother's eyes and nose.

But the more I handle it, the more inanimate the handbag becomes. It refuses to speak of my grandmother's life, except of that moment when, forced to discard her belongings, she pressed it and the handkerchief into Elizabeth's hands. The handbag was left behind. It has come to me because it could not travel with her, and it was saved because she could not be saved.

At Treblinka, where Omama perished, no camp buildings have been preserved and there are only monuments. But I have visited Auschwitz, where one can see not only the buildings but also carefully presented evidence of what happened there, and I have stared at the large pile of suitcases that are on display, carried there by those who were killed. And for me as for others, the size of the pile is horrifying, and one can see how each case is one case, with a characteristic look and maybe a printed name, and yet each case is also part of the pile, and the pile is huge but smaller by far than anything that could represent the truth.

And Omama's handbag is a part of that horror, because while one wants the size of the pile to be noticed, each individual story becomes submerged in that pile and is lost. So one kind of understanding, which is an understanding of scale, erases another kind of understanding, which is an understanding about individuality, and the numbers overwhelm us, so that my grandmother's cruel death becomes many deaths, and her story many stories. And the handbag

I now possess is not, as at first I thought it was, a part of her, but a symbol of what happened to so many.

My father never spoke to me of Valerie's death and I do not know what nightmares he endured. But all my life, or so it feels, I have lived with the uncompleted story of my grandmother's life and have needed to complete it. I have wanted to cross the years and miles.

I have consistently avoided the task. I have avoided it despite the fact that out there in the wider world there has been no shortage of material and encouragement. Books and films have proliferated; remembrance and testimony have been promoted. I have read, watched and listened, perhaps out of a sense of duty, perhaps in the hope of discovery. I have been fed by others' stories, and I have fed myself through reading and research, thinking perhaps that the story I am seeking would emerge already formed, making no demands on my imagination or feelings, so that the work would not lie in its creation but in its assimilation, and in continuing to live with it thereafter.

But the more the horror is publicly recognised, the more remote it feels. I feel not closer to but further from my grandmother's death.

My grandmother was cruelly killed. My grandmother was brutally murdered. I try these and other phrases on my tongue. They are not the words with which I usually end the story. I usually say, 'My grandmother died in the Holocaust' or 'My grandmother died in Treblinka.' I speak of the swathe cut across my family tree, death after death recorded in 1942, 1943, 1944. I take it for granted that this will be understood, that this is the case with many other families, that the horror is known and (politely) need not be specified.

But if I wish to complete her story, I must tell a story that is not polite, a story my father would not have wanted to be told. I must picture what happened from the moment she was taken off the train to the removal of her body from the gas chamber.

It is not my grandmother's voice that demands this story's telling. What, after all, is gained? Can it honour her, to tell the truth?

63

Omama

The train did not pull into a station at Treblinka because there was no station building, only a building made to look like a station, which was in fact a storehouse for the belongings of those who arrived.

Omama was moved off the train and her belongings, whatever they were, were taken from her. She was taken to some barrack buildings.

In the barrack building, she had to undress. I picture her thin, elderly body and the slight stoop of her shoulders.

Was it cold? Did she shiver? Did she know what lay ahead?

Her head was shaved. I picture her beautiful face, and the wispy long hair. Before it could be cut, she must have had to unpin it. I picture her hands, unpinning her hair as Heinrich must have watched her do, reaching round towards the back of her head.

When her head was shaved and she was naked, an SS man opened a door which led to the road from the barracks to the gas chambers. Omama walked this road.

How many walked with her? Did she see her cousin, Olga Krafft? Or Charlota Duschak, the rabbi's wife?

Omama entered the gas chamber. The door was closed. The motor that pumped the gas into the chamber was started. It must have made a noise.

I imagine now the smell, the cries, the fighting for air, the struggle, the pain, the prayers, the collapse.

I picture my grandmother's beautiful old body.

64

Russell Square

y father described my birth as a noisy, slightly comical event. I was born at home and was first presented to him, as he came into the bedroom, red-faced and bawling. This was a different experience to the more worrying but quieter and more dignified birth of my sister, by Caesarean section, in 1946.

My father had married my mother, Olive Britton, in the summer of 1943. They had met in the Yorkshire Dales in 1942, she on a walking holiday with her sister from Kent, he escaping for a weekend from Bradford.

Their wedding photograph is reticent, quiet and well behaved. A small group of relatives and friends gathered in London to celebrate the event, which took place at the registry office in Russell Square.

By the time of the Russell Square wedding in 1943, Hansi Pick had been transported to Theresienstadt. Her mother Anna was with her. The following September, Anna was transported to Auschwitz.

There is no record of Hansi being transported onwards from Theresienstadt. There were 1,021 people on her transport from Prague to Theresienstadt, and 239 of these were liberated. I do not know if Hansi was one of them or, even if she was, whether she survived.

And so, having appeared late and unexplained in the story, Hansi disappears. My father never spoke of her, and since I knew nothing of her, I did not ask questions. For over forty years, her affectionate letters were stored along with those from Omama, untouched and unread, and even now it is hard to know how to respond to their simple warmth.

In my parents' wedding picture, Olive's family rubs shoulders with the shipwrecked from Europe. Her parents, her sister, her brother and her sister-in-law are all there. So far, they have lived uneventfully through the war. Now the youngest in their family has fallen in love and brought them into contact with another, more eventful world that, at the time this photo is taken, they intend to do their best to accommodate. In time, however, it will become apparent that these two worlds do not meet, and it may be that Olive herself does not wish for them to meet, and that her marriage is an escape from a family in which she does not feel altogether comfortable.

At the time Rudi places the ring on her finger, Olive does not know whether her mother-in-law is alive or dead. She cannot know what may be asked of her in the future, and she commits herself just the same, well dressed, elegant, smiling at the camera with quiet confidence.

Where does her confidence come from? Is it her Englishness that she feels will see her through? The simplicity of love? Rudi's willing dependence? His need for ordinary domesticity, for meals on the table, washing on the line, and, in time, some noisy English babies?

On 15 October 1945, which would have been Omama's seventy-first birthday, Rudi wrote to a contact in Czechoslovakia: 'The news we have had about my mother from many good friends for the last few months has left us in no doubt as to her fate.'

65

The Journey

My father and I set out together on a journey. At first, he led and I followed. It was a journey full of love and fun. There were jokes most of the way.

The direction of our journey was away from the past. Holding to what was good and discarding what he felt would only taint the future, he kept his eyes and mine fixed firmly on the horizon. His plan was to create a new world, an English world (as it happened), a world connected with the past but still unburdened, a world in which I and my sister could move freely, achieve what we wished to achieve, and be the kind of grandchildren of whom our grandmother would have been proud.

He did not reinvent or anglicise himself, as others in a similar position did. Our forward-looking present still celebrated all that he treasured from the past. We lived among a wealth of possessions from the old country, and a store of memories. From childhood, I learned to cherish the past and respect my unknown, never-met family.

As I grew older and wanted to know more, I wrote to him with questions, and he replied with evocative memories of family, Podersam and Prague. But typically, in these letters he would break off abruptly, and a reminiscence would be interrupted by the words, 'But that was long before the tragedies that followed . . .' In one particular letter, he ended by saying, 'But all that took place before you were born. And after that, there was no need for me.'

That was how he saw it. From the time of his mother's death, the deaths of others, and his own survival, his purpose was clear: to send his own children forward into the world as free of the past's burden as he could contrive it to be. After that, there was no need for him.

So limits were set around my knowledge of the past. Some boxes were opened, and others remained firmly closed. And looking back, it is hard to say whether it was my father who tacitly forbade their opening, or whether it was I who hesitated to ask about what lay inside. On reflection, it would have been hard to ask because of my own ignorance. And in any case, it seemed to me then as though my father was my only appropriate source of information about the past, and all that he could tell me would be all that I would want to know. He was the gatekeeper – that was his right.

Then, in my late twenties, I visited Prague for the first time, just over forty years after my father had left. He himself had never returned, and he did not intend to do so.

He was then in his mid-seventies. He was fit and vigorous for his age and talked about living for many more years. He spoke of this frequently and fought the smallest signs of ageing or physical debility. This was all the more noticeable because my mother, though twelve years younger than him, was becoming increasingly unwell, and increasingly disinclined to fight her symptoms. My father tried to support her, but he found her lassitude and depression so difficult to understand that he hardly knew how to begin. For my father, the greatest compliment one could pay him was to say he looked young.

He wanted me to visit Prague, and also Podbořany, but at the same time he attempted to deter me, saying 'You'll find nothing there,' 'What's the point?' 'Must you go?' I did not know what imperative was urging me on, but it was not idle curiosity. I knew I could honestly say to him, 'Yes, I must' and I felt that this was what he wanted to hear. I was aware that he often contradicted himself. 'You'll find nothing there' would be followed by instructions and directions, which would be followed by 'But what's the point?' He was by turns enthusiastic and nervous, pleased and a little irritable.

And in the time around this trip, and through the conversations it engendered, my footsteps began to falter, and so, I think, did his, and the direction of our journey changed. We began to travel back towards the past.

As I travelled from Prague airport towards the city centre, I looked out of the bus window at vistas of ugly concrete tower blocks. It was not what I was expecting and I was glad my father was not with me. But when I reached the centre, I found a city almost untouched by time, the city of my father's youth, lying in wait for me. There was his school in the Kinsky Palace in the old town square, his lodgings at *Die Schwarze Rose* on the Graben, the coffee house and wine bar where Heinrich took him for term-time treats. There was the town hall where Franz and Edith married, the flat where the family found lodging in 1938, the cemetery where Berta and Heinrich were buried. It was all there, decrepit, overgrown but little changed. I paced the city with my eyes on cobblestones my father had also trodden, or gazing up at the roof line and skyscape of the early twentieth century and before.

This astonishing discovery of my father's Prague was lucky for me – but unlucky for Prague. It was the time of the Russian occupation. Depression rather than a spirit of preservation kept the buildings unchanged, the shops empty of merchandise, and the street lights so dim that one could almost imagine the city in the days before electric lighting. In Podbořany, signs of decay were still more evident – and much less evocative. The Kohner shop was still standing, but with grass growing from a corrugated iron roof, and the shop front battered and changed beyond recognition. Only the first-floor windows, and a large oak door with decorative panelling of which my father was particularly proud, made me certain that this was the same building.

I was a little ahead of the influx of European and American visitors, all bent on discovering their roots, and my presence in Podbořany caused interest and a little amazement. At the post office, where I explained the reason for my visit and asked for directions to what had once been Ringstrasse, the woman behind the counter immediately abandoned her work and came out to show me the way. She, and others who joined in the search, were enthusiastic, voluble and kind – but not, so far as I could feel, even remotely connected with the world I was looking for. In Podbořany, it seemed, that world was gone.

Its absence revealed my intentions to me more than any discovery might have done. I felt frustrated and angry. Maybe I had believed, for far too much of my life and seduced by my father's stories, that the past was waiting for me, intact. The discovery that it was not, and that the world I had come to find was not just lost but had been deliberately destroyed, was shocking.

It took time before I realised what these feelings meant. I had to return to England and reflect on what I had seen before my thinking began to change. I appreciated only very slowly how little I knew, and how what I knew was sentimental and selective, and not a story at all.

On that first visit to Podbořany, had I but known it, there was probably much I could have seen. It would not have made a story, but it would have told me much that I later longed to know. Soon afterwards, the shop and house were demolished, and the *Garten* was covered over. On that first visit, I could probably have entered the shop, and maybe even have walked through the accommodation on the floor above. I wandered in the *Garten*, or on land that I thought I could identify as the *Garten*, but although the photos I took show the bridge over the Sauerbach, Friedrich Löwy's barn, and broken pieces of the ornamental wall, at the time I did not recognise these landmarks and simply gazed on them as ruins, more grateful for their survival than curious about their significance.

I was not yet in a position to make discoveries. This was only the beginning, the point at which I began to realise all that I did not know and all that my father had not told me.

In the years after that first visit to Prague and Podbořany, I spent long periods of time researching the family's past. My father died eight years later, and we had had little time to share information. I did most of the work without him, saddened but accepting that this was an enterprise of my own. My relationship with the past was not his, nor his mine. The connection and completeness I sought was not what he had envisaged for me, although when he was confronted with it – 'I must go' – he understood.

His own task, to travel involuntarily backwards at the end of his life, was sadder by far. It was impossible for him, as he grew older, to avoid reflection on his life, and while there was much of which he was proud, less-wanted memories also pressed upon him and could not be denied.

66

Your Hand in Mine

I think of my father's hands as working hands – a gardener's hands, a violinist's hands. They were strong and square. He wore a gold signet ring, dull and scratched.

I am seated beside my father. My hand, as it often was, is held in one of his. I know the feel of his hand. The skin is slightly leathery.

Omama wears a spotted blouse, fastened at the collar by a brooch decorated with a menorah. She too is seated beside me. I put out my hand to feel the smooth fabric of her blouse, the paper-softness of her cheek – but they are beyond my touch. And so too is the feel of her hand, as she slips it into mine.